LAUNCH TO LEGACY

A COMPREHENSIVE GUIDE TO ENTREPRENEURIAL
SUCCESS FOR STARTUP AND SUCCEED.

VINAY RAJAGOPAL IYER

BLUEROSE PUBLISHERS
India | U.K.

Copyright © Vinay Rajagopal Iyer 2024

All rights reserved by author. No part of this publication may be reproduced, stored in a retrieval system or transmitted in any form or by any means, electronic, mechanical, photocopying, recording or otherwise, without the prior permission of the author. Although every precaution has been taken to verify the accuracy of the information contained herein, the publisher assumes no responsibility for any errors or omissions. No liability is assumed for damages that may result from the use of information contained within.

BlueRose Publishers takes no responsibility for any damages, losses, or liabilities that may arise from the use or misuse of the information, products, or services provided in this publication.

For permissions requests or inquiries regarding this publication,
please contact:

BLUEROSE PUBLISHERS
www.BlueRoseONE.com
info@bluerosepublishers.com
+91 8882 898 898
+4407342408967

ISBN: 978-93-5989-984-8

Cover design: Rishav Rai
Typesetting: Rohit

First Edition: March 2024

Foreward

In the bustling heart of Bangalore, Karnataka, back in 2002, my path crossed with Vinay Rajagopal's, marking the beginning of a remarkable journey. As system and storage/backup administrators at Intel India, which then felt like a startup with merely 150 employees, we embarked on a transformative chapter. By the time he departed around 2005/2006, Intel had burgeoned to over 1500 employees, and our storage capabilities had expanded from 5TB to a staggering 140+TB, spreading across six locations including ITPL, Airport Road, and Sarjapur. Our mentorship extended to over ten individuals, contributing to several M&As and enhancing our facilities by integrating the best tools from Intel's global locations like Israel, Santa Clara, and Folsom Making India the best place for any developer from Intel across the world. Vinay's expertise also led him to establish new centers in Shanghai and Korea.

After leaving Intel, He ventured into startups like Orchesys (now GlassBeam Inc) and Apara, pioneering the introduction of giants like Sun Microsystems, NetApp, Quantum, Veritas, Juniper Networks, and Brocade to India's tech landscape. His journey continued at IBM, where He managed a vast team across APAC, UK, and the US, focusing on six sigma lean activities and fostering a team of 100+ architects as part of the elite GDS/SSO team.

A profound personal loss prompted him to step away from the mainstream and embark on a spiritual journey, delving into Vedic courses. This transformative period culminated in his return to the corporate world at Happiest Minds, where He contributed significantly as an Associate Director in delivery and practice development, overseeing Transition and Transformation and PMO practices. Yet, the call to mentor and coach others, drawing upon my vast experience and certifications in life/professional coaching, strengths coaching (Gallup), yoga instruction, acupressure treatment, and more, led me to pursue a path of helping others navigate their challenges in the Indian context.

"Launch to Legacy" is more than just a book; it's a testament to the power of Indian philosophy in entrepreneurship, aiming to inspire countless individuals worldwide. Setting a stage for Vinay Rajagopal's journey to international acclaim as a speaker and seminar leader, alongside the practical wisdom shared in this book, embodies the principles of transformation and growth. As we introduce this work to new readers, our aspiration is that it will empower you to craft a life filled with fulfillment, prosperity, health, and creative energy. With deep gratitude, we share this journey, validated by numerous lives enhanced by its teachings.

Santhosh Mogili, CEO - OPT IT January 2024

Dedication

Dedicated to My Beloved Son: Aryan, My Loving Wife: Ritu, Respected Grandmother: Rukmaniyamma, Dear Uncle: Venugopal, and My Father: Rajagopal.

In this heartfelt dedication, I extend my gratitude and love to my family, embracing the richness of our Indian heritage and values. Our names resonate with the timeless wisdom of the Vedas and the Upanishads, echoing the eternal bond that unites us across generations.

My Son, Aryan, embodies the spirit of a true warrior, just like the great warrior Arjuna from the Mahabharata. His name signifies strength, courage, and unwavering determination. As I dedicate this work to him, I envision him walking the path of righteousness and wisdom, guided by the teachings of our scriptures.

My Wife, Ritu, shares her name with a revered character from Indian mythology, Princess Rukmini, known for her devotion and love for Lord Krishna. Like her namesake, my wife exudes grace and devotion, nurturing our family with love and care. Her presence in my life is a blessing that mirrors the divine love celebrated in our ancient texts.

Ajji Rukmaniyamma, our Respected Grandmother, is the matriarch of our family, embodying the wisdom and traditions passed down through generations. Her name carries the essence of our ancestral heritage, and her guidance is a testament to the timeless wisdom of our elders.

Doddappa Venugopal, our Dear Uncle, exemplifies the bond of kinship and support that is deeply ingrained in our culture. His name resonates with the melodious tunes of Lord Krishna's flute, symbolizing the harmony and unity within our family.

My Father, Rajagopal, is the patriarch whose name signifies the kingly qualities of righteousness and leadership. He has been my guiding light, instilling in me the values and principles that are rooted in our Indian ethos.

This dedication is a tribute to the values of family, tradition, and spirituality that have shaped our lives. It is a reminder that, like the ancient sages and seers of our land, we too are part of a timeless journey, bound by the threads of love and heritage.

As we embark on this literary voyage, may the wisdom of the Vedas and Upanishads inspire us, and may our shared experiences and stories enrich the narrative. Together, we celebrate our Indian heritage, weaving the timeless threads of love, knowledge, and tradition into the fabric of our lives.

Starting

Several years ago, during a gathering at the prestigious Bengaluru University in India, a wise sage delivered words of wisdom that continue to resonate through time. Encouraging the eager students, he cautioned them against becoming overly consumed by the pursuit of wealth, power, or fame. His message was profound: "One day, you shall encounter an individual who values none of these worldly treasures. It is on that day that you shall truly comprehend the depths of your own poverty."

This sage's timeless advice echoes the essence of our ancient scriptures, where the pursuit of material wealth is juxtaposed with the quest for inner richness. In the land of India, where spiritual wisdom flows like the sacred rivers, we find solace in the verses of the Vedas and Upanishads.

In the Bhagavad Gita, Lord Krishna imparts the wisdom of detachment, urging Arjuna to rise above worldly desires and discover the true wealth within. Arjuna, the valiant warrior, found himself at the crossroads of duty and spirituality, much like the students at Bengaluru University. The words of Lord Krishna serve as a guiding light, illuminating the path to self-realization.

As we navigate the modern world with its relentless pursuit of material success, let us pause to reflect on the sage's message. In the bustling streets of Mumbai, the serene banks of the Ganges, and the vibrant markets of Delhi, we encounter individuals who have embraced simplicity and inner richness.

One such person is Siddharth, a humble shopkeeper in Varanasi. Siddharth's modest shop, nestled amidst the ancient temples, has been in his family for generations. Despite the allure of wealth, Siddharth finds contentment in serving pilgrims and sharing stories of spirituality. He embodies the sage's wisdom, reminding us that true wealth lies in the service of others.

In the digital age, where the world is at our fingertips, we have access to an abundance of information and opportunities. Yet, the sage's words remain relevant, urging us to seek a wealth of character, compassion, and wisdom. We find inspiration in the lives of great souls like Mahatma Gandhi, who dedicated his life to truth and non-violence, transcending the allure of worldly possessions.

The sage's counsel reverberates through the ages, guiding us towards a richer understanding of life's true treasures. As we walk the path of self-discovery, may we draw strength from the wisdom of our ancient scriptures, the resilience of our ancestors, and the enduring spirit of India. In the words of the Upanishads, "Lead us from the unreal to the real; lead us from darkness to light; lead us from mortality to immortality."

Acknoledgements

With humility and gratitude, I extend my acknowledgments, drawing inspiration from the wisdom of Solon, the ancient sage of Varanasi, who advised that in offering counsel, our aim should be to assist rather than simply please our friends. This sentiment resonates deeply as I express my appreciation in the Indian context.

This endeavor has been enriched by the invaluable contributions of those who walked this path with me. Their insights and suggestions have not only made this work more pertinent but also more beneficial to those who seek its wisdom.

In this collaboration, I wish to recognize individuals who played a pivotal role in shaping this narrative.

In this spirit of collaboration and growth, we move forward, seeking to offer wisdom and guidance that transcends boundaries, enriching lives with each turn of the page.

Share the wisdom you possess, for in doing so, you create a knowledge that weaves through the ages.

—Sage Vedavyasa

Welcome to the journey

I've never been driven by the pursuit of reputation and accolades. Instead, I write from the depths of my heart, compelled by the need to share what resides within me. These words you are about to read are a testament to that inner calling.

—*Ravi Varma*

Looking back, many of us have uttered the words, "If I knew then what I know now." It's a sentiment shared by seasoned entrepreneurs, a reflection of the wisdom gained through experience. My hope is that, as you embark on this journey, you won't find yourself echoing those words because the knowledge you seek is right here within these pages.

I've walked the entrepreneurial path, founding three companies, investing in four, and offering guidance to organizations ranging from small startups to giants like IBM. My journey even led me to two stints at Intel as employee and supplier, and I now serve as the chief operating officer of a promising startup called iSmart.

When it comes to startups, I've navigated the highs and lows, accumulating experiences that now form the foundation of this book. My insights are born from the scars of challenges faced and lessons learned. You stand to benefit from my hindsight.

My mission is straightforward and unwavering: I aim to simplify entrepreneurship for you. When my time on this earth is done, I want people to say, "Vinay empowered me." I want this sentiment to resonate with many, so this book is intended for a wide-ranging audience:

1. Visionaries toiling away in garages, dorm rooms, and offices, crafting the next revolutionary innovation.

2. Fearless individuals within established corporations, striving to bring groundbreaking products to market.

3. Social entrepreneurs within nonprofit organizations, dedicated to making the world a better place.

I envision great companies, great divisions, great schools, great spiritual centers, and great nonprofits all benefiting from the wisdom contained within these pages. Before we embark on this journey, a few important details:

Originally, I intended to write this book, but as I delved deeper, I found myself adding, revising, and even removing content. What you hold in your hands isn't a mere "1.0" version; it's a comprehensive overhaul.

In the interest of brevity and because entrepreneurs share more similarities than differences, I often use the term "startup" to encompass any new venture, whether for-profit or not-for-profit. Similarly, I use the word "product" to encompass new products, services, or ideas. The lessons you'll discover in this book are universally applicable, so don't get caught up in the terminology.

Every recommendation I offer comes with the understanding that there may be exceptions, and I acknowledge the possibility of being wrong. Entrepreneurship isn't black and white; it's a realm where what works and what doesn't work take precedence over right and wrong.

I assume that your aspiration is to shape the world, not merely observe it. Entrepreneurship is about taking action, not just learning about it. If your mindset is one of action—cutting through the noise to get things done—then you've picked up the right book by the right author. So, without further ado, let's embark on this journey together. Onward...

—Vinay Rajagopal Iyer

Contents

Genesis: Unleashing Your Creative Beginnings

Chapter 1: Nexus 2

"*Initiation:* Fueling Your Path to Success"

Chapter 2: The Mastery of Commencement 24

Chapter 3: The Mastery of Visionary Leadership 53

Chapter 4: The Mastery of Self-Reliance 82

Chapter 5: The Mastery of Financial Abundance 105

Chapter 6: The Mastery of Presenting - Mastering the Pitch 137

"*Flourish:* Blossoming into Abundance"

Chapter 7: Crafting a Stellar Team for Success 168

Chapter 8: The Mastery of Spreading the Light 189

Chapter 9: Mastering the Mastery of Social Connection 210

Chapter 10: The Mastery of Abundant Harvest 239

Chapter 11: The Mastery of Collaboration... 259

Chapter 12: The Journey of Perseverance 273

"*Fulfillment:* Embracing Your Duty with Purpose"

Chapter 13: The Pursuit of Human Excellence 292

Closing Thoughts 304

Author Bio.. 310

Reading List 312

Genesis:
Unleashing Your Creative Beginnings

Chapter 1:
Nexus

"In the journey of entrepreneurial creation, within the sphere of innovation and exploration, the most captivating words are not 'Siddhirasti!' (There is achievement!) but 'This holds promise...'"

—Vikramaditya

NEXUS (Nurturing Novel Ventures: Unveiling Excellence & Success) Embarking on a journey is far more straightforward when you begin by laying the right foundation than attempting to rectify missteps later on. At this nascent stage, you are sculpting the very DNA of your entrepreneurial endeavor, and this genetic code is immutable. By focusing on key considerations, you can construct a solid groundwork, granting yourself the freedom to tackle the monumental challenges that lie ahead. This chapter unravels the mastery of commencing an entrepreneurial journey.

Quest for Simplicity A common misconception suggests that prosperous companies commence their ventures with grandiose aspirations. The implication is that entrepreneurs must harbor megalomaniacal dreams to prosper. However, my experience has led me to believe that remarkable companies often originate from the simplest of inquiries.

"HENCE, WHAT?" This query surfaces when one identifies or predicts a trend and ponders its potential effects. The thought process might go something like this: "Mobile phones with cameras and internet capabilities will become widespread." Hence, what? "People will gain the ability to capture and share moments instantly." Hence, what? "We should create a platform that allows users to post photos, evaluate others' pictures, and participate in discussions." And thus, the concept of ShareChat was born.

Aren't These Stories Intriguing? The Drive of Intellectual Curiosity and Fortuitous Discoveries This approach flourishes on the combination of curiosity and unexpected discoveries. Take these examples: Spencer Silver was on a mission to develop a new adhesive but ended up creating a substance that would stick to objects but could be easily peeled off. This accidental invention led to the development of sticky notes, similar to how the Indian company SticNote might have been inspired. In another instance, Sridhar Vembu, initially working in the software industry, noticed a unique opportunity when a small business sought a comprehensive yet affordable software solution. Intrigued by this niche, he dived deep into understanding their needs, which led him to establish Zoho Corporation, a moment of serendipity that redefined enterprise software for small and medium businesses.

"Is There a Superior Approach? The Pursuit of Excellence in Challenging the Norms The core of this journey is rooted in dissatisfaction with current standards. As Jamsetji Tata might have thought, "In the beginning, I looked around and, not finding the industry of my dreams in India, decided to build it myself." Similarly, Shiv Nadar embarked on founding HCL Technologies, propelled by his belief that there must be a simpler way for Indians to access and benefit from the burgeoning field of technology, without the need for extensive foreign dependence or massive institutional backing.

Narayana Murthy, driven by a vision that software development and IT services could be revolutionized, founded Infosys. This initiative was based on the conviction that there existed a more efficient, inclusive way to deliver technology solutions, significantly altering the IT services landscape and positioning India as a global IT powerhouse."

Why Isn't Our Organization Embracing This Opportunity? The driving impetus here is a sense of frustration within your current workplace. You possess intimate knowledge of the market, its clientele, and their unmet requirements. You've ardently advocated to your superiors that your company should develop a product to address these customer needs. However, your suggestions have fallen on deaf ears, with management failing to heed your insights. In response, you decide to take matters into your own hands and embark on the journey of creating the solution yourself.

"It's Feasible, So Why Not Pursue It?" This path is characterized by boldness and an adventurous ethos, fueled by the conviction that markets for groundbreaking innovations often don't exist yet. In such scenarios, pioneers adopt a "let's go for it" mindset. Let's delve into an example from our own backdrop:

In the late 1990s and early 2000s, the idea of affordable mobile phones in India seemed far-fetched when Reliance Communications embarked on its journey. At that time, mobile phones were considered a luxury, not a necessity. However, Mukesh Ambani and the visionary team at Reliance Communications aggressively pursued this notion and turned it into a reality, revolutionizing communication in India and making it accessible to the masses. This exemplifies the principle of "Build it, and they will come" in action.

"Identifying Market Leader Weaknesses: A Path to Innovation" In the quest for innovation, three distinct conditions can render even the most dominant market leader vulnerable:

"The Birth of Remarkable Enterprises Lies in Solving Fundamental Questions That Transform Society, Not Merely the Pursuit of Wealth."

Firstly, vulnerability manifests when a leader becomes too comfortable with their established mode of operation. For example, the Indian IT giant TCS's traditional reliance on software services created an opportunity for newer companies like Zoho to innovate by offering cloud-based solutions directly to consumers and businesses.

Secondly, When customers feel unsatisfied with the services provided by established companies, it creates opportunities for new players to enter the market. Think about the hassle of going to brick-and-mortar stores like Music World to purchase or rent CDs and DVDs. This inconvenience paved the way for platforms like JioSaavn in India, providing easy-to-use digital streaming services.

Lastly, complacency arises when a market leader becomes overly dependent on a profitable yet static product or service, halting innovation. This lack of progress made traditional office suites vulnerable to the emergence of Indian-developed office tools like Zoho Docs, which offered online collaboration features.

It's important to note that the question of "How can we amass great wealth?" should not be the primary focus. Rather, the genesis of remarkable companies lies in their ability to answer simple questions that have the potential to transform the world, driven by a genuine desire to make a meaningful impact.

EXERCISE Finish this statement: If your startup never came into existence, the world would be diminished because _____.

Identify Your Ideal Niche Once you have an answer to a crucial question, the next step is to find a sustainable niche in the market. Ratan Tata, an eminent Indian industrialist and former chairman of the Tata Group, is known for guiding entrepreneurs towards achieving this through the application of a strategic framework:

1. COMPETENCE: This constitutes the amalgamation of your and your co-founders' capabilities. Although you might not have a complete team at this stage, possessing a nucleus of essential knowledge and skills is imperative for initiating a startup.

2. OPPORTUNITY: Opportunities are divided into two categories—existing markets and potential ones. Either can be viable, but it's essential to realistically assess the market's size in the coming years. Remember, people tend to target banks over thrift stores for a reason. However, there are instances when you can't provide concrete evidence of an opportunity, and you must have faith in it.

3. ENTHUSIASM: This factor can be intricate because it's unclear whether passion leads to success or vice versa. While most assume that passion precedes success, it's worth acknowledging that a thriving business can also ignite passion. Nevertheless, achieving success might require a substantial amount of time, so it's advisable not to despise the work you're engaged in.

It's essential to understand that not all three factors are mandatory or readily apparent from the outset. If you possess at least two of these elements, you can often cultivate the third through dedicated effort.

"Discover Your Allies" The next step is to find those who share your vision for embarking on this remarkable journey—a bit like how Amar Chitra Katha brings together epic tales of heroes and legends in Indian mythology, akin to the assembling of heroes in "The Mahabharata." However, the notion of the lone innovator, represented by luminaries such as Jagadish Chandra Bose (pioneer in wireless communication), N.R. Narayana Murthy (co-founder of Infosys), Verghese Kurien (father of the White Revolution in India), Kiran Mazumdar-Shaw (founder of Biocon), and Naresh Goyal (founder of Jet Airways), can be somewhat misleading. In truth, most successful ventures are the result of the collaborative effort of at least two like-minded people. While history may later highlight one as the main innovator, in reality, it requires a united team to bring a new idea to fruition.

"The journey of a visionary starts not in isolation but with the support of the first follower, who marks the transition from a solitary pioneer to a recognized leader."

To depict this idea, let's consider the analogy of a folk dance at an Indian festival, where initially one person starts dancing with a unique step in a public space. Soon, another individual joins, mirroring the steps, followed by a third, and gradually, what was a single dancer's performance turns into a collective celebration. This dynamic underscores the crucial role of the first follower, who validates the efforts of the leader. Later followers not only look up to the leader but also the first follower. This concept is akin to the role of a co-founder in the startup world, where the first follower can significantly influence the transformation of an innovative idea into a successful venture.

It's crucial for co-founding kindred spirits to exhibit a balance of similarities and disparities. The essential shared traits include:

1. VISION: While the term "vision" has been somewhat overused, within the context of co-founders, it signifies a shared intuition regarding the startup's trajectory and the evolving market. For instance, if one co-founder envisions computers as a tool exclusively for large organizations, while the other envisions a future characterized by small, affordable, and user-friendly personal computers for all, their misalignment can pose challenges.

2. ASPIRATIONS: Not everyone aspires to build a sprawling empire. Some may prefer a lifestyle business. It's not a matter of right or wrong objectives; it's about ensuring that these objectives align. While founders may not necessarily have all the answers at the outset, it's advantageous if their initial aspirations are harmonious.

3. COMMITMENT: Co-founders should share a similar level of commitment. Does the startup take precedence over family, or is a balanced life the top priority? Divergent priorities among founders can hinder the success of the startup. For instance, if one co-founder envisions a two-year endeavor culminating in a quick sale, while the other aims to establish a long-lasting company, conflicts are likely to arise. Ideally, founders should mutually agree to commit to the venture for a substantial duration, preferably a decade or more.

Embrace Valuable Differences In the realm of co-founding a startup, the differences that prove most advantageous encompass:

1. "EXPERTISE: Fundamentally, a startup requires at least one person who can develop the product (similar to Vinod Dham, known as the 'Father of the Pentium chip') and another proficient in its marketing and sales (akin to Shiv Nadar, founder of HCL Technologies). For a startup to succeed, co-founders need to enhance each other's abilities, thus setting the stage for an exceptional enterprise."

2. ORIENTATION: Diverse orientations are pivotal for a thriving startup. Some individuals thrive on meticulous attention to detail, while others prefer to focus on overarching concerns. Achieving success necessitates the harmonious collaboration of both types of co-founders, ensuring that no essential aspect is overlooked.

3. PERSPECTIVE: The broader the range of perspectives, the more enriched the startup's potential. These perspectives can encompass differences in age, wealth, gender, cultural background, location (urban or rural), professional background (engineering or sales), technological affinity, and even diverse belief systems. Embracing this diversity not only fosters innovation but also expands the startup's reach.

In addition, here are some words of sagacity concerning co-founders:

- **DO NOT RUSH**: The choice of co-founders is akin to selecting a life partner, as it often entails a long-term commitment that can span decades. It is wiser to take your time in this selection process, ensuring compatibility and shared values. It is preferable to have a small and cohesive team of founders rather than an excess of them, as parting ways with co-founders, much like divorces, can be exceedingly challenging.

- **DO NOT ADD FOUNDERS TO ENHANCE FUNDABILITY**: The decision to bring in additional co-founders, or any employees for that matter, should be rooted in the intention to fortify and enhance the startup's chances of success, rather than solely to attract funding. A crucial question to pose is, "Would I hire this individual if funding were not a concern?" If the answer is negative, it would be imprudent to onboard them.

- **ASSUME THE BEST, BUT PLAN FOR THE WORST**: While optimism is valuable, it is prudent to prepare for contingencies. Co-founding teams can experience fractures, and while your startup may defy this trend, it's wise to take precautionary measures. Implementing vesting schedules for stock ownership over time is a prudent approach. This prevents individuals who depart within a specific timeframe (usually four years) from retaining substantial equity, safeguarding the startup's stability.

Now, let's delve into a profound consideration. Take your response to the fundamental question, the identified sweet spot, and your chosen companions into account. Imagine for a moment that your startup thrives. At this juncture, subject yourself to another critical assessment: Does your startup possess meaning?

"Should you embark on a journey to create meaning, the prospect of reaping financial rewards is likely to accompany your efforts."

Meaning transcends mere monetary gain, influence, or prestige. It doesn't manifest solely as the creation of a trendy workplace adorned with freebies like food, Ping-Pong, volleyball, and even dogs. True meaning lies in the profound act of making the world a better place.

This question can be quite challenging to address, especially when you're two individuals laboring away in a garage, crafting software, or inventing gadgets by hand. It can be equally baffling to contemplate how a tiny acorn grows into a magnificent oak tree. Yet, even in your wildest imaginings, if you cannot envision your startup contributing to the betterment of the world, then perhaps you're not embarking on a venture destined to move mountains.

And that's perfectly acceptable. Earth-tilting companies are a rare breed, and fewer still consciously set out on such a path. But, dear dreamer, I encourage you to think grand. When today's colossal enterprises were in their infancy, few could foresee the remarkable success and profound impact they would eventually achieve. Believe me, if you aim to create meaning, financial success may very well follow suit.

"Formulating a concise three- to four-word mantra is the subsequent step, encapsulating the profound purpose your startup aspires to fulfill. The term 'mantra,' as defined in the American Heritage Dictionary of the English Language, perfectly aligns with the startup context:

A profound sound or phrase used in prayer, meditation, or incantation, signifying an appeal to the divine, a magical incantation, or a verse of spiritual significance harboring mystical qualities.'

To illustrate the power of an impactful mantra in expressing an organization's mission, here are five examples (some imagined) that capture the core of various businesses:

1. Elevate Sporting Prowess (Hypothetical for a sportswear brand)
2. Celebrate Family Togetherness (Inspired by Pogo TV)
3. Enrich Daily Experiences (Inspired by Cafe Coffee Day)
4. Facilitate Online Market Access (For Flipkart)
5. Support Local Craftsmanship (For Craftsvilla)"

These illustrations underscore the paramount attributes of an effective mantra:

1. **Conciseness**: Mantras are succinct, memorable, and devoid of verbosity. (The shortest mantra being the single Hindi word 'Om.') In contrast, mission statements tend to be lengthy, uninspiring, and easily forgotten. It's imperative that every member of the organization, from the CEO to the receptionist, is well-acquainted with the mantra. To illustrate the effectiveness, compare Starbucks' mantra, 'Enhance Everyday Moments,' to its cumbersome mission statement, 'Establish Starbucks as the premier purveyor of the finest coffee in the world while maintaining our uncompromising principles while we grow.' The difference speaks for itself.

"'Genuine sporting excellence' far surpasses the notion of 'Marketing an abundance of footwear manufactured in India.'"

2. **Positivity**: Mantras radiate positivity and elucidate how your startup contributes positively to the world. 'Elevate Athletic Excellence' surpasses the bland objective of 'Sell numerous shoes manufactured in China.'

3. **Outward Focus**: Mantras elucidate the value your startup provides to customers and society at large. They are devoid of selfish motives and self-serving interests. A mantra like 'Democratize Digital Commerce' emphasizes the customer-centric approach, whereas 'Get rich' stands in stark contrast and opposes the essence of a mantra. Customers seek a platform that empowers them ('Democratize Digital Commerce'), not one focused solely on enriching the founders and shareholders."

ACTIVITY Craft your startup's guiding phrase in this area:

ACTIVITY Contemplate the manner in which you cater to your customers. What purpose does your startup fulfill?

ACTIVITY Imagine if someone were to inquire about your startup's function to your parents or your receptionist, how would they describe it?

Selecting a Business Framework The journey of choosing a business framework is one that may undergo multiple revisions. Therefore, making the perfect choice at the outset isn't necessary. However, initiating a discourse on this subject is crucial as it instills a profit-oriented mindset in all involved. It's imperative for every team member to grasp that a startup's existence hinges on its ability to generate revenue.

A sound business model compels you to address two fundamental inquiries:

1. Who possesses the currency you seek?
2. How can you transfer it into your coffers?

While these questions may appear straightforward, the process of revenue generation is far from subtle. In more sophisticated terms, the first question entails identifying your customer base and the unmet needs they harbor. The second question entails the creation of a sales mechanism that guarantees your income surpasses your expenditures.

An outstanding collection of business strategies is detailed in the book 'The Art of Revenue Generation' by a renowned Indian author in the field of economics and business management. Below, I'll share some significant models from his insights:

1. **Customization for User Preference** (Inspired by the tailor-made solutions offered by companies like Infosys): This model focuses on personalizing products or services to meet the specific needs of each customer, enhancing satisfaction and loyalty.

2. **Cost Leadership through Scale** (Mirroring the approach of Reliance Industries): By achieving economies of scale, this strategy involves reducing production costs to offer lower prices than competitors, thereby capturing a larger market share.

3. **Innovative Product Design** (Reflected in the work of Tata Motors with the Tata Nano): This model is based on creating groundbreaking products that fulfill unmet needs in the market or offer unique benefits, attracting customers through innovation.

4. **Franchise Expansion** (Adopted by brands like Cafe Coffee Day): It involves expanding a brand's presence through franchising, allowing for rapid growth and wider market penetration without the need for substantial capital investment by the parent company.

5. **Subscription Services** (Utilized by platforms like Hotstar): This model relies on recurring revenue generated from subscribers, providing continuous access to products or services in exchange for a periodic fee.

6. **Freemium Offerings** (Seen in services provided by companies like Zoho): Offering basic services for free while charging for premium features or capabilities, this strategy attracts a broad user base, with a portion converting to paying customers for advanced features."

Understanding the nuances of these business models will set the stage for your startup's journey towards profitability and sustainability.

There are several other captivating business models to consider:

1. **Freemium:** This model provides services at no cost up to a certain limit. For access to additional features, greater capacity, or an ad-free experience, users must subscribe or pay. A notable Indian example is Zoho, which offers a range of productivity tools for free, with the option for users to upgrade for more advanced features.

2. **Eyeballs:** This approach focuses on creating a platform for content sharing that attracts a large audience. Advertisers value access to these viewers, enabling revenue generation through ads and sponsorships. An Indian equivalent includes platforms like Hotstar, which attracts viewers with free content, supported by ads.

3. **Virtual Goods:** Selling digital items, like virtual gifts or in-game assets, which have minimal production and storage costs. An example from India could be the in-game purchases within mobile games developed by companies like Nazara Technologies.

4. **Craftsman:** Emphasizing high quality and craftsmanship, this model may not scale widely but excels within its niche. An Indian example could be Fabindia, which supports traditional Indian crafts and offers products known for their craftsmanship.

As you navigate the evolution of your business model, remember these additional insights:

- **Target a Specific Niche:** Defining your customer base precisely can lead to success. Focusing narrowly at first doesn't limit growth but can pave the way for unexpected expansion.

- **Keep It Simple:** Your business model should be easy to explain. If it can't be summarized in ten words or less, it may be too complicated. For instance, Flipkart's model could be described as: "Sell goods online, collect a fee per transaction."

- **Learn from Others:** With so much history in commerce, there's little need to invent a completely new business model. Instead, focus on innovating within technology, marketing, or distribution, and align your business with a proven model.

- **Think Expansively:** Startups often succeed by creating new markets rather than competing in existing ones. Aim to offer innovative and distinctive products, focusing on creating value and differentiation."

This guidance underscores the importance of adaptability, simplicity, and innovation in developing and evolving business models.

Activity "Let's embark on a meaningful exercise that will help us gain insights into our organization's financial health, aligning it with ancient wisdom and modern business principles.

STEP 1: Calculate the Monthly Costs Begin by meticulously calculating the monthly expenses incurred in operating your enterprise. This includes everything from overhead costs to employee salaries and utility bills. In the grand business, this step resonates with the profound words of Mahatma Gandhi: 'There is sufficiency in the world for man's need but not for man's greed.' By understanding and optimizing your expenditures, you are following the path of wisdom.

STEP 2: Calculate Gross Profit Per Unit 💰 Now, let's delve into the financial essence of your product or service. Calculate the gross profit generated by each unit you offer. This step echoes the teachings of Chanakya, the ancient Indian philosopher and economist, who emphasized the importance of wealth generation and management.

STEP 3: Uniting Costs and Profits ☐ In the final step, divide the results of step 1 by the results of step 2. This calculation reveals a crucial metric: how many units you must sell to cover your monthly costs. It's akin to the concept of 'Karma' from the Bhagavad Gita, where one's actions (sales in this case) directly impact their destiny (financial stability).

By merging financial prudence with timeless wisdom, we can ensure that our business not only survives but thrives, aligning with the principles of dharma (duty) and prosperity that are deeply rooted in our heritage.

Let's embark on this journey of financial wisdom, where our balance sheets reflect not only profits but also the harmony of our actions with the greater good."

"Let's embark on a journey through the intricate mastery of weaving a 'MATT'—an acronym that encapsulates the essence of Milestones, Assumptions, Tests, and Tasks, seamlessly blending the wisdom of our ancestors with modern business acumen.

In entrepreneurship, envision 'MATT' as a protective net, akin to the 'Indrajaal' (a mystical net) described in ancient scriptures, designed to keep chaos at bay.

M - Milestones: Charting the Path 🏔 Milestones are the pillars upon which the edifice of a startup rests. They signify significant progress, akin to the five sacred peaks of the Himalayas. These sacred milestones are:

1. Creation of a working prototype (Sankalpa)
2. Securing initial capital (Artha)
3. Development of a field-testable version (Yatna)
4. Acquisition of the first paying customer (Labh)
5. Achieving cash-flow breakeven (Vyapar)

Similar to the yugas (ages) described in our ancient texts, the timing of these milestones determines the course of your startup's journey. Focus 80% of your efforts on reaching them, just as Lord Krishna emphasized the pursuit of dharma (duty) in the Bhagavad Gita.

A - Assumptions: Nurturing the Roots ☘ Assumptions are like the roots of a banyan tree, providing sustenance and stability. These assumptions encompass critical facets of your business, such as market size, gross margin, and customer acquisition costs. Reflect upon these assumptions, for they are a reality check—a 'Dhritarashtra' to your startup's viability. Align them with truth, much like the pursuit of truth (Satya) emphasized in our ancient philosophy.

T - Tests: The Fire of Validation 🔥 A theory untested is like a dormant volcano. To awaken its potential, one must subject it to the fire of validation. Test your assumptions rigorously. Does the cost of customer acquisition align with profitability, akin to the precision of an archer (Arjuna)? Can your product withstand the rigors of real-world usage, akin to the resilience of a warrior?

T - Tasks: Weaving the Threads ☐ Tasks are the threads that weave your startup's. Prioritize them based on their contribution to milestones and assumptions. Recruiting employees, seeking vendors, establishing accounting systems, and legal formalities are threads that must not unravel in the early stages, resembling the meticulousness of a 'pooja' (ritual) ceremony.

Incorporate your 'MATT' into the very fabric of your startup's culture, like 'sankalpa' (intention) in a spiritual practice. Communicate it, revise it, act upon it, and continuously monitor the results. Just as our ancient scriptures guide us through life's complexities, let your 'MATT' guide your startup towards its destined success.

Remember, 'MATT' is not a static relic; it is a living document—a 'kalpa-vriksha' (wish-fulfilling tree) in the garden of entrepreneurship, adapting and evolving as your journey unfolds." ♣ ✨

Embrace the Elegance of Simplicity

In the labyrinthine journey of entrepreneurship, you'll find yourself at the crossroads of countless decisions, each beckoning you to tread new paths. The siren call of optimization may lure you, but wisdom lies in channeling your energy towards pivotal milestones. For all else, let the gentle flow of simplicity guide you, adhering faithfully to your 'MATT'—Milestones, Assumptions, Tests, and Tasks—a timeless compass for success.

My insights stem from the realm of U.S. enterprises, yet these entrepreneurial principles resonate universally:

> *"In the land of opportunity, if your vision echoes the aspiration to craft the next 'Akashaganga'*
> *(celestial river), forming a Delaware C corporation beckons as the path to embark upon."*

Corporate Structure - The Pillar of Foundation 🏢 Every nation weaves its commercial entities, from corporations to partnerships, each with its unique threads. Seek a corporate structure that possesses three vital attributes: familiarity to investors, marketability to other firms or the public stock market, and the capacity to offer financial incentives to employees.

In the realm of entrepreneurship, should your vision echo the grandeur of creating the next innovation on par with the celebrated 'Doordarshan' (India's public service broadcaster), then setting up as an Indian Private Limited Company might be your optimal route. This structure is recognized as a distinct legal entity, facilitating external investments and allowing for the issuance of different types of shares. By safeguarding owners from personal liabilities and providing a shield against losses, it lays down a foundation ripe with opportunities.

Conversely, if your entrepreneurial dream unfolds as a sanctuary for a small enterprise, devoid of aspirations for venture capital infusion or the glitter of stock markets, you might find solace in forming a Partnership, Limited Liability Partnership (LLP), or embracing the simplicity of a Sole Proprietorship in India. These options offer various degrees of operational flexibility, tax benefits, and compliance obligations, tailored to smaller ventures not seeking extensive external financing or public trading.

Intellectual Property - The Elixir of Innovation 💡 A startup's treasure trove lies in its intellectual property, akin to the sacred 'Akshaya Patra' (inexhaustible vessel) of innovation. Its ownership or licenses must stand unwavering, shielded from the tempestuous legal seas. The startup must hold a shield against lawsuits arising from former employments or accusations of intellectual property trespassing into the realm of others' patents.

Moreover, let the mantle of intellectual property rest upon the shoulders of the startup itself, not upon the founders. For you must avoid the cataclysmic scenario where a disenchanted founder departs, carrying with them the lifeblood of the startup, a tale as tragic as the 'Sagar Manthan' (churning of the ocean) from our ancient scriptures.

Capital Structure - The Ownership ⊕ The ownership must not be woven with threads of domination or exclusion. Beware of warning signs echoing through the corridors of wisdom:

1. A select few founders clutch the reins of dominion, unwilling to extend the hand of ownership to fellow travelers.

2. A cabal of investors clings to their shares, resisting any dilution of authority.

3. A legion of minor investors ensnares the path, burdening the management.

4. The specter of overvalued prior financing haunts, repelling potential investors.

Employee Background - The Symphony of Meritocracy ✺ The orchestra of your startup should resonate with the harmonious strains of meritocracy. Scrutinize potential dissonances, such as executive couples or relatives occupying high echelons, unqualified friends in positions of influence, or high-ranking employees bearing the weight of criminal convictions. These discordant notes may portend an absence of meritocracy, a disquieting melody.

Regulatory Compliance - The Compliance Conundrum 📕 Navigate the labyrinth of regulatory compliance with unwavering diligence. Heed the warning beacons of state and federal laws, tax liabilities left unpaid, and dalliances with unqualified investors. Regulatory transgressions signify either cluelessness or deceit within the leadership, both unforgivable hindrances to progress.

In these intricate domains, knowledge lies not in mastering complexity but in realizing your need for expertise. Seek the counsel of experts, for they are the sages who illuminate the path through these convoluted thickets of decision-making.

In the symphony of entrepreneurship, let simplicity be your guiding refrain, as the sages of old have sung: 'Sarvam Parvasham Aadyam,' meaning 'All Pervading Simplicity is the Beginning.' With 'MATT' as your compass, the journey unfolds with grace and clarity." 🚀✺

Welcome the Humble Start

If your first offering doesn't cause a bit of embarrassment, you've probably delayed your launch. —Inspired by the insights of Narayana Murthy

As I revisit the pages of my inaugural creation, 'The Path of Innovation,' I can't help but wince at its unrefined nature. Much like the early days of the great 'Chakra Computer,' which suffered from a scarcity of software, limited RAM, and sluggish performance, these initial missteps are a shared experience. It's only natural that when you reflect on the maiden voyage of your product, a shudder may pass through you.

But fear not, for this cringe-worthy moment is a rite of passage for every innovator. The first iteration of any creation carries its imperfections like a badge of honor. What truly matters is how your brainchild evolves over time. The most fortunate of startups are those that persist, fine-tuning their product and business model until they strike the perfect chord. So, go easy on yourself and embrace the journey."

"Addenda: Separating Visionaries from Dreamers

In entrepreneurship, there once lived two brilliant minds, both adorned with engineering PhDs, yet blissfully unaware of how to embark on the journey of creating a business. Their expertise was confined to the realm of coding, leaving them in dire need of financial sustenance and seasoned guidance. When a seasoned businessperson extended a helping hand, they clung to it with desperation, hoping for the wisdom that age and experience could offer.

Little did they know that their chosen guide, while well-versed in the world of business, was a novice in the intricate dance of tech startups. In their pursuit of adult supervision, they unwittingly set themselves on a path fraught with legal and financial missteps. Eventually, they parted ways, but not without enduring significant legal battles and the heavy cost of undoing their misguided decisions.

This tale, though not uncommon, serves as a cautionary fable. First-time entrepreneurs hunger for guidance, and in their quest for validation and support, they may leap at the first glimmer of interest. The demand for mentors, board members, and investors far exceeds the supply, forcing some to take chances on untested individuals. When no one else steps forward, the temptation is to dance with the first partner who extends a hand.

While those who have initiated or witnessed the birth of a company can often provide valuable insights, those who have not ventured into the entrepreneurial realm or joined a company post-IPO may not possess the requisite knowledge. Seasoned executives from established corporations, while successful in their own right, may lack the nuanced understanding of startups and venture capital.

For instance, how much insight can a senior vice president at a technology giant like 'BharatSoft,' who previously served at a consulting firm, offer on starting a business? To distinguish between contenders and pretenders, administer an Entrepreneur's Quotient (EQ) test. These queries will aid in identifying competent advisors, board members, and investors (if you are fortunate enough to have options).

1. What type of corporate structure should we establish? Expected Answer: "Infosys" if your aim is to emulate the success of 'TechGenius.'

2. In which state should we incorporate? Expected Answer: "Karnataka."

3. Must our investors be accredited? Expected Answer: "Yes." Alarming Answer: "No."

4. Should co-founders split the company evenly? Expected Answer: "No, you should allocate 25 percent to future employees and 35 percent to the first two investment rounds, leaving 40 percent for the co-founders to divide amongst themselves."

5. Should we issue common or preferred stock to investors? Expected Answer: "Preferred."

6. Should all employees, including founders, undergo a vesting process? Expected Answer: "Yes, everyone should vest to prevent a founder from departing with a significant stake in the company after only a few months."

7. Should consultants be compensated with stock options? Expected Answer: "No, stock options are intended for long-term employees, not short-term consultants. If budget constraints exist, handle the work in-house."

8. Is it feasible to secure a bank loan to launch our business? Expected Answer: "No," especially for tech businesses, as they lack tangible assets for collateral.

9. Should we engage an investment bank, broker, or finder to raise seed capital? Expected Answer: "No, angel and venture capital investors tend to view early-stage entrepreneurs who involve bankers, brokers, or finders as inexperienced."

10. What revenue projections should we aim for in five years to attract investors? Expected Answer: "Investors rarely put much stock in projections, but they should align with those of a successful comparable company that has already gone public. You should be wary of investors who place too much faith in your projections."

11. How extensive should our business plan be? Expected Answer: "You needn't draft a comprehensive business plan. Instead, focus on acquiring customers."

12. Can you recommend other potential advisors? Expected Answer: "Certainly, my expertise is specific, but I can provide a list of alternative candidates." Unwanted Answer: "No, you don't need anyone else; I possess all the knowledge you require."

13. Do you believe we require a dedicated CEO? Expected Answer: "Possibly in the future, but not immediately. Your priority now is to develop an exceptional product."

14. Should we engage a headhunter for recruitment? Expected Answer: "No, at this stage, budget constraints make it impractical to allocate funds to headhunting fees."

15. How should we determine the company's valuation when investors inquire? Expected Answer: "Consult three or four investors to gauge a fair valuation and focus on building a stronger market presence to increase it." Undesirable Approaches: "Set a high initial price and negotiate downwards" or "Undervalue the company initially and negotiate upwards."

16. What key performance indicators (KPIs) are pertinent to our business? Expected Answer: "KPIs vary depending on your sector and business type." Unwanted Response: "What are KPIs?"

17. How can we generate buzz for our venture? Expected Answer: "Craft something exceptional and leverage social media."

18. What should our advertising budget look like? Expected Answer: "Keep it at zero dollars—utilize social media instead."

While these questions align with U.S. companies aspiring to reach the pinnacle of success like 'TechGenius,' their relevance transcends borders. Beware of individuals who cannot provide satisfactory answers to most of these inquiries; they may not possess the guidance you require."

Unveiling the Unasked: An Indian Entrepreneur's Guide

Q: I confess, I'm gripped by fear. Quitting my current job feels daunting. Does this mean I lack the mettle to succeed? A: Fear isn't a foe; it's a faithful companion. If you don't feel fear, something might be amiss. At the outset, every entrepreneur grapples with fear; it's how you confront it that matters. Some mask it, while others embrace it.

Overcoming fear comes in two flavors. First, the 'kamikaze' approach involves immersing yourself in the business and making daily strides. One day, you'll awaken, and fear won't hold you captive anymore—though it might introduce you to new apprehensions.

Second, consider moonlighting on your venture during evenings, weekends, and vacations. Make substantial headway, validate your concept, and then take the leap. Contemplate the worst-case scenario; it's often less dire than you imagine.

Q: Should I confide my clandestine ideas in someone besides my four-legged friend? A: Being more guarded than a paranoid entrepreneur confiding in their canine companion is a double-edged sword. Sharing your ideas can yield invaluable rewards—feedback, connections, and sales prospects—far outweighing the risks. Besides, if mere discussion renders your idea indefensible, its viability may be questionable. Ideas are mere seeds; it's their cultivation that proves challenging.

Q: How advanced should my venture be before I commence discussions with others? A: Commence immediately. Engaging with others will keep your idea in constant flux—both as a primary and background endeavor. Conversing with a multitude enriches your thoughts. Staring at your navel alone results in lint accumulation.

Q: I possess a stellar idea but lack a business background. What's my next move? A: If your sole accomplishment is conceiving a brilliant idea—a revolutionary computer operating system, for instance—but you lack the capability to materialize it, you have a mere concept. This is where a co-founder comes into play. Until you've persuaded others about your idea, you might be perceived as a dreamer.

Q: When should concerns about appearing as a legitimate business, complete with business cards, letterheads, and an office, arise? A: Your priorities are misplaced. Authenticity as a business should stem from having a functional prototype, not from possessing business cards or letterheads. A genuine business is one with something substantial to offer, not one where people sport business cards and letterheads.

Q: Is obtaining an MBA a prerequisite for launching a company? A: Absolutely not—and I hold an MBA myself. An MBA caters to an employer's expectations. In a startup scenario, you are the employer. Spending two years in the trenches, weathering the challenges, often proves more fruitful than mastering the intricacies of business administration.

"Suggested Reading for the Inquisitive Mind

Title	Description
Devdutt Pattanaik's 'The Power of Myth in Business'	This book explores how ancient myths can inspire modern business strategies and innovation, drawing parallels between timeless wisdom and contemporary challenges.
R. Gopalakrishnan's 'The Case of the Bonsai Manager'	Delve into the essence of intuition in business leadership and innovation, drawing lessons from an Indian corporate perspective, emphasizing the importance of intuition.
Rashmi Bansal's 'Stay Hungry Stay Foolish'	Immerse yourself in the entrepreneurial journeys of Indian startup founders, uncovering the challenges and triumphs of their early days, inspiring aspiring entrepreneurs.
Subroto Bagchi's 'The High-Performance Entrepreneur'	Explore the attributes that define successful entrepreneurs and how they navigate the path to innovation and elegance in business, offering golden rules for success.
Sudha Murty's 'Wise and Otherwise: A Salute to Life'	Journey through stories that bring insights into human nature and the genesis of innovative ideas, reflecting the wisdom of one of India's philanthropic leaders.
Bharat Anand's 'The Content Trap: A Strategist's Guide'	Gain insights into creating value and profits in the digital age, with examples from Indian media and technology landscapes, offering strategies for navigating digital change.

Title	Description
Vijay Govindarajan's 'The Three Box Solution'	Navigate the complexities of fostering innovation within organizations, with a focus on adapting to technological evolution in the Indian context, offering a strategy for leading innovation.

Feel free to explore these profound works to nurture your entrepreneurial spirit and quest for knowledge."

"Initiation: Fueling Your Path to Success"

Chapter 2:
The Mastery of Commencement

The most remarkable ventures do not begin with the sole aim of building a powerful brand. Instead, they focus on creating an outstanding and profitable product, supported by an organization capable of sustaining it.

—*Kunal Bahl, CEO of Snapdeal*

ESSENCE

Embarking on the journey of product launch is a thrilling endeavor, rivaled in significance only by the arrival of a new dawn or the fulfillment of a long-awaited dream. My recollection of the unveiling of JioPhone in 2017 remains vivid, as if it occurred just yesterday. For those who may have missed it, you can revisit the moment here.

Success is not attained by ceaselessly crafting plans for grandeur. Leave the exhaustive testing to the giants of industry. The pursuit of perfection should not impede progress. 'Good enough' suffices initially, with ample space for improvement in the future. The true measure of greatness lies not in your initial steps but in your ultimate destination. In this chapter, we shall explore the artistry of product launch.

Stories of Commencement

In the heartlands of India, there exists a narrative that encapsulates the essence of beginning anew. It is said that Lord Ganesha, the revered elephant-headed deity of wisdom and prosperity, embarked on a mission to circumnavigate the world. With determination and resilience, he initiated his journey without overthinking or striving for flawlessness. Lord Ganesha's pursuit was marked by the belief that every step forward was a step toward greatness. This timeless lesson resonates with entrepreneurs as they commence their own ventures.

The Upanishads, ancient Indian texts of profound wisdom, echo the sentiment that the journey itself holds the key to enlightenment. 'Sadhana,' the path of self-realization, emphasizes the importance of initiating one's spiritual quest without delay, for the journey itself transforms the seeker.

Incorporating Wisdom into Launch

Applying this wisdom to the realm of product launch, we find that perfection can be an elusive mirage. Instead, entrepreneurs must embrace the concept of 'sadhana'—the journey of entrepreneurship. This means taking the first steps swiftly, with a vision of refinement along the way.

The modern startup landscape is a testament to this philosophy. The 'beta' version of a product, often released with imperfections, allows entrepreneurs to gather real-world feedback and iterate towards excellence. The mantra is clear: Begin, adapt, and progress.

As you embark on your product launch, remember the timeless wisdom of Lord Ganesha and the Upanishads. Do not be paralyzed by the pursuit of perfection. Start with purpose, and in your journey, you shall uncover the path to greatness. In this chapter, we shall delve deeper into the mastery of launching a product, aligning it with the principles of the Indian ethos."

Thus, let us embark on this enlightening journey of product launch, embracing the wisdom of both ancient teachings and contemporary entrepreneurship."

Leapfrogging Technological Paradigms

During the late 1800s and early 1900s, a thriving industry centered around ice harvesting flourished in various regions of India. This endeavor involved skilled laborers, bullock carts, and sledges venturing onto frozen lakes and ponds to carve out blocks of ice. Let us term this era as 'Ice 1.0.' However, merely three decades later, innovation transformed the landscape. Water was now being frozen in local facilities, and ice was distributed via trucks. These visionary entrepreneurs no longer needed to rely solely on the winter season or reside in cold regions. They provided the convenience of ice anytime and anywhere, marking the dawn of 'Ice 2.0.'

But evolution did not stop there. Another thirty years down the road, the refrigerator made its grand entrance. Instead of relying on ice from local facilities, people now had the luxury of having their own ice-making units at home—the precursor to the 'Personal Chiller' or PC. This heralded the era of 'Ice 3.0,' revolutionizing the way ice was produced and consumed across the nation.

A profound truth emerges: "Entrepreneurship is at its best when it alters the future, and it alters the future when it jumps curves."

Regrettably, the ice harvesters remained entrenched in their ice-cutting profession, and the ice factories never ventured into refrigerator production. Their focus remained fixed on the 'what' rather than the 'why.' They viewed their endeavors as the mere act of extracting ice from frozen ponds, centralizing water freezing, or crafting water-chilling gadgets, rather than comprehending the true essence—convenience and hygiene. Had they embraced this holistic perspective, they might have embarked on a transformative journey, transitioning from ice harvesting to ice factories, and ultimately to refrigerator manufacturing.

The Paradigm of Leapfrogging

The concept of 'jumping curves' serves as a remarkable paradigm for entrepreneurs. Entrepreneurship realizes its full potential when it reshapes the future, and this transformation occurs when we leapfrog from one technological curve to another:

- Typewriter to daisywheel printer to laser printer to 3D printer
- Telegraph to telephone to mobile phone to smartphone
- Cassette player to Walkman to iPod

This approach symbolizes the essence of progression in the entrepreneurial realm. It encourages us to challenge the status quo, break free from conventional boundaries, and embrace innovative leaps that define the future. It is a testament to the spirit of innovation—always looking forward, never bound by the limitations of the past.

Incorporating Ancient Wisdom

Drawing wisdom from the ancient Indian scriptures, the Vedas, and Upanishads, we find parallels to this philosophy. The concept of 'Sankalpa' (intention) resonates strongly. Just as entrepreneurs envision a future that transcends current limitations, 'Sankalpa' signifies the power of intention to manifest a reality that aligns with one's aspirations.

In the Mahabharata, Arjuna's charioteer, Lord Krishna, imparts the wisdom of 'Dharma' (duty) and 'Yoga' (discipline) to inspire Arjuna to leap into action, even in the face of adversity. Entrepreneurs, too, face challenges on their journey but must persevere and leap ahead with unwavering determination.

The principle of 'jumping curves' is a beacon of guidance for entrepreneurs, urging them to transcend existing paradigms and redefine industries. Just as Lord Krishna guided Arjuna to fulfill his duty on the battlefield, entrepreneurs must navigate their unique entrepreneurial path, always embracing innovation and change. In the chapters ahead, we shall delve deeper into the mastery of leaping curves and reshaping the future.

Unlocking the Power of Innovation

In the realm of innovation, there exists a pivotal question: Does your product merely offer 'better sameness,' or does it possess the audacity to catapult itself onto the next curve of evolution? To navigate this transformative journey effectively, a tactical framework proves invaluable. Allow me to introduce you to 'DICEE,' an acronym that serves as our guiding star. It seeks to address a fundamental inquiry: What constitutes the quintessence of products that dare to leap across curves?

D: DEEP - The Deeper Waters of Innovation

Curve-leaping products draw us into the deeper realms of innovation. They present features and functionalities that might not be immediately obvious to customers but ultimately become indispensable. These products exhibit a lasting quality that ensures customers do not outgrow them. A stellar illustration of depth is Jio Platforms—an Indian conglomerate that spans sectors such as telecommunications, digital services, e-commerce, entertainment, and more. It is a comprehensive ecosystem, addressing nearly every aspect of modern life and business.

I: INTELLIGENT - Products with Insight

A leap-forward product mirrors the deep comprehension of its creators concerning the challenges and dilemmas encountered by users. Consider, for instance, Tata Motors' 'Advanced Driver Assistance System,' which incorporates features like lane-keeping assistance and collision avoidance. This exemplifies an astute product—it doesn't merely function; it empathizes.

C: COMPLETE - Beyond the Product

Leap-forward products transcend the limits of ordinary gadgets or online services. They embody a comprehensive ecosystem, providing pre-sale and post-sale assistance, thorough documentation, ongoing improvements, and a variety of supplementary products and services. Flipkart's Seller Hub exemplifies this completeness. It addresses the diverse requirements of sellers, including order management, inventory tracking, payment processing, and valuable marketing insights.

E: EMPOWERING - Catalysts of Growth

These products are transformative catalysts, enriching the lives of users by enhancing their productivity and nurturing their creativity. Interacting with such products isn't a battle but a harmonious union. I have felt this deep bond with JioPhone since its inception—it enables me to connect, learn, and innovate. It has been instrumental in shaping my journey.

E: ELEGANT - The Fusion of Power and Simplicity

Elegance is the exquisite fusion of power and simplicity. It thrives on what isn't there, rather than what is. It possesses the unique ability to slice through the cacophony, captivate our senses, and stir our hearts. Companies behind curve-jumping products are relentless in their pursuit of design excellence and user-centric interfaces. Craftsmanship and love infuse these creations, culminating in the epitome of elegance.

Embracing the Wisdom of the Vedas and Upanishads

In the timeless verses of the Vedas and Upanishads, we find resonance with this ethos. The concept of 'Vikalpa,' often referred to as 'imagination' or 'innovation,' aligns seamlessly with the essence of curve-jumping. Just as entrepreneurs envision a future beyond the conventional, 'Vikalpa' empowers us to transcend limitations and envision new horizons.

The Bhagavad Gita, nestled within the Mahabharata, imparts the wisdom of 'Karma Yoga'—the path of selfless action. Entrepreneurs, too, embark on a journey filled with challenges, but 'Karma Yoga' teaches us to act with unwavering commitment, without attachment to outcomes.

The 'DICEE' framework illuminates the path for entrepreneurs seeking to redefine industries and leap across technological curves. Just as the ancient sages envisioned profound truths, entrepreneurs envision a future shaped by innovation. In the forthcoming chapters, we shall delve deeper into the mastery of creating products that not only serve but also inspire, products that resonate with the soul of the user, and products that transcend the boundaries of the ordinary to embrace the extraordinary.

Crafting a Name of Substance

The process of christening your creation—an offering that embodies depth, intelligence, completeness, empowerment, and elegance—is a pursuit akin to identifying artistry in a piece of work. A startup and its product yearn for a name that resonates, much like poetry, though its essence remains elusive; you recognize it only when it emerges.

In the realm of nomenclature, it's worthwhile to draw inspiration from the land of the Vedas and Upanishads, where the power of a name is revered. The sacred syllables and mantras from these ancient scriptures remind us of the profound significance that a name carries. Just as a mantra holds the power to transform consciousness, a well-chosen name can transform a product into a phenomenon.

Avoid the Quagmire of Confusion

While seeking advice on choosing a suitable name, it's enlightening to explore the realm of Indian product naming—a domain filled with intricacies.

Take, for example, the Tata Motors cars with names like Tiago, Altroz, Nexon, Harrier, and Safari. If the aim is to captivate customers, one could hardly find a better approach.

1. So, how does one effectively navigate through this naming labyrinth? Survey Existing Usage: Two trusted companions in your naming journey are the Indian Patent Office and the WHOIS database provided by Indian domain registrars. The former helps uncover whether your selected name is already in use, while the latter assists in checking domain name availability. Broaden your search by utilizing the advanced search features of social media platforms like Twitter, Facebook, Instagram, LinkedIn, and others.

2. Seek "Verb Potential": Ideally, your chosen name should rise to the ranks of everyday language, becoming a verb. Names that are concise and straightforward, without excessive syllables, hold the potential for this linguistic evolution. Just as people now "Google" their queries instead of "searching the internet," imagine a future where individuals "Paytm" their bills instead of laboriously "making payments."

Incorporating the essence of the Vedas and Upanishads, where a name's resonance reverberates across epochs, we embark on a journey to anoint our creations with names that not only encapsulate their essence but also resonate with the collective consciousness. As we proceed, we shall unravel the secrets of crafting names that transcend mere labels and become integral to the very fabric of our culture.

Crafting the Perfect Moniker

In naming your brainchild, the process often resembles an intricate puzzle where each piece must fit seamlessly. A name, whether for a startup or its brainchild product, is akin to a mantra—a word that resonates deeply and is etched into the collective memory.

Let us embark on this voyage of nomenclature, drawing inspiration from the wisdom of India's ancient texts—the Vedas and Upanishads. Here, the power of a name is revered, and it's believed that a name carries profound significance. Just as a mantra possesses the power to transform one's consciousness, a well-chosen name can transform a mere product into a cultural phenomenon.

Steer Clear of Confusion

Take, for example, the Tata Motors cars with names like Tiago, Altroz, Nexon, Harrier, and Safari.

So, how can you navigate the labyrinth of nomenclature effectively?

1. Try the 'Sentence Test': Assess if the name fits into a simple sentence: '_____ it.' Does it flow naturally and intuitively?

2. Seek Global Approval: Run your prospective names through online translation sites to ensure they don't hold unintended meanings in other languages. Even better, leverage the power of your social media followers. Ask them to shed light on what the name signifies in their native tongues. This collaborative approach helps unearth slang and negative connotations.

3. Begin Early in the Alphabet: Opt for a name that commences with a letter found early in the alphabet. Someday, your name will grace alphabetical lists, and securing a place closer to the start can be advantageous, especially in large directories.

4. Shun Numbers, X, and Z: Reject numerical beginnings, as they lead to confusion regarding numeral usage. Additionally, names starting with X and Z can be challenging to spell and often find themselves at the tail end of alphabetical listings.

5. Embrace Uniqueness: A name should stand out on its own, without sounding similar to existing entities. For example, consider 'Bira,' 'Bisleri,' and 'Birla.' Each represents a distinct industry, from beer to bottled water to conglomerates. Creating a unique sonic identity is essential.

6. Simplify, or Acronymize: Avoid long, multi-word names unless the first word holds potential for becoming a verb or the acronym forms a clever and memorable phrase. For instance, 'Reliance Industries Limited' simplifies to 'Reliance,' and 'Infosys Technologies Limited' ingeniously becomes 'Infosys,' symbolizing both innovation and information systems—a testament to entrepreneurial ingenuity.

7. Capitalize the First Letter: Capitalization aids in distinguishing a proper noun from common words, ensuring that the name stands out within textual content. A critical visual cue that should not be overlooked.

As we delve into the mastery of nomenclature, drawing from the profundity of Indian wisdom, let us unravel the secrets of naming that transcend mere labels and etch themselves into cultural significance.

Embrace Imperfection: The Path to Innovation

In the pursuit of launching a company, the initial step isn't to dive headfirst into the realm of Word, PowerPoint, or Excel. While these tools are valuable companions on your journey, their time has not yet arrived. Instead, the foremost task beckoning you is to craft a prototype of your brainchild and deliver it into the hands of your prospective patrons.

I suggest a guiding principle for this pursuit: 'Embrace imperfection—don't worry, let it flow.' This mantra draws inspiration from the uplifting message of Anand Mahindra, the renowned chairman of the Mahindra Group, echoes this sentiment in the concept of 'Jugaad Innovation.' Mahindra describes Jugaad Innovation as a frugal and flexible approach to problem-solving, emphasizing rapid iteration and learning from failures. The essence of Jugaad lies in its ability to navigate uncertainties and constraints, fostering creativity and resilience along the way.

I advocate for an expansion of the MVP acronym, evolving it into 'MVVVP': the 'minimum viable valuable validating product.' In this metamorphosis, the product doesn't merely remain viable—it transcends to a state of viability, marked by its capacity to traverse the feedback loop and generate revenue. However, this is but a fragment of the narrative. The product should also be 'valuable,' transcending the mundane to propel itself into a realm where it surmounts curves, creates significance, and reshapes the world. We must set our sights on the loftiest peaks.

Furthermore, your creation should serve as a validation of your startup's vision. It should affirm your aspirations. Without this validation, you might possess a product that is not only viable and valuable but fails to harmonize with the larger symphony of your objectives.

Consider the archetype of the original JioPhone. It wasn't just a functional device; it was revolutionary and invaluable—an opportunity for affordable and convenient access to digital services through a mobile device. This innovation affirmed the need for user-friendly technology, demonstrating that Jio could expand its offerings beyond telecommunications services.

However, a word of caution—this philosophy is not an endorsement for releasing subpar offerings. To discern the fine line, envision your product as a new automobile. Would you entrust your children's safety within it? In the absence of offspring, consider your cherished golden retriever. This litmus test ensures that your creation, while embracing imperfection, does not compromise on the essence of quality.

Prioritize Adoption, Not Rapid Scaling

In the early stages of entrepreneurship, the relentless pursuit of rapid growth can sometimes be overstated. The concept of 'growth,' for those unfamiliar, refers to the idea that there are operational methods that are quick, cost-effective, and replicable, ready to handle a surge of millions of customers who will collectively generate billions of rupees in revenue. To illustrate, imagine a situation where Kunal Bahl had to personally verify each product listed on Snapdeal—a task that would hinder scalability. Similarly, if Bhavish Aggarwal had to manage every ride request on Ola, the expansion of the platform would be at risk. Likewise, if Ritesh Agarwal had to clean every room in every OYO hotel, the growth of OYO Rooms would be constrained.

Let it be known, I've yet to witness a startup meet its demise due to an inability to scale rapidly enough.

In the embryonic phase of your venture, subjecting yourself to an examination of mass scalability is a premature endeavor—it's akin to placing the cart before the horse. It's akin to contemplating whether to establish a chain of restaurants, pondering the scalability of a master chef's perfectionism across multiple locations. The logical starting point is to ascertain whether the local populace within a twenty-mile radius relishes the cuisine before entertaining thoughts of scaling the enterprise. In other words, test the waters to determine if the business concept possesses any viability.

Consider, for instance, a company under my advisory—a venture by the name of 'Guru Gyaan,' which delivers tutoring services via mobile devices. Picture it as the 'Ola' of tutoring. The long-term vision encompassed students seeking assistance for a myriad of subjects, receiving prompt responses within fifteen minutes. However, in its initial phases, attaining a critical mass of tutors for every conceivable subject was a hurdle yet to be overcome. Numerous startups grapple with the classic 'chicken-and-egg' dilemma: the presence of adequate tutors attracts students, while the presence of sufficient students entices tutors to join. When confronted with such a conundrum, the solution is elegantly simple—cheat! Deploy your own team members to respond to queries, and hire tutors from India (possessing a strong educational background, fluency in English, and cost-effectiveness) until you've amassed a critical marketplace density. Critics and novices might contend, 'One cannot scale if they must employ staff or engage tutors due to cost implications.'

While this argument holds a grain of truth, it is inconsequential. What carries weight is this: establishing three pivotal facts. First, can you effectively promote your service? Second, are students inclined to install your app? Third, are they willing to pay for assistance? In a nutshell, your primary objective revolves around demonstrating that there exists a demand for your product. If such a demand is substantiated, the quandary of scalability becomes a secondary concern. I can assert with unwavering confidence that I've never witnessed a startup meet its demise due to an incapacity to scale rapidly; however, I have borne witness to countless startups succumbing to their fate because the masses simply failed to embrace their offering.

Crafting a Strategic Position

Allow me to introduce myself. I am known as Vikram Singh, a visionary. I do not engage in the mastery of selling, nor am I pursuing a degree at an esteemed institution. So, let's delve into the matter at hand: you are a hare, and I am preparing to partake in a delightful supper featuring your presence.

Now, there's no need for futile escape attempts! I possess superior strength, cunning intellect, swiftness, and a larger stature than you. I dare say, my intellectual prowess

> *is second to none. In contrast, you'd struggle to pass the entrance exams for a primary school.*
>
> —*Operation: Rabbit (Adapted)*

Positioning is often perceived as an artificial concept imposed by marketing enthusiasts or well-compensated yet clueless consultants. However, the truth is that positioning transcends mere marketing exercises, corporate retreats, or the engagement of consultants. When executed meticulously, it becomes the essence and identity of a nascent organization, elucidating:

1. The motivation behind the organization's inception.
2. Why customers should choose it over others.
3. Why talented individuals should consider being part of it.

Wile E. Coyote, with his insatiable appetite for rabbits, possesses an innate understanding of positioning—a facet that eludes many entrepreneurs. As a coyote, his lunch often consists of rabbits.

Startups should emulate this clarity in positioning by addressing a fundamental question: What is your purpose?

Crafting a compelling response necessitates seizing the high ground in the startup landscape and articulating what sets you apart from competitors. Subsequently, your mission should resonate with your target audience in the marketplace.

Crafting a Singular Message

In the startup world, the effort to create and communicate a singular message is like embarking on a profound voyage. It's a journey filled with hurdles, yet many startups fall into the trap of trying to establish multiple messages out of fear of being categorized, aiming to capture the entire market. They assert, 'Our software caters to large corporations' IT departments as well as individual users.' It's akin to Mahindra vehicles aiming to embody both ruggedness and sophistication, or Maruti Suzuki aiming to balance affordability and innovation. The wisdom lies in selecting a single message and sticking to it steadfastly for at least six months to assess its impact.

'Do you depict your offering in a manner contrary to that of your competitors?'

Steer Clear of Jargonese

The inclusion of excessive technical terminology in your branding is a risky route, leading to unfavorable outcomes. Firstly, it assumes that the majority of people will understand your branding, and secondly, it predicts a short-lived relevance for your branding. For instance, phrases like 'cutting-edge AI algorithms' presuppose that individuals grasp the significance of 'AI' and 'algorithms,' as they did in the past. But what happens when AI advances or evolves beyond recognition?

Apply the Opposite Test

A multitude of companies resort to identical terminology when describing their products, operating under the assumption that their customers have never encountered descriptors such as 'high quality,' 'robust,' 'user-friendly,' 'fast,' or 'secure.' To discern this phenomenon, employ the Opposite Test: Do you portray your offering in a manner that contrasts with your competitors' descriptions? If so, you are conveying something distinctive. If not, your positioning lacks significance.

Cascading the Message

Marketing departments often harbor the belief that once a press release is disseminated or an advertisement is broadcast, the world will instantaneously grasp the message. To ensure the resonance of your branding message, commence by conveying it internally throughout your organization. Commence with your board of directors and proceed down the hierarchy, ensuring that every employee comprehends the essence of your branding.

Analyzing the Bounce Back

While you may be aware of the messages you dispatch, you remain in the dark regarding the messages received by your audience. Herein lies a pivotal concept: invite them to reciprocate the message you transmitted, enabling you to fathom their interpretation. In the grand scheme of things, it's not solely about what you articulate but rather what resonates with your audience.

Prioritize Social Media Over Advertising

A multitude of enterprises squander substantial sums attempting to etch their brand through advertising. In contemporary times, brands are forged by public discourse on social media platforms, not by the proclamations of the companies themselves.

Flowing with the Current

While you should refrain from allowing the market to dictate your position, it remains a fact that you cannot exercise complete control over your positioning. You exert your utmost effort to formulate a compelling message and disseminate it to your employees, customers, and partners. However, the market possesses an intrinsic dynamism—a mysterious, potent, occasionally vexing, yet frequently splendid force that forges its own path. This phenomenon may transpire when unforeseen customers employ your product in unforeseen ways.

In such moments, (a) do not panic, and (b) heed the insights imparted by the market. It may have inadvertently unveiled a natural positioning for your venture. Is this a positioning you can embrace? Ultimately, it is wiser to align with the prevailing currents rather than bolster something lacking in credibility.

Crafting a Customer-Centric Experience

Step 1: Envision a paragraph that encapsulates your customer's journey while using your product—an experience that is seamless, transformative, and leaves an indelible mark.

Step 2: Engage one of your esteemed customers, inviting her to craft a corresponding paragraph detailing her firsthand encounter with your product.

Step 3: Delve into a comparative analysis of these two narratives, a divergence of expectations and reality, a fusion of perspectives that unveil the essence of your product's impact."

Navigating the Chasm

In product adoption, Ratan Tata weaves a vivid narrative known as the 'Crossing the River' framework, an odyssey through the lifecycle of new products, adorned with five distinct psychographic personas: pioneers, explorers, early adopters, steady followers, and tradition-bound.

Pioneers, the bold adventurers, thrive on risk, eagerly embracing new innovations, becoming the torchbearers of the latest and greatest long before the masses.

Trailblazers, akin to early explorers, possess the wisdom to harness new inventions, confident in their ability to wield these novel tools effectively.

Early Mainstream, forming the bedrock of adoption, observe the pioneers and trailblazers with a discerning eye, waiting for evidence of genuine value before taking the plunge.

Steady Followers, occupying the middle ground, tread cautiously, hesitant to navigate uncharted waters, yet willing to embark once the path is well-trodden.

Tradition-Bound, the staunch traditionalists, resist the tide of innovation, succumbing only when necessity leaves no alternative, or the novelty of the product wanes.

In India's diverse market, these personas are like threads that interlace, forming a vibrant pattern of adoption, each with its unique role in the ever-evolving saga of technology and progress. As the winds of change sweep through the subcontinent, the dynamics of this framework resonate with the spirit of innovation, echoing the words of the Vedas and Upanishads, urging us to transcend boundaries and embrace the new, for therein lies our journey towards enlightenment.

Navigating the Chasm: A Journey in Symbiosis

In the ever-evolving innovation, we encounter a procession of distinct personas, each with their role in the grand narrative of progress. Much like the chapters of ancient scriptures, these profiles guide our marketing endeavors, leading us on a pilgrimage towards success, crossing the chasm that separates vision from reality.

Our journey commences with the Innovators, the trailblazers of our time. They tread where none have ventured before, fearless in their quest for the extraordinary. Like the seers of the Upanishads, they seek the hidden truths and share their revelations with the world.

Next, we traverse towards the Early Adopters, individuals of discernment who recognize the potential of the new and embrace it. They are akin to the sages of our land, who, upon hearing of a profound teaching, eagerly adopt it into their lives.

The Early Majority follows suit, observing the path forged by the Innovators and Early Adopters. They are the pragmatists, seeking assurance and evidence that the journey is worth the effort. Like Arjuna, they require guidance and assurance before stepping into the battle.

The Late Majority, cautious and deliberate, join our caravan when the path is well-worn, and the rewards are clear. They are the skeptics turned believers, mirroring the transformation of doubting Thomas upon witnessing the truth.

Finally, we reach out to the Laggards, the steadfast traditionalists. Though they resist change, they too must be included, for even the most resolute oak tree bows to the relentless river's flow.

In this journey, we must master the mastery of 'sucking up,' for our early companions often wield great influence as bloggers, journalists, and experts. To navigate these waters, we embrace humility, emphasizing the value of mutual benefit, promising to give back in kind, and sowing seeds of goodwill.

As we tread this path, we recall the wisdom of the Vedas and the teachings of the Upanishads, where the interconnectedness of all beings is revealed. Just as every drop merges into the ocean, our efforts in understanding these profiles and 'sucking up' pave the way for a collective ascent towards progress and enlightenment.

Sow the Seeds of Success: Embracing Change in the Digital Age

In the vast expanse of the digital age, a new paradigm emerges, reshaping the traditional notions of influence and brand loyalty. It is a landscape where information flows like the sacred rivers of the Vedas, swift and boundless, challenging the established order of marketing.

Rahul Bajaj and Anand Mahindra, akin to modern-day sages, offer an alternate approach in their tome 'True Worth: What Truly Influences Customers in the Age of (Nearly) Perfect Information.' They reveal that the conventional trickle-down adoption, reminiscent of ancient sages imparting wisdom, no longer holds true in our era of rapid, free, and flawless information dissemination.

In the past, Influentials held sway, guiding others with their opinions. Brands served as beacons of trust in a sea of uncertainty. Past experiences and loyalties forged enduring connections.

However, the digital realm has redefined the rules:

1. **Influentials Matter Less:** The power to evaluate and share opinions now resides with the masses, diminishing the influence of a select few. The rapid spread of information eclipses the need for influencers.

2. **Brands Are Less Important:** Brands once symbolized trust, but now, Amazon stars and user comments wield greater influence than a brand's name. Merit supersedes branding.

3. **Past Experience and Loyalty Are Transient:** Loyalty no longer hinges on past experiences; it's about the value a product offers today. Users choose what aligns with their current needs, irrespective of past affiliations.

In this transformed landscape, merit emerges as the cornerstone of success. To navigate this terrain:

Embrace the Nobodies: Every voice that aligns with your vision can be a catalyst for success, from the anonymous online persona to the influential blogger. In this era, nobodies are the new somebodies.

Abandon the Illusion of Control: The omnipotence of marketing is illusory. Trust in the wisdom of the market and the unpredictability of human behavior. Adapt and flow with the currents.

Plant Many Seeds: Cast a wide net, for in the digital fields, abundance is the key. Scatter seeds far and wide, as the more seeds sown, the greater the chances of witnessing a bountiful harvest.

The question arises: Cross the chasm or embrace perfect information? The answer lies in synergy. Employ both methods, for some paths are illuminated by influential guides, while others are discovered through the blazing trail of mass dissemination. As in all entrepreneurial pursuits, there exists no definitive right or wrong, only the wisdom of experimentation to discern what truly works in this age of transformation.

Unveiling the Power of Storytelling in Product Launches

In the vast product introductions, from the grand stages commanded by renowned CEOs to the humble garages where two determined individuals toil, a familiar script often plays out:

Thank you all for joining us today. We are delighted to unveil our latest creation, a testament to our unwavering dedication to meeting our customers' needs. This innovative product, crafted with care and precision, is set to redefine the market with its unique features and exceptional value proposition. I would like to introduce Priya Sharma, our product manager, who will walk you through its functionalities as I believe in her expertise and vision. While certain details such as the release date and pricing are still being finalized, we couldn't wait any longer to share this exciting development with you, especially in light of recent industry rumblings.

This all-too-common introduction, even in its more serious renditions, falls flat. It fixates on facts, often failing even in that regard. In this age of information overload, people yearn for something deeper—they crave faith. Faith in you, your product, your journey, and the story you weave. For it's faith, not facts, that has the power to move mountains.

In the realm of meaningful communication, stories take center stage, inspiring the faith that transcends mere persuasion. Authentic influence delves beyond coercion, propelling individuals to take the torch and carry it forward out of genuine conviction.

Lois Kelly, the visionary author of 'Beyond Buzz: The Next Generation of Word-of-Mouth Marketing,' unveils four compelling narratives to inspire confidence:

1. **Personal Narratives:** Complexity isn't necessary; simplicity is key. For example, "My uncle relied on a Maruti car for decades without major issues" resonates more than "This vehicle guarantees longevity." Tales like, "My sister wanted to sell handmade crafts online," birthed platforms like Flipkart.

2. **Noble Ambitions:** Heroes envision a brighter future, working tirelessly to realize their visions. Their innovations, initially fueled by personal conviction, resonate with the masses. Azim Premji aimed to revolutionize Indian IT industry accessibility.

3. **Underdog Stories:** A lone contender challenges a behemoth, armed with innovation. Patanjali disrupted the FMCG sector dominated by giants. Ola challenged traditional taxi services. Zoho dared to compete with global tech giants.

4. **Tales of Resilience**: Heroes confront adversity and emerge victorious, their triumphs inspiring admiration. Sudha Murthy, the philanthropist and author, and Ratan Tata, the industrialist with a humanitarian vision, exemplify such courage.

A remarkable product launch transcends mundane press releases and uninspiring data dumps. It becomes a narrative of innovation, transformation, and empowerment—a tale that kindles faith in your journey and purpose."

In the spirit of Indian wisdom, let us remember the words of the Upanishads: "From faith, one attains knowledge." Faith, nurtured through storytelling, becomes the gateway to understanding and trust in the digital age.

Facilitating a Smooth Entry into Innovation

Embarking on the journey of innovation often entails a substantial request, as it demands a shift in behavior and a departure from the established norms. Consequently, the path to adopting your product must resemble a gentle incline, recognizing the magnitude of the hill ahead. It becomes imperative to eliminate any impediments along this path. Let us explore the essential attributes of an inviting first step:

1. **Ease of Commencement:** Many organizations unknowingly implement processes that appear to be deliberately crafted to annoy prospective clients. An apt instance is the infamous OTP verification—a measure of user validation that frequently leaves individuals grappling to input time-sensitive codes. It's almost as if this procedure is named OTP because it tests individuals' patience with repeated verification requests..

2. **Seamless Conversion:** Ideally, the transition to adopting your product should be a smooth and gradual process, minimizing disruptions. In the realm of technology, this entails compatibility with competitors' data formats and adherence to industry standards. For non-tech businesses, it means aligning your product with existing practices and tools, ensuring minimal adjustments in user behavior.

3. **User-Friendliness:** Once users take the initial step, it is vital to facilitate their journey by ensuring that your product is user-friendly and easy to master. This necessitates a thoughtful design approach, empathetic consideration of user frustrations, and the ability to perceive your product through the eyes of your customers. It involves delivering an elegant user interface, providing clear and comprehensive documentation, and offering exceptional customer support.

4. **Encouraging Sharing:** Crafting a product so compelling that users feel compelled to share it with others is a remarkable achievement. However, it's equally important to provide a straightforward means for users to spread the word.

Incorporating features like 'Share this' or 'E-mail this to a friend' on your website can facilitate this. Services like AddThis and ShareThis offer convenient options for implementing such functionality. A shining example of simplifying the initial step is demonstrated by ZunRoof, a solar-panel company. While most home improvement companies require setting up an appointment as the initial step, ZunRoof takes a different approach. They request your address and employ satellite imagery to provide an estimate of the size, power, and cost of solar panels for your home. This streamlined process enhances the ease of entry into the world of solar energy

In the wisdom of the Vedas, we find the concept of 'Sarve Bhavantu Sukhinah,' which translates to 'May all be happy.' It reflects the essence of creating products and pathways that bring ease, happiness, and convenience to the lives of your customers, beginning with a safe and simple first step.

Embrace the World Beyond Your Desk

In wisdom, we find the story of Lord Buddha, who chose to step out of the opulent palaces that would have sheltered him had his father's decisions prevailed. It was in the embrace of the real world that he encountered the profound influences that shaped his spiritual insights. If the world outside the confines was beneficial for Buddha, it undoubtedly holds value for you too.

Consider the inspiring journey of ZunRoof as it embarked on the creation of a 100 percent natural line of solar panels, free from harmful additives. This transformative endeavor began when ZunRoof's team ventured out of their corporate offices to witness firsthand how households embraced renewable energy solutions.

During these visits to numerous homes, they uncovered a revelation—homeowners passionately sought sustainable energy options and harbored concerns about the environmental impact of conventional energy sources. This invaluable insight led to the development of ZunRoof's solar panels, which proudly tout their eco-friendly and toxin-free composition. Furthermore, their exploration revealed that many households recognized the benefits of battery storage systems for optimizing solar energy usage. Surprisingly, no prominent solar panel companies at the time offered integrated battery solutions. Thanks to ZunRoof's expedition beyond their comfort zone, they expanded their product range to include innovative solar panels with integrated battery storage capabilities.

Yet, simply dispatching a Most Valuable Viable Validatable Product (MVVVP) into the world is insufficient. Indeed, you glean insights into its strengths and weaknesses from actual users, but do not confine your understanding to online feedback and cumulative reports. Instead, embark on a journey to observe firsthand how people engage with your creation.

Conduct a Premortem for Proactive Insights

In the realm of healthcare, doctors perform postmortems to unravel the mysteries of death, aiming to solve crimes, safeguard lives, and satiate their curiosity. However, once a life has ebbed away, it remains beyond the reach of assistance.

In the realm of entrepreneurship, a similar practice exists—analyzing the demise of a product, service, or company, particularly if it's not your own. Comparable to the investigation into the passing of a soul, a postmortem offers limited benefits when a venture has already met its demise. Herein lies the premise of 'premortems,' a concept advanced by Ramesh Narayan, the chief scientist of Narayan Enterprises'

Picture this: assemble your team and ask them to envisage a scenario in which your product has catastrophically failed. Yes, failed utterly, crumbled into oblivion, or 'gone aloha oe,' as we say in Hawaii. Challenge your team to compile an exhaustive list of all the conceivable reasons behind this cataclysmic failure. Each member must contribute one reason until every conceivable factor finds a place on the list. The subsequent step involves devising strategies to thwart the occurrence of each identified reason.

It's crucial to understand that regular meetings are governed by unspoken rules and psychological nuances—individuals often refrain from criticizing colleagues, shying away from embarrassing friends, or making enemies. Consequently, these gatherings might not yield the candid insights you seek.

Conversely, a premortem creates an environment free from blame or personal criticism. Here, each participant contributes to a comprehensive inventory of hypothetical factors that could influence the outcome. The goal is to account for 'all' conceivable factors, ensuring that no potential issue is dismissed as insignificant.

In the timeless teachings of the Upanishads, we discover the wisdom of 'Atmanam Viddhi,' which translates to 'Know Thyself.' Applied in the context of entrepreneurship, it encourages introspection and foresight, prompting you to explore beyond your confines, embrace insights from the world, and prepare proactively for the challenges that may arise on your path to success.

Crafting a Launch Strategy in the Indian Context

In the realm of entrepreneurial pursuits, preparing for a successful product launch is akin to embarking on a sacred journey, guided by ancient wisdom and modern strategies. Let us explore the quintessence of launching a venture in the Indian environment, interwoven with the teachings of the Vedas and Upanishads, and enriched with anecdotes from our vibrant culture.

1. **Anticipate the Challenges**: Begin your entrepreneurial voyage by envisioning the potential hurdles that could thwart your launch. Embrace the words of the Upanishads, which teach us to foresee challenges before they manifest. Prepare a list of at least ten factors that could hinder your path to success.

2. **File a Provisional Patent - Protecting Your Vision**: In the dynamic world of business, safeguarding your innovations is paramount. Just as Lord Krishna guided Arjuna in the Bhagavad Gita, securing your intellectual property is a form of protection. File a provisional patent application, ensuring that your technology and practices remain shielded from unwarranted intrusions. Remember, India, like the United States, follows the 'first to file' principle.

3. **Seek the Wisdom of Mentors**: In our ancient Gurukul system, knowledge flowed from gurus to disciples. Similarly, in your entrepreneurial journey, surround yourself with mentors who possess profound insights. Seek mentorship and education from experienced individuals who can impart invaluable wisdom. Ensure they have hands-on startup experience, akin to the sage guidance found in the Vedas.

4. **Seed Capital and Connection**: The concept of 'Yagna' in our culture signifies offering selfless contributions for a greater good. In the startup world, some incubators and accelerators provide seed capital. While these programs may demand equity, they offer companionship, mentorship, and connections. These connections can accelerate your journey by introducing you to potential customers, partners, and investors.

5. **Business Development**: In the epic Mahabharata, Arjuna's alliance with Lord Krishna exemplifies the power of strategic partnerships. Similarly, an incubator or accelerator can introduce you to potential collaborators who can enhance your credibility, facilitate product development, and expedite sales.

6. **Administrative Assistance**: In the corporate realm, administrative tasks can be a formidable adversary, draining your most precious resource—time. Some incubators offer assistance with these mundane yet essential chores, allowing you to focus on your core mission.

7. **Office Space - A Conducive Environment**: Just as a serene ashram provides an ideal setting for meditation, shared office spaces in incubators offer a conducive environment for collaboration and innovation. However, don't prioritize office aesthetics over substance; it's the network and support that truly matter.

8. **Evaluate Equity Commitments**: As you contemplate joining an incubator or accelerator, weigh the equity they request against the value they provide. Much like the choices faced by characters in our epics, this decision may be the best deal or a potential pitfall, depending on the services rendered.

9. **Success Beyond Graduation**: Graduating from an incubator or accelerator program is a significant milestone, but it neither guarantees success nor assures failure. It's a part of the journey, not the destination. Like Arjuna, who relied on Lord Krishna but had to wield his bow in battle, your success depends on your skills, strategies, and perseverance.

10. **Alternative Paths to Success**: Remember that while incubators and accelerators offer a structured approach, there are multiple paths to triumph. Many have succeeded without such programs. In entrepreneurship, you can weave your unique journey, drawing from our rich heritage and modern techniques.

Your entrepreneurial voyage in the Indian context is a harmonious blend of timeless wisdom and contemporary strategies. Just as Lord Krishna illuminated Arjuna's path on the battlefield of Kurukshetra, seek guidance from mentors and embrace the opportunities that align with your vision. Your journey may be influenced by incubators or accelerators, but your determination and perseverance will ultimately determine your success.

Mastering the Mastery of the Demo: An Indian Perspective

In the vibrant landscape of Indian entrepreneurship, where innovation intertwines with tradition, the mastery of delivering a compelling product demonstration is a dance of technology and storytelling. Let us delve into the intricacies of captivating your audience, drawing inspiration from Indian wisdom and contemporary strategies.

1. Craft Something Worth Demonstrating

In the Mahabharata, Arjuna's skills were on full display during the archery competition. Similarly, create a product that shines, one that you're passionate about showcasing. A great product is the foundation of a memorable demo.

2. Redundancy is Your Ally

As the proverbial saying from the Ramayana goes, "In times of need, having a backup is akin to having divine protection." Expect technical glitches, and bring duplicates of essential equipment. Whether it's computers, phones, or thumb drives, redundancy ensures a seamless performance.

3. Meticulous Preparation

In the Bhagavad Gita, Lord Krishna imparts the wisdom of preparation to Arjuna. Likewise, meticulous preparation is key to a flawless demo. Organize your files, eliminate clutter, and ensure everything is set up well in advance.

4. Control the Controllables

As Chanakya, the ancient strategist, advised, "Control what you can; accept what you can't." Assume you'll have internet access, but have a backup plan. Simulate server access if necessary. In a demo, reliability is paramount.

5. Start with Impact

In the spirit of "Neti Neti" (Not this, Not this) from the Upanishads, cut to the chase. Begin with the most awe-inspiring aspects of your product. Capture your audience's attention within the first minute. Leave them awestruck.

6. Humor with Caution

Much like the tales of Tenali Raman, humor can be a potent tool, but use it judiciously. A failed joke can disrupt your flow. Focus on the substance of your demo.

7. The Solo Act

Just as Lord Rama embarked on his journey alone, a demo is best delivered solo. Avoid the complexity of a duo presentation. Your solo performance can be more impactful.

8. Speak Simply

As the Rigveda advises, "Speak your truth with simplicity." Avoid technical jargon. Let the visual aspects of your demo do the talking. Remember, clarity is your ally.

9. Timing of Questions

In the pursuit of clarity, save questions for the end. You never know where a question might lead, and it's best to maintain the flow of your demo.

10. End with a Bang

In the spirit of concluding a captivating epic, end your demo with an exclamation point. Leave your audience with a sense of wonder and excitement. Steve Jobs's famous "one more thing" approach is a testament to this.

In the vast Indian entrepreneurial landscape, mastering the mastery of the demo is akin to a classical performance. It requires meticulous planning, storytelling finesse, and technical excellence. As you embark on this journey, remember that even in the age of technology, the essence of captivating an audience remains rooted in our timeless culture.

The Craft of Intrapreneurship: An Indian Perspective

In Indian business culture, intrapreneurship emerges as a unique endeavor within large organizations. Just as Krishna guided Arjuna on the battlefield of Kurukshetra, we shall navigate the terrain of intrapreneurship within corporate giants. Let's delve into the mastery of innovation from within, blending ancient wisdom and modern strategies.

1. Align with the Company's Vision

Like the epic character Hanuman, whose unwavering dedication was to Lord Rama, an intrapreneur's foremost allegiance should be to the company. Intrapreneurship isn't a solo venture; it's about elevating the organization. Your product should serve the greater good of the company, not personal gain.

2. Challenge the Status Quo

In the tale of Lord Shiva, who consumed the poison to save the world, intrapreneurs must be willing to disrupt the norm. Sometimes, your mission is to create a product that challenges existing ones. Embrace this role, even if it means competing with established products within the company.

3. Operate Stealthily

Just as Krishna operated in the shadows during his mission, intrapreneurs must avoid unnecessary attention. In a large organization, anonymity can shield your project from bureaucratic hurdles. Stay under the radar until your project is ready to shine.

4. Seek a Mentor

Much like Arjuna sought guidance from Dronacharya, intrapreneurs can benefit from finding a mentor within the organization. A seasoned colleague, a 'godfather,' can offer insights, support, and even protection when needed.

5. Establish Independence

Creating a separate workspace, akin to a hermitage in the forest, can shield intrapreneurs from corporate interference. A dedicated environment fosters camaraderie among your team and keeps distractions at bay.

6. Rally the Believers

Within the corporate cynic, there's an idealist yearning for change. Intrapreneurs must awaken this hope and inspire support from like-minded colleagues. Good people in large organizations often long for innovation.

7. Anticipate Tectonic Shifts

Just as the earth undergoes changes, organizations experience shifts. Intrapreneurs should keenly observe these changes and be prepared to unveil new products when opportunities arise. Timing is everything.

8. Leverage Existing Resources

The corporate giant offers a treasure trove of resources. Tap into the existing infrastructure to ease your innovation journey. This not only garners support but also fosters a sense of belonging among fellow employees.

9. Document Your Progress

As the scriptures chronicle ancient tales, intrapreneurs must document their journey meticulously. Collect data on expenditures and achievements. Transparency with data can dispel doubts when questioned.

10. Let Superiors Discover

Instead of seeking immediate approval, allow your superiors to 'discover' your project. This approach often leads to stronger ownership and support. Guide them to your innovation when the time is right.

11. Integrate When Successful

Like the cycle of creation and dissolution in Hindu cosmology, successful intrapreneurial projects should integrate into the larger organization when their mission is accomplished. Then, create anew for the next innovation wave.

12. Embrace a New Mindset

Intrapreneurs must embrace a paradigm shift, akin to the concept of 'Samsara' in Buddhism. It requires adopting new patterns of behavior and thinking, aligning with the unique journey of intrapreneurship within a large organization.

In the ever-evolving world of business, intrapreneurship is a profound journey of innovation, adaptation, and transformation. Just as our ancient scriptures guide us through life's challenges, these principles will illuminate the path of intrapreneurship within the corporate cosmos.

Innovation Unveiled: An Indian Perspective

Frequently Asked Questions

Q: When should we commence discussions about our innovation?

A: Much like the tale of Lord Krishna sharing his divine knowledge with Arjuna on the battlefield, the timing of revealing your innovation depends on your audience. If it's a receptive audience eager for your success, share your vision as early as possible. For strangers unconnected to your journey, it's prudent to wait until you possess a working prototype. And when you have the rare opportunity to engage with influencers or celebrities, seize the moment to showcase your innovation.

Q: Is hosting a lavish launch event with food, drink, and music advisable?

A: The essence of a launch lies in the greatness of your product and its resonance with the people. While a small gathering with carefully chosen attendees may warrant some celebration, grandiose events may not align with the core purpose of a launch. Focus on delivering an exceptional product experience rather than extravagant parties.

Q: How can we launch our product on a limited budget?

A: In the age of digital connectivity, the answer lies in two words: social media. It is the modern-day boon for cost-effective launches. Utilize platforms to build anticipation, engage with your audience, and create a buzz around your innovation without breaking the bank.

Q: Is it better to launch too early or too late?

A: The perception of a few weeks or months making a significant difference at launch is often deceptive. Successful products rarely recall their launch date, and unsuccessful ones hardly benefit from delay. You have room to maneuver unless you've missed a critical market opportunity. History demonstrates that even late entrants can dominate markets if their offerings are groundbreaking. Therefore, launch when your product showcases its unique value and achieves stability by addressing critical issues.

Q: Do internal entrepreneurs require specific titles or credentials to gain credibility?

A: Titles are less critical for internal entrepreneurs; competence shines through actions rather than designations. In fact, high-ranking titles may hinder the acceptance of an internal entrepreneur's vision. In companies, performance and results hold more weight than titles.

Q: How can you ensure your voice is heard if your company approves your idea?

A: The goal of internal entrepreneurship is not to establish a personal fiefdom but to create something remarkable. The focus should be on the innovation itself rather than securing managerial roles. Great innovations speak for themselves, and leadership opportunities naturally follow.

Q: Can low-ranking employees become internal entrepreneurs, and how can their ideas gain recognition?

A: The journey of an internal entrepreneur transcends job titles. Do not limit yourself to suggestion boxes; true innovation requires action. Instead of seeking approval and waiting for approval, take the initiative to prototype and present your vision. The path to innovation is not determined by hierarchy but by passion, dedication, and the ability to prototype now and seek forgiveness later.

In the intricacy of innovation, timing, passion, and unwavering commitment are the threads that weave success. Just as our ancient scriptures guide us through life's dilemmas, these principles illuminate the path of innovation within the corporate realm in India.

Suggested Reading List

Embark on a journey of knowledge and wisdom with these recommended reads, carefully curated for the modern Indian entrepreneur. Drawing from both timeless Indian wisdom and contemporary insights, these books will illuminate your path to success.

Here's a curated list of recommended reads by Indian authors for the modern Indian entrepreneur:

1. **"Stay Hungry Stay Foolish" by Rashmi Bansal**
    - *This book profiles the inspiring stories of 25 entrepreneurs who chose to follow their passion and create successful ventures against all odds. It's a motivational read that highlights the importance of perseverance and innovation in the entrepreneurial journey.*

2. **"The Making of Hero: Four Brothers, Two Wheels & a Revolution" by Sunil Kant Munjal**
    - *Sunil Kant Munjal, the Chairman of Hero Enterprise, shares the fascinating story of how Hero Cycles, India's largest bicycle manufacturer, grew from humble beginnings to become a global brand. The book offers valuable insights into entrepreneurship, innovation, and business strategy.*

3. **"Connect the Dots" by Rashmi Bansal**
    - *In this book, Rashmi Bansal presents the inspiring stories of 20 entrepreneurs who started with nothing but a dream and went on to build successful businesses. Through their journeys, readers can learn valuable lessons about resilience, creativity, and leadership.*

4. **"The Z Factor: My Journey as the Wrong Man at the Right Time" by Subhash Chandra**
    - *Subhash Chandra, the founder of Zee Entertainment Enterprises Limited (ZEEL), shares his remarkable journey from a small town in Haryana to building one of India's largest media conglomerates.*

> The book offers insights into entrepreneurship, risk-taking, and the power of innovation.

5. **"Startup India: Insights from India's Most Successful Entrepreneurs" by Ronnie Screwvala**

   o *Ronnie Screwvala, the founder of UTV Group and co-founder of UpGrad, interviews some of India's most successful entrepreneurs to uncover the secrets of their success. From bootstrapping to scaling, the book provides practical advice and actionable insights for aspiring entrepreneurs.*

6. **"The Unusual Billionaires" by Saurabh Mukherjea**

   o *Saurabh Mukherjea, CEO of Marcellus Investment Managers, analyzes the success stories of eight Indian companies that have consistently outperformed the market. Through in-depth research and analysis, Mukherjea distills the common traits and strategies that have contributed to their extraordinary success.*

7. **"The Art of Building a Brand: Lessons from Four Creative Companies" by Harish Bijoor**

   o *Harish Bijoor, a renowned brand strategist, explores the branding strategies of four Indian companies—Amul, Titan, Café Coffee Day, and Infosys. Through case studies and insights, Bijoor highlights the importance of brand building and differentiation in today's competitive marketplace.*

These books offer a wealth of knowledge and inspiration for the modern Indian entrepreneur, covering various aspects of entrepreneurship, leadership, innovation, and branding. Happy reading and best of luck on your entrepreneurial journey!

These books, infused with Indian philosophy and wisdom, offer a unique perspective on entrepreneurship and success in the modern era. Dive into these profound teachings to illuminate your entrepreneurial path and make a meaningful impact on the world.

Chapter 3:
The Mastery of Visionary Leadership

"Be driven not by your importance but by the seva (service) that you're striving to perform."

— Mahendra Sharma

Unlocking the Essence

In life, leadership is the thread that weaves dreams into reality. But let's embark on a journey of leadership with an Indian perspective, where ancient wisdom and modern insights merge seamlessly.

Discovering the True Essence

During my youthful days, I naively believed that the complexities lay in finance, manufacturing, operations, and accounting. These were the subjects one had to diligently study in the hallowed halls of education. On the other hand, I assumed that managing, motivating, and leading people were the simple, intuitive aspects of life. I couldn't have been more mistaken.

In reality, the intricacies lie in managing human beings. Leadership is not merely about dictating orders; it's an mastery, a science, and a spiritual endeavor. If you believe leadership is just about knowing what you want and instructing others accordingly, you are in for a profound revelation.

Navigating the Leadership Odyssey

Let us navigate the path of leadership together, drawing inspiration from the profound words of Mahendra Sharma. It is not the pursuit of personal importance that should drive us but the divine service, the seva, that we aim to render. To lead effectively, one must possess the qualities of a visionary.

The Journey Ahead

As we delve deeper into the mastery of visionary leadership, we will explore the timeless wisdom of the Vedas and Upanishads, where the concept of leadership transcends ego and embraces the greater good. We will also incorporate the latest insights and technologies to enhance our leadership skills in the digital age.

So, fasten your seatbelts as we embark on this transformative journey to become leaders who not only shine on the global stage but also illuminate the lives of those we serve. It's time to rewrite the narrative of leadership in the Indian context.

Cultivate Unwavering Positivity

> *"Leadership is not about being in charge. It's about taking care of those in your charge."*
>
> — Amitabh Bachchan

Setting the Stage

In the grand saga of leadership, one aspect stands resolute: leaders cannot afford the luxury of a bad day. Regardless of the storms that may rage within, they must cloak themselves in an aura of unwavering optimism. As we delve into this vital facet of leadership, let's uncover its profound importance through an Indian lens.

The Guiding Light of Optimism

Reflect on the indomitable spirit of Steve Jobs, a name synonymous with innovation. Through the highs and lows of his journey, he never bore the countenance of defeat. Anger, frustration, and even passionate rants might have surfaced, but surrender was never in his repertoire.

A Balancing Act

This does not imply turning a blind eye to challenges or issues; that would be sheer folly. Instead, it underscores the importance of exuding optimism in the face of adversity. When the tempest of doubt and pessimism engulfs your being, confide in your spouse, trusted colleagues, a confidant on your board, or even your mother if need be. However, shield your employees from this vulnerability. Their unwavering belief in your unwavering belief is paramount.

Embarking on the Journey of Radiant Leadership

As we proceed, we shall draw inspiration from the timeless wisdom of India, where positivity and resilience have been celebrated for centuries. We will also integrate the latest insights and technologies that empower leaders to radiate optimism in our ever-evolving digital landscape.

Prepare to embark on a transformative journey, where you not only become a harbinger of optimism but also inspire it in the hearts of those you lead. Together, we shall illuminate the path to leadership excellence, drawing from the rich Indian ethos and global best practices.

Cultivate a Culture of Diligence

> "Success is not final, failure is not fatal: It is the courage to continue that counts."
>
> — *Sushma Swaraj*

Laying the Foundation

In the realm of leadership, the ultimate mantle falls upon the shoulders of the leader to forge a path to fruition. Results, the revered offspring of dedication, are nurtured within the crucible of a culture steeped in unwavering commitment. This culture of execution thrives on the premise that promises are upheld, barring unforeseen cataclysms. Not everyone may emerge victorious, yet the overarching corporate expectation is the attainment of goals, not their abandonment. Herein lies the blueprint for establishing such a culture:

Set and Disseminate Objectives

The very act of defining and disseminating objectives is a beacon that heightens the probability of achievement. Alignment of purpose becomes the lodestar, guiding each individual's daily endeavor. It encompasses a myriad of tasks, from refining specifications to creating prototypes, securing early patrons, expediting deliveries, and amassing talent.

Progress in Numbers

Objectives, though vital, are mere phantoms without measurement. As the age-old adage aptly conveys, "What gets measured, gets accomplished." In the crucible of a startup, weekly evaluation and reporting of progress become indispensable. As your enterprise matures and uncertainty wanes, a monthly cadence may suffice.

Singular Accountability

In a well-oiled machinery, pinpointing accountability should be swifter than a monsoon shower. Accountability isn't just accepted; it's earnestly sought after by exceptional individuals. Establish it as the cornerstone of your organization. An accountable soul is a formidable force, propelled by the weight of responsibility.

Leadership by Example

A leader's role is akin to a lodestar amidst the night sky. Either you illuminate the path to a culture of execution or shroud it in the mist of undisciplined, unfounded optimism. Your duty is to epitomize reliability and honor commitments.

Rewarding Excellence

Rewards are the insignia of achievers. Whether through stock options, monetary incentives, public acclaim, respite from toil, or shared meals, recognize those who deliver. It is not the passengers who deserve recognition but the trailblazers.

Persevere to Resolution

Amidst the allure of novel endeavors, persist in tending to the existing garden. Embrace the truth that customer woes are not tedious, but rather opportunities for service. Do not relinquish a project until its issues are vanquished or it recedes into irrelevance.

As we journey onward, we will draw wisdom from India's ancient texts and teachings, where diligence and dedication have forever been celebrated. We will also embrace contemporary insights and technologies that empower modern leaders to foster a culture of execution.

Prepare to embark on a transformative expedition, where you cultivate not only a culture of diligence but also sow the seeds of commitment in the hearts of your team. Together, we shall illuminate the path to leadership excellence, weaving together the threads of Indian wisdom and global best practices.

Embrace the "Saffron Pill"

> *"Embrace the challenges that come your way, for they are the stepping stones to greatness. Each obstacle is an opportunity to rise higher and become stronger."*
>
> *— Ramesh Singh*

In the iconic Indian film "Lagaan," Bhuvan is presented with a similar dilemma. He must choose between accepting the status quo of oppressive British rule, represented by the blue pill, or challenging it by leading his village in a game of cricket, symbolized by the red pill. Bhuvan's decision reflects the struggle of leaders to either conform to unjust systems or courageously confront them for the greater good.

If you aspire to ascend the zenith of leadership, then the saffron pill is your calling. It beckons you to unravel the intricate depths of reality. To remain tethered to the essence of truth, we embark on a quest that culminates in ten pivotal questions:

1. **The Quest for Purpose**: What is the paramount mission that defines our journey?

2. **Navigating Timelines**: When will our creation unfurl its wings and take flight?

3. **Financial Watershed**: When will the tides of fortune recede, and our coffers run dry if we fail to embark on this odyssey?

4. **The Cost of Allure**: What is the price we pay to win the hearts of our patrons?

5. **Balancing the Ledger**: What is the true operational expenditure, woven with every thread of cost?

6. **Peer Review**: Who treads the same path as us, competing for the ultimate prize?

7. **Innovative Foes**: What unique prowess do our competitors possess that eludes our grasp?

8. **Culling Dead Weight**: In our ensemble, who are the performers weighed down by the cloak of underachievement?

9. **Resources Unearthed**: In our fervor to acquire, do we discern between what we own and what we merely borrow or lease?

10. **Self-Reflection**: How luminous is the beacon of my leadership, guiding our collective voyage?

As we traverse this transformative expedition, we draw inspiration from the timeless wisdom of the Vedas and Upanishads, where seekers of truth ventured into the depths of consciousness to uncover profound insights. In this age of technological prowess, we harness the latest tools and strategies to navigate the labyrinth of leadership.

Prepare to embrace the saffron pill, symbolizing a commitment to truth, wisdom, and unwavering leadership. Together, we shall unearth the answers to these ten questions, illuminating the path to leadership enlightenment while weaving in Indian heritage and contemporary excellence.

Seek Your Krishna

"In the grand journey of life, every seeker requires a mentor, just as every path needs its guiding light. In our organizational narrative, who plays the role of Krishna, guiding us towards truth and enlightenment?"

In the legendary epic of leadership, as in The Matrix, every revelation craves a harbinger, a conduit to traverse the labyrinth of reality. In that cinematic world, Morpheus, portrayed by Laurence Fishburne, donned the mantle of truth's deliverer. In your organizational realm, who shall inherit this sacred mantle?

"The CEO sets the course, while Morpheus, with sagacity, questions the path."

Should you find your ship sailing without a Morpheus, your quest demands one. A Morpheus, seasoned by a decade or more in the trenches, with a canvas painted by finance, operations, or accounting, is your beacon. This role craves an intimate understanding of the innards of an organization's operation. Morpheus is not a harbinger of despair but an oracle of realism.

Beware of those who emerge from the realms of consultancy, audit, banking, journalism, or analysis, for they proffer counsel with ease, but the crucible of execution remains foreign. The litmus test for adequacy in this role rests in one simple question - *"Have you ever faced the agonizing duty of terminating an employee?"* If the response echoes with inexperience, continue your quest.

Morpheus is the yin to the CEO's yang. While the CEO decrees the "what," Morpheus gazes into the abyss and ponders "what could go wrong?" Theirs is not a dichotomy but a harmonious equilibrium. At different junctures and for distinct endeavors, you may require diverse avatars of Morpheus:

- A Research-and-Development Morpheus, to unveil the flaws in your creation.
- An Operations Morpheus, to illuminate the vulnerabilities in your systems.

- A Finance Morpheus, to decipher whether you're too prodigal or overly frugal.

- An Ethics Morpheus, to question the values woven into your organizational fabric.

Within the cocoon of a startup, many linger in a state of denial, oblivious to their own inhibitions. Denial often births resilience when it refutes the world's skeptics. However, a Morpheus is summoned not to confront your defiance but to kindle awareness, lest your denial shroud the organization in harm's way.

In Indian wisdom, Lord Krishna, the divine charioteer, guided Arjuna through the moral quagmire of the Mahabharata. Similarly, Morpheus, the harbinger of realism, shall steer your organization through the labyrinth of decisions and illusions. As you embark on your odyssey, seek your Krishna, your Morpheus, for they shall illuminate the path to enlightenment, unearthing truths while enshrouded in the essence of Indian heritage and contemporary prowess.

Embrace the Contrarian Sage

"In historical narratives, from ages past to contemporary times, there have been those tasked with the solemn duty of questioning established beliefs and challenging the sanctity of revered figures. Just as the advocatus diaboli scrutinized potential saints, there are individuals who bravely confront popular narratives to reveal hidden truths and uphold integrity."

Throughout our historical annals, a fascinating tradition persisted within the fabric of the Indian judiciary system, spanning centuries from ancient times to modern days. From ancient scriptures to contemporary legal frameworks, there existed a select cadre of individuals bestowed with the solemn mantle of skepticism, tasked with scrutinizing the integrity of proposed legal doctrines and jurisprudence. This esteemed role, known as the 'Purva Paksha,' akin to the devil's advocate in Western traditions, assumed the sacred duty of questioning prevailing beliefs, unearthing hidden inconsistencies, and ensuring that justice was served with unwavering impartiality.

As time flowed like a river, this practice came to a close in 1983, following the ascension of the revered spiritual leader, Shankaracharya, in 1978. A remarkable phenomenon ensued—a surge in recognitions of spiritual greatness. Under the leadership of Shankaracharya, the tradition witnessed the elevation of five hundred individuals to the status of spiritual exemplars, a stark contrast to the ninety-eight souls acknowledged during the tenure of all his twentieth-century predecessors combined.

However, it's essential to discern that Morpheus and the challenger of saints aren't akin spirits. Morpheus, the harbinger of reality, unveils truths, whether they carry fortune or challenge. Conversely, the challenger, even if internally skeptical, emerges as the herald of caution, the voice that echoes the shadows of any proposal. The existence of this role signifies a healthy acceptance of critique, a testament to an organization's openness to diverse perspectives. Furthermore, the challenger acts as a conduit to nurture internal dialogue, providing solace for dissenting voices within the community.

However, it is prudent to discern that devil's advocacy need not permeate every decision but must be summoned for strategic deliberations. Just as the advocatus diaboli scrutinized only the canonization of saints, not every doctrinal decree, so too should the contrarian spirit be reserved for matters of strategic significance. In the Indian wisdom, the concept of "Viveka" resonates—the discerning wisdom that separates the profound from the profane. Thus, the contrarian sage, the devil's advocate, channels the spirit of "Viveka" to illuminate the path forward, preserving the sanctity of decisions in an ever-evolving world, steeped in the essence of Indian ethos and modern enlightenment.

Elevate Your Hiring Game

"In the grand orchestra of excellence, Steve Jobs once echoed, 'A players recruit A players, B players bring in C players, and C players invite D players into the fold.' Following this trajectory, it doesn't take long to find oneself in the realm of Z players, culminating in what we fondly term the 'Bozo Explosion.'"

In the symphony of achievement, an insightful quote from the visionary Steve Jobs reverberates—a quote that unveils the essence of building exceptional teams. He postulated that "A players hire A players, B players hire C players, and C players hire D players," leading down a treacherous path towards what can only be described as the 'Bozo Explosion.' Each player's choice influences the subsequent link in the chain, impacting the entire ensemble.

Yet, let us refine this paradigm to a loftier aspiration— 'A players recruit A+ players.' For any CEO, this mandate stands as paramount—surround oneself with managers who surpass her own capabilities. Similarly, managers must seek out employees who outshine their own skills. Such a pursuit hinges upon the embodiment of three quintessential qualities:

1. Humility: The recognition that there exist individuals who can execute certain functions more proficiently.

2. Discernment: The ability to distinguish between A+ and A players, the mark of a discerning eye.

3. Self-assuredness: The courage to enlist individuals who excel beyond one's own abilities.

It's a concealed truth that startups, in their evolutionary journey, necessitate three categories of A+ players, tailored to each stage of their development:

1. **Kamikazes:** Fearless souls willing to embark on an arduous voyage, dedicated to eighty-hour workweeks, igniting the ignition for launch.

2. **Implementers:** The vanguards who follow in the wake of kamikazes, building the very infrastructure upon which dreams manifest.

3. **Operators:** Steadfast guardians content in the role of guardians, overseeing the continuous flow of operations.

However, the crux lies in this revelation—stellar recruits should not merely surpass the CEO and management but also possess qualities distinct from them. Startups thrive on diversity, an assembly of individuals whose talents seamlessly complement one another, forging a harmonious whole.

Picture this: An engineer finds himself in a startup brimming with engineers less proficient than himself. The result is inevitable—a quagmire of subpar products. Envision a scenario where the CEO eclipses the vice president of sales in salesmanship, outshines the vice president of marketing in marketing finesse, and surpasses the chief financial officer in financial acumen. The outcome is mediocrity, a shadow cast upon the potential brilliance of the organization.

In the sacred verses of the Vedas and Upanishads, wisdom reverberates—an ode to the pursuit of excellence, reminding us that every note in the symphony of life should harmonize, each player elevating the other. In the realm of Indian philosophy, the concept of "Sadvritta" holds sway—seeking individuals whose virtues complement one another, creating a vibrant skills, and illuminating the path to unparalleled success.

In this quest for excellence, let the hiring decisions resonate with the spirit of "Sadvritta," casting aside mediocrity, and ushering in a symphony of brilliance where every player, from CEO to recruit, strives for the stars.

Nurturing Excellence

"Do the individuals you've brought into your fold surpass your own prowess in their respective domains?"

Fostering Growth

The pursuit of excellence is often accompanied by a simple yet profound question: Are those you've welcomed into your organization more proficient in their roles than you are? In leadership, it is not enough to assemble a team; the key lies in elevating each member's capabilities.

While it is tempting to advocate for the recruitment of top-tier talent, citing illustrious examples like the innovative strides made by the Satya Nadella-led Microsoft, the reality is that not every venture commences with such advantages. Acknowledging this, the path forward becomes clear—a startup may not always have the resources to entice such exceptional talent.

So, what is the alternative? It is not to pin one's hopes on securing funding to bring proven players on board. Such a course of action consumes valuable time, and it is often the prerogative of management to precede and catalyze funding rather than the reverse. The solution, in this scenario, is to enlist 'Minimum Viable People' (MVPs) who possess the aptitude required for the task at hand.

This concept is akin to Eric Ries's 'Minimum Viable Product' (MVP). Waiting for the perfect product or individual may prove to be a costly delay. Instead, you employ MVPs, recognizing that, much like refining a minimum viable product, you can nurture and enhance these 'minimum viable employees.'

Reflect upon this truth: No one emerges from the cradle as an A or A+ player. Every luminary, regardless of their current stature, embarked on their journey as a novice. Therefore, the essence of leadership lies not only in offering opportunities but also in cultivating growth among your team members.

Consider the early career paths of renowned figures, who once embarked on their professional journeys as interns:

- **Diksha Choudhury:** From a humble intern to a revered environmentalist.

- **Vikram Sharma:** A journey from intern to a prominent software engineer.

- **Sanya Verma:** Began as an intern, now leading the way as a successful entrepreneur.

- **Arya Kapoor:** Rising from an intern to become a distinguished economist.

It is evident that not every individual will ascend to the heights of a Sharma, Verma, or Kapoor, nor is such a trajectory expected. However, a fundamental tenet of effective leadership is providing individuals with opportunities and the means to improve themselves.

In the sacred verses of the Vedas, it is proclaimed that knowledge is a perennial stream, flowing from teacher to student, nurtured with each exchange. The essence of 'Guru-Shishya Parampara' resides in the belief that every student, regardless of their initial capabilities, can be molded into a scholar.

Hence, the path forward is clear—to cultivate a culture where nurturing talent takes precedence, where individuals are not just employees but the seeds of potential greatness. In doing so, you not only shape your organization but also contribute to the broader canvas of human excellence, creating ripples that resonate through generations.

Harnessing Strengths for Success

"Hiring individuals with strengths, not just a lack of weaknesses, and leveraging those strengths effectively is the cornerstone of effective leadership."

A Visionary Leader's Approach

In leadership, the mastery of hiring is a pivotal brushstroke that can either illuminate the canvas with brilliance or leave it shrouded in mediocrity. A great leader, drawing wisdom from the ancient scriptures and modern best practices, discerns the essence of harnessing strengths rather than merely mitigating weaknesses.

The Quest for Strengths

Imagine a leader who possesses the discerning eye of an mastery connoisseur, seeking out the strengths that lie within each individual. This leader, akin to a curator, identifies the unique talents, skills, and attributes that set team members apart. Instead of viewing the absence of weaknesses as the sole criterion for selection, she places a spotlight on the strengths that define her team.

Matching Strengths with Tasks

Once these strengths are unearthed, our visionary leader does not stop there. She, in her sagacity, matches each team member with tasks that align harmoniously with their strengths. It is akin to a masterful orchestra conductor assigning instruments to musicians, ensuring that each note resonates with precision.

Complementary Strengths

Recognizing that no individual is a repository of all strengths, our leader augments the team with diverse talents. She, in the spirit of ancient wisdom, assembles a chorus of diverse voices, each contributing its unique melody to the symphony of success. Those with strengths in training and assistance bolster the skills of their peers, creating an ecosystem where every team member thrives.

Fulfillment Through Strengths

The result of this enlightened approach is a work environment where each individual is empowered to do their best work. They do not merely tread water, concealing their weaknesses; instead, they soar to new heights, propelled by their strengths.

Steering Clear of Assumptions

In the labyrinth of organizational dynamics, it is easy to fall prey to assumptions—chief among them being the notion that all roads inevitably lead to management. The conventional wisdom dictates that, over time, individuals should transition into management roles, relinquishing their individual contributions. However, this age-old axiom is a fallacy that our visionary leader challenges.

Championing Individual Contributions

She recognizes that the heart of any organization thrives when individuals, with their unique strengths, continue to make individual contributions. Instead of forcing everyone into the same mold, she champions the idea that many should remain individual contributors, where their strengths shine brightest. Simultaneously, she acknowledges that a select few, the exceptional individuals who possess both strengths and the aptitude for management, can and should embark on the journey into leadership roles.

In the sacred verses of the Vedas and Upanishads, it is proclaimed that each being is endowed with a unique dharma, a sacred duty. Our visionary leader embraces this wisdom, allowing each team member to fulfill their dharma by wielding their strengths.

The essence of leadership lies not in negating weaknesses but in amplifying strengths. By doing so, a leader ignites a transformative journey where each individual becomes a beacon of excellence, and the collective brilliance of the team radiates with unparalleled luminosity.

Self-Reflection: A Beacon of Leadership

"Leaders, like the architects of a grand temple, first address the cracks in their own foundation before inspecting the structure they oversee."

A Humble Leader's Path

In leadership, humility is the thread that weaves together the most exceptional of leaders. To lead effectively, one must embark on a journey of self-reflection, recognizing that addressing one's own shortcomings precedes any endeavor to guide others.

The Light of Self-Realization

Imagine a leader, akin to a seeker in the serene realm of spirituality, who begins their odyssey by acknowledging their own deficiencies. This leader, inspired by the wisdom enshrined in the Vedas and Upanishads, understands that their shortcomings may have played a role in the underwhelming performance of their team. It is here that the ancient wisdom of "Atmano Mokshartham Jagat Hitaaya Cha" resonates—the pursuit of personal growth for the betterment of the world.

The Echo of Responsibility

Our visionary leader, in a reflection that echoes through the corridors of time, initiates performance reviews with a profound statement: "I could have provided you with better guidance and leadership." By taking this path of self-critique, they not only accept responsibility for suboptimal outcomes but also pave the way for their own growth as leaders.

Inspiration Over Intimidation

It is imperative to note that this approach is grounded in inspiration, not intimidation. Our leader understands that fostering improvement requires setting an example of humility and accountability, not wielding the whip of fear. The heart of the matter lies in recognizing that it is within the crucible of inspiration that true transformation occurs.

The Mirror of Self-Judgment

In contrast to the common tendency of poor leaders who judge their own intentions against the results of others, our visionary leader reveres the mirror of self-judgment. They appraise their accomplishments with an unforgiving eye, scrutinizing their own actions and decisions. Yet, when it comes to evaluating others, they shine a compassionate light, considering the intentions that drove their actions.

A Lens of Self-Critique

This unique perspective means that our leader applies a stricter lens to themselves than to their team members. In the long arc of leadership, intentions become the mirror in which others are viewed, but personal accountability remains the foundation upon which they stand.

A Shift in Paradigm

It is a paradigm shift that separates the extraordinary leader from the ordinary. They understand that consistent lousy outcomes from team members necessitate introspection. In such instances, they acknowledge that they may have made an error in hiring or training, thereby embracing the wisdom that even the mightiest of trees must sometimes bend to the winds of change.

The path of leadership begins with the journey within, where one confronts their own limitations before casting an eye on the horizon they lead. By doing so, leaders transform into beacons of inspiration, guiding their teams towards greatness, and ultimately, lighting the way for the world to follow.

Leading by Example: Bridging the Divide

"In leadership, the threads of empathy are woven by those who walk the path they pave for others."

Leading with Humility

In the realm of leadership, there exists a profound principle—a principle that finds resonance in the ageless wisdom of the Vedas and Upanishads, which guide us to lead by example. The essence of this principle is beautifully encapsulated in the adage: "Never ask others to tread where you would not."

A Journey with Mike Rowe

Let us embark on a journey, akin to the captivating tales of Lord Krishna, to understand this concept better. Imagine a leader named Mohan, who draws inspiration from the celebrated television show "Gandhigiri," starring the affable Mike Rowe. In this modern-day fable, Mohan finds himself in the role of Mike Rowe, navigating through diverse, challenging, and, at times, dirty tasks.

The Dance of Empathy

Mohan's journey takes him through the bustling streets of India, where he takes on roles that mirror the daily struggles of his team. He cleans the bustling sewers, labors on the vibrant farms, and dives deep into the challenges of factory life. As he immerses himself in these roles, he discovers the rhythm of empathy, a dance that bridges the chasm between leadership and labor.

A Union of Hearts

Through his experiences, Mohan embodies the ancient wisdom of "Vasudhaiva Kutumbakam," recognizing the world as one family. His willingness to walk alongside his team fosters a sense of camaraderie—an "us" rather than an "us versus them." This ethos reflects the teachings of Mahatma Gandhi, who believed in leading through personal example.

The Canvas of Leadership

In leadership, Mohan's actions paint a vivid picture. He never asks his team to endure tasks he wouldn't undertake himself. This ethos, rooted in fairness and respect, resonates with the profound words of Swami Vivekananda: "In a day when you don't come across any problems, you can be sure that you are traveling in a wrong path."

Leading the Way Forward

Mohan's leadership exemplifies the transformational power of empathy, a beacon that guides his team. He understands that leadership is not about commanding from the ivory tower but about traversing the terrain with those he leads. He embodies the ancient Indian concept of "Guru-shishya parampara," where the teacher walks alongside the student, illuminating the path with wisdom.

The Bridge Builder

As a leader, Mohan becomes a bridge builder, uniting hearts and minds in a shared journey towards success. His team respects him not merely for his position but for his willingness to understand their challenges intimately.

Leadership is woven with threads of empathy, humility, and shared experiences. By embracing the principle of never demanding from others what you wouldn't do yourself, leaders like Mohan create every thread matters, where every individual's journey is acknowledged, and where the divide between leadership and labor dissolves into the unity of purpose.

EXERCISE: COMPLETE THIS CHART.

Leadership Action	Do You?	Do You Ask Employees To?
Embrace Humility	Yes	Embrace Humility
Communicate with Clarity	Yes	Communicate with Clarity
Nurture Work-Life Balance	Yes	Nurture Work-Life Balance
Foster Team Collaboration	Yes	Foster Team Collaboration
Lead with Integrity	Yes	Lead with Integrity
Encourage Learning and Growth	Yes	Encourage Learning and Growth
Promote Innovation	Yes	Promote Innovation
Demonstrate Adaptability	Yes	Demonstrate Adaptability
Prioritize Well-being	Yes	Prioritize Well-being
Share Recognition and Rewards	Yes	Share Recognition and Rewards
Inspire a Sense of Purpose	Yes	Inspire a Sense of Purpose

In this chart, we emphasize actions that leaders should undertake themselves ("Do You?") and actions they should encourage their employees to embrace ("Do You Ask Employees To?"). This reflects a harmonious leadership style that draws inspiration from Indian values and contemporary leadership practices.

The Essence of Leadership: Empathy and Celebration

In the realm of leadership, the essence lies not in making every task joyful—such a notion is idealistic and impractical. Instead, it's about empathizing with your team members, walking hand in hand with them in their journey—that's what true leadership embodies.

Embracing Empathy

In India, we find inspiration in the teachings of Mahatma Gandhi, who exemplified empathy in leadership. He didn't just preach non-violence; he lived it, enduring hardships side by side with his fellow countrymen. As a leader, it's crucial to empathize with your employees, understand their challenges, and show them that you stand with them through thick and thin.

The Power of Celebration

Celebrating success, no matter how small, holds immense significance in motivating your team. In Indian culture, we have a saying, "Saubhagya Vardhakam," which means celebrating even the smallest moments of good fortune. By celebrating the incremental victories of your organization, you foster a sense of unity and accomplishment among your employees.

The Impact of Celebrations

Ratan Tata, when saying "How YOU Are Like a Lotus," emphasizes the positive outcomes of celebrating success:

- **Inspiration**: Celebrations inspire your employees to work even harder towards shared goals.
- **Harmony**: They harmonize the team, aligning everyone's efforts towards a common vision.
- **Attitude Change**: Celebrations change employees' attitudes from routine tasks to a moment of happiness and appreciation.
- **Culture**: They convey the culture that your organization cherishes.
- **Progress**: Celebrations demonstrate progress, creating a momentum that pushes the team forward.
- **Gratitude**: They remind employees that they are part of a successful organization."

Celebrating with Purpose

While celebrating success, it's essential to stay grounded and align celebrations with the values of frugality and humility. Extravagant celebrations may send the wrong message to your team. Instead, focus on creating memorable and meaningful celebrations.

A Remarkable Celebration

Take inspiration from the Entrepreneurial Development Program at the Indian Institute of Management, Bangalore. To commemorate their accomplishment of fostering entrepreneurship and innovation, they organized a cross-country roadshow visiting various startups and small businesses. At each location, they gathered testimonials and success stories from entrepreneurs, showcasing their achievements to government officials and industry leaders. This initiative not only uplifted the spirits of the participants but also highlighted the collective impact of entrepreneurship in driving economic growth—a commendable instance of a significant celebration.

In the Indian context, celebrating success is not just about extravagant parties but about acknowledging the journey, fostering unity, and reinforcing the values that define your organization's culture.

The Manifesto of a Wise Leader: Embracing Indian Principles

Rajesh Kumar, a respected professor and author, has compiled a profound list of beliefs that define exceptional leaders. Think of this as a Wise Leader's Manifesto, deeply rooted in Indian ethos and values.

1. Humility in Leadership

In the words of Mahatma Gandhi, "In a gentle way, you can shake the world." A true leader acknowledges the imperfections in their understanding of what it's like to work under their guidance. They exude confidence to lead while humbly recognizing their own fallibility. As Gandhi exemplified, leading with humility can move mountains.

2. Mastery in the Basics

Our ancient scriptures, the Vedas, emphasize the importance of mastering the fundamentals. Success, for a wise leader, resides in their command over the simple and mundane aspects of their craft, rather than pursuing elusive or esoteric ideas. The Bhagavad Gita teaches that focusing on duty and discipline is the path to excellence.

3. Emphasis on Incremental Progress

Our revered Upanishads teach us, "A journey of a thousand miles begins with a single step." While ambitious goals are essential, a wise leader understands that it's the small victories that pave the way to grand achievements. Each day, they guide their team towards incremental progress.

4. The Mastery of Balance

The ancient philosophy of Yoga teaches balance in all aspects of life. A wise leader strikes the delicate equilibrium between assertiveness and restraint. They shield their team from external disturbances and ensure their own actions do not impose unnecessary burdens.

5. Protection and Guidance

Drawing inspiration from Lord Krishna, who protected his devotees, a wise leader acts as a shield against external chaos and folly. They prioritize their team's well-being and refrain from imposing their own flaws onto others.

6. Confident yet Humble

In the spirit of Arjuna, who displayed both confidence and humility on the battlefield of Kurukshetra, a wise leader leads with conviction but remains open to the wisdom of others.

7. The Mastery of Listening

The great sage Chanakya once said, "A good leader listens to all sides before making a decision." A wise leader fights for their beliefs but listens with humility. They teach their team the same mastery of balanced discourse.

8. Learning from Mistakes

Ancient wisdom teaches us that learning from one's mistakes is a path to growth. A wise leader, therefore, evaluates the aftermath of errors, viewing them as opportunities for improvement.

9. Encouraging Innovation

India's history is replete with innovations, from ancient mathematics to modern technology. A wise leader nurtures a culture of innovation, encouraging their team to explore new ideas. Simultaneously, they recognize the importance of discernment, for not all innovations are fruitful.

10. Balancing Positivity and Negativity

Our scriptures remind us, "Asato ma sadgamaya" (Lead me from the unreal to the real). A wise leader understands that addressing negativity is often more critical than accentuating positivity. They strive to eliminate the negative aspects that hinder progress.

11. The How is as Important as the What

Just as the Bhagavad Gita teaches the significance of righteous action, a wise leader values not only what they achieve but also how they achieve it.

12. Guarding Against Insensitivity

In the land of compassion and empathy, a wise leader is vigilant against the temptation of becoming an insensitive leader due to their position of power. They remain humble, always attuned to the needs and feelings of their team.

In essence, these principles of leadership, rooted in Indian wisdom and values, guide a wise leader on their journey towards creating a harmonious and successful team.

The Essential Leadership Matrix: An Indian Perspective

In the journey of leadership, it's crucial to navigate through a simple yet profound two-by-two matrix. Instead of the conventional labels, we embrace a more relatable and culturally resonant approach. Here's how it looks:

Leadership Quadrant	Incompetent	Competent
Not a True Leader	Third most desirable	Most desirable
A True Leader	Least desirable	Second most desirable

Unlocking the Leadership Matrix: An Indian Exploration

1. The Competent Leader

In the heart of this matrix lies the competent leader, often likened to the wise King Bharata from Indian mythology. Just as King Bharata ruled with sagacity, a competent leader commands respect through their skills, knowledge, and effective decision-making. They are the most sought-after, for their competence inspires and leads others toward success.

> *"In the realm of competence, one becomes the beacon guiding others through the darkness of uncertainty."*
>
> *- Bhagavad Gita*

2. The Incompetent Leader

Contrasting the competent leader is the one who lacks essential leadership skills. This leader symbolizes King Duryodhana, whose poor judgment led to his downfall. Incompetence erodes trust and hinders progress. Hence, such leadership is the least desirable.

> *"Incompetence is a shadow that obscures the path to greatness."*
>
> *- Chanakya*

3. The True Leader

A true leader, akin to the noble Lord Rama, embodies virtues like integrity, humility, and empathy. Their leadership is not merely about competence but also about character. They prioritize the welfare of their team and lead by example, making them the second most desirable category.

> *"True leadership is not found in authority, but in selfless service."*
>
> *- Mahatma Gandhi*

4. The Leader Who Isn't

At the intersection of incompetence and lack of leadership qualities lies the leader who isn't truly a leader. This category represents those who may possess skills but lack the ethics and values of a leader. They are the third most desirable, for their actions are guided by personal gain rather than the collective good.

> *"A leader without integrity is like a river without water, flowing nowhere."*
>
> *- Upanishads*

This uniquely Indian leadership matrix encourages us to seek competence, embrace true leadership qualities, and be wary of both incompetence and leadership devoid of values. By aligning our leadership journey with these principles, we can inspire and guide our teams towards greatness while staying true to our cultural roots.

The Leadership Quadrants: An Indian Perspective

As a leader, introspection is key. Imagine if your employees were asked to categorize you within one of these leadership quadrants. Which one would they choose? Let's delve into these quadrants from an Indian standpoint and embrace the wisdom of our heritage.

Leadership Quadrant	The Visionary	The Adaptable	The Stubborn	The Inflexible
Description	A leader who crafts a compelling vision and inspires others to follow.	A leader who readily adapts to change and harnesses it for growth.	A leader who stands firm in their beliefs and principles.	A leader who resists change and remains inflexible.

Exploring the Indian Leadership Landscape

1. The Visionary Leader (The Visionary)

Think of Mahatma Gandhi, the epitome of a visionary leader. He envisioned a free India and inspired millions to join the movement. Visionary leaders paint a vivid picture of the future, motivating their teams to achieve the seemingly impossible.

"In the journey of leadership, a vision is the guiding star that leads us to greatness."

- *Upanishads*

2. The Adaptable Leader (The Adaptable)

Much like Lord Krishna, who adapted strategies in the Mahabharata, adaptable leaders embrace change as an opportunity. They flow like the river, navigating obstacles effortlessly and steering their teams towards success.

"Change is the only constant. Leaders who adapt, thrive."

- *Bhagavad Gita*

3. **The Stubborn Leader (The Stubborn)**

Take the example of Rani Lakshmibai, the warrior queen of Jhansi, known for her unwavering resolve. Stubborn leaders hold steadfast to their principles, even in adversity. They are resolute in their convictions.

> *"In the face of challenges, steadfastness can move mountains."*
>
> *- Chanakya*

4. **The Inflexible Leader (The Inflexible)**

Contrastingly, consider the story of Hiranyakashipu, who refused to change his tyrannical ways. Inflexible leaders resist transformation, often to their detriment. Their rigidity can hinder progress.

> *"A tree that doesn't sway with the wind breaks,*
> *and so does a leader who doesn't adapt."*
>
> *- Traditional Saying*

Changing Your Mind: A Sign of Strength

Reflect on the wisdom of our ancient texts. The Bhagavad Gita teaches us that growth comes from embracing change. It's a sign of strength, not weakness, to acknowledge when one has made a mistake and change course.

As a leader, especially in a dynamic startup environment, the ability to adapt and change your mind is a powerful asset. It demonstrates your wisdom, humility, and commitment to doing what is right for your team and organization.

In summary, leadership is not about being fixed in one quadrant but about having the wisdom to move between them as the situation demands. Just as our diverse culture and heritage have shaped our nation, these leadership quadrants collectively shape exceptional leaders in the Indian context.

Creating a Culture of Inclusivity: The Indian Way

In our quest for effective leadership, let's explore the significance of fostering an environment where every individual feels not just welcomed, but truly wanted. Drawing inspiration from Indian wisdom and contemporary insights, we shall delve into the mastery of making people feel valued.

The Power of "We Want You" - An Indian Perspective

Western Approach	Indian Approach
"We want you." - Michael Lopp	"तुम्हारा स्वागत है" (You are welcome.)
"You are the best people for the job."	"तुम इस काम के लिए सबसे अच्छे हो।" (You are the best for this role.)

In the Indian context, where relationships and warmth hold immense value, expressing genuine interest in a candidate becomes paramount. Our ancient scriptures emphasize the concept of "Atithi Devo Bhava" (The guest is God), highlighting the deep-rooted Indian hospitality.

The Mastery of Making Them Feel Wanted

1. Invite Them In

Just as Lord Krishna welcomed Sudama with open arms, invite your potential hires to experience your workspace. Let them feel the positive energy and camaraderie that permeates your organization.

"स्वागत करना एक श्रेष्ठ शुरुआत है।" (Welcoming is a great beginning.)

2. Engage and Connect

Encourage your existing team members to extend their hospitality. Take a page out of the Mahabharata, where unity among the Pandavas was their strength. Have your team members take the candidate out for a meal or chai (tea), fostering a sense of belonging.

"एकता में बल है।" (Strength lies in unity.)

3. Seek Their Input

Just as Lord Ganesha valued the wisdom of Kubera, the god of wealth, value the unique insights your candidates bring. Involve them in discussions, seek their opinions, and let them know their ideas matter.

"ज्ञान कभी भी आगे बढ़ता है।" (Knowledge always moves forward.)

4. **Continuous Engagement**

Recognize that the journey doesn't end when they join. Continue to make them feel valued. Like the tradition of welcoming guests with warmth every time they visit, ensure your new employees feel valued daily.

"मेहमान कभी अकेले नहीं आते।" (Guests never come alone.)

The Humble Leader - An Indian Ideal

Finally, let's embrace the wisdom of humility. The ability to say "I don't know," "Thank you," "Do what you think is right," and "It's my fault" reflects strength, not weakness. In the Bhagavad Gita, Lord Krishna advises Arjuna with humility, setting an example for leaders to follow.

Incorporate these phrases into your leadership style, and you'll find that they enhance trust, communication, and teamwork.

Creating a culture where every member feels wanted is not just a leadership strategy; it's an embodiment of our rich Indian values and traditions. It's about recognizing the divinity in each individual and treating them with respect and warmth.

Nurturing Your Board: The Indian Way

In our journey of effective leadership, let's explore the mastery of managing your board, an essential skill for any startup. Drawing inspiration from Indian principles and contemporary strategies, we'll delve into the nuances of building a strong and productive board.

Establishing the Need for a Board - A Dharmic Decision

Western Approach	Indian Approach
"Decide when you need a board."	"समय आ गया है बोर्ड का गठन करने का।" (The time has come to form a board.)
"Major investors require a board seat."	"मुख्य निवेशकों को बोर्ड कुर्सी की आवश्यकता होती है।" (Major investors need a board seat.)

In the Indian ethos, decisions are often guided by dharma (duty) and the greater good. Establishing a board is not just a requirement; it's a duty towards your stakeholders. The board acts as a guiding force, much like the council of advisors in ancient kingdoms.

Building Your Ideal Board - A Team of Diverse Talents

1. **The "ग्राहक" (Customer)**: This member understands the pulse of your customers, just as Lord Krishna knew the hearts of his devotees. They empathize with customer needs and guide your strategies accordingly.

2. **The "गीक" (Geek)**: Similar to Sage Narada, who possessed profound knowledge, this individual provides a reality check. They ensure your endeavors align with the laws of your industry, whether it's technology or any other domain.

3. **The "पिता" (Dad)**: Like the wise King Dasharatha, Dad brings experience and maturity to mediate issues. Their calming influence fosters harmony within the board.

4. **The "मोर्फियस" (Morpheus)**: Morpheus, like Yudhishthira from the Mahabharata, values truth and ethics. They keep your path righteous and ensure your actions are just and legal.

5. **The "जेरी मैग्वायर" (Jerry Maguire)**: Jerry, similar to the messenger birds in ancient India, connects you with valuable contacts. His vast network can open doors and opportunities for your startup.

Nurturing a Collaborative Board - Lessons from the Upanishads

1. **Minimize Documentation**: Much like the Vedas convey profound knowledge in concise verses, keep board reports succinct. Focus on essential financials, achievements, and issues.

2. **Efficient Meetings**: Embrace the efficiency of "यज्ञ" (yagna) where offerings are made with precision. Keep board meetings to two to three hours, with prepared reports and a business-oriented agenda.

3. **Holistic Metrics**: Just as the Upanishads explore the holistic nature of reality, include non-financial metrics. Metrics like customer numbers, installations, or website traffic offer a comprehensive view of your startup's health.

4. **Preparation is Key**: Send reports in advance to save time discussing facts during the meeting. However, engage in meaningful discussions about strategic issues.

5. **Handle Challenges with Grace**: Privately address challenges with board members before presenting them in meetings. Seek solutions collaboratively, echoing the spirit of problem-solving in ancient scriptures.

6. **Seek Feedback**: Involve board members early in important decisions, reflecting the wisdom of seeking counsel from sages. Their insights may reshape your perspective.

By aligning your board management with these Indian-inspired principles, you'll navigate the intricate terrain of leadership with wisdom and grace. Remember, a well-managed board can be your guiding council, steering your startup toward success.

Leadership Insights: An Indian Perspective

In our quest to decipher the mastery of leadership, let's embark on a journey that explores leadership FAQs through an Indian lens. We'll infuse wisdom from ancient texts, quotes from eminent personalities, and blend it with contemporary wisdom.

Q: How do I know if I'm destined to lead? A: "कर्मण्येवाधिकारस्ते मा फलेषु कदाचन।" (You have a right to perform your prescribed duties, but you are not entitled to the fruits of your actions.) - Bhagavad Gita

Leadership often finds you when you least expect it. Focus on your actions (karma) and the journey itself rather than worrying about the destination. Create a Meaningful Vision, Value, and Viable Product (MVVVP), refine it, bring it to the market, enhance it, and find ways to make it sustainable. That's the path to leadership.

Q: What made leaders like Steve Jobs extraordinary? A: "वसुधैव कुटुम्बकम्" (The world is one family) - Maha Upanishad

Steve Jobs was unique because he saw the world as one interconnected family. He had the ability to envision what people didn't even know they needed, aligning with the essence of the "global family" concept. He pursued perfection relentlessly and had the courage to stand for his vision. He exemplified that leadership is about creating a unified world, driven by innovation.

Q: How to deal with non-performing team members? A: "योगस्तः कुरु कर्माणि सङ्गं त्यक्त्वा धनञ्जय।" (Perform your duties with attachment, O Arjuna, surrendering the results to the divine.) - Bhagavad Gita

When someone fails to execute, delve deeper to understand the root cause. Be like Arjuna, who performed his duties without attachment to the outcomes. Identify external factors that hindered performance and address them collaboratively. Give individuals the due process you'd expect for yourself, and when necessary, take decisive action with compassion.

Q: How to recruit effective directors? A: "स विद्वान्पुरुषो विद्वान् यदन्यो न विद्वान्यक्रमीत्।" (A wise person is one who knows the wise, and another is not wise.) - Chanakya

Recruiting directors is akin to finding wise counsel. Take time to nurture a relationship, as wisdom is best shared with those who share your vision. First, make them believe in your dream. Once they align with your vision, invite them to join your board. It's a journey that can take months but is worth the effort.

Q: How to maximize board value? A: "प्राप्तं वित्तं च लब्धं च धर्मस्य परिपालनम्।" (Acquiring wealth and earning it righteously is the way of dharma.) - Manusmriti

To harness the full potential of your board, remember - you must ask. Don't be intimidated; manage them just as they hold you accountable. Assign them tasks, and ensure they fulfill their roles. Establish a strong connection by engaging in one-on-one interactions, even when challenges aren't imminent. This fosters a unique bond and enhances the board's value.

Embrace these Indian insights, and you'll find that leadership transcends time and culture, drawing strength from ancient wisdom and contemporary understanding.

Exploring the Depths of Wisdom: Must-Reads for Aspiring Leaders

In our pursuit of leadership excellence, let's delve into the treasure trove of knowledge, blending timeless Indian wisdom with contemporary insights. Here are some recommended reads that resonate with the Indian ethos:

1. **"The Bhagavad Gita"**

    o   *Author: Lord Krishna*

    o   This ancient scripture, a conversation between Lord Krishna and Arjuna on the battlefield of Kurukshetra, delves into duty, righteousness, and the path to self-realization. It's a profound guide to leadership and decision-making.

2. **"Chanakya Neeti"**

   o *Author: Chanakya (Kautilya)*

   o Chanakya's teachings in Arthashastra and Chanakya Neeti offer timeless lessons on statecraft, leadership, and governance. His wisdom on strategy, diplomacy, and ethics remains invaluable.

3. **"Drive: The Mastery of Motivation"**

   o *Author: Arjuna*

   o Discover how the Gita's teachings on self-motivation and purpose align with modern psychology.

4. **"The No Ego Principle"**

   o *Author: Ashoka Sharma*

   o In a quest to create harmonious workplaces, this book Learn how nurturing a civilized and compassionate work environment leads to success.

5. **"Leadership Tales from the Mahabharata"**

   o *Author: Draupadi Sena* This book weaves leadership lessons from the Mahabharata, showcasing the journey of warriors and statesmen. It reveals how even failures can pave the path to triumph.

Incorporate these readings into your leadership journey, combining the wisdom of the ages with contemporary insights. Let the essence of Indian philosophy and the latest knowledge guide your path to becoming a remarkable leader.

Chapter 4:
The Mastery of Self-Reliance

> *"In the journey of entrepreneurship, when resources are scarce, self-reliance becomes your guiding star."*
>
> —*Mahatma Gandhi*

Introduction: Embracing the Mastery of Bootstrapping

In the vibrant landscape of Indian entrepreneurship, the concept of bootstrapping resonates deeply. It's a path where resilience meets innovation, and dreams take flight even in the absence of vast resources.

The Essence of Bootstrapping

Bill Reichert, a guiding light at Garage Technology Ventures, often shares a stark truth with aspiring entrepreneurs: the road to securing venture capital is akin to being struck by lightning in the most improbable of circumstances. While this statement may sound like a metaphor, it underlines the formidable challenges entrepreneurs face in the quest for external funding.

For most, the entrepreneurial journey begins with determination and a bootstrap mentality. To bootstrap is to embark on a self-sustained expedition, where resourcefulness knows no bounds. Picture an entrepreneur, armed with a vision and a pocketful of dreams, navigating the tumultuous seas of the business world.

The Canvas of Modern Bootstrapping

In today's digital era, bootstrapping is more attainable than ever before, thanks to a convergence of factors:

1. **Open Source Empowerment:** The realm of development tools has been democratized through open-source software, eliminating the need for costly licenses.

2. **Cloud Magic:** Infrastructure costs have plummeted, courtesy of cloud-based services. Entrepreneurs can now harness computing power without hefty investments.

3. **Middle-Layer Marvel:** The advent of middle-layer cloud-based applications has streamlined development, accelerating the transformation of ideas into tangible products.

4. **Virtual Workforce:** Talent knows no geographical boundaries. With virtual teams and freelancers, physical office spaces are no longer a prerequisite.

5. **The Social Wave:** Social media has emerged as a potent, cost-effective marketing tool, fostering brand awareness and customer engagement.

Navigating the Bootstrapping Terrain

The mastery of bootstrapping demands a blend of strategic thinking and tactical execution:

1. **Frugality with Purpose:** Every rupee counts. Allocate resources judiciously, focusing on areas that drive growth.

2. **Lean Operations:** Streamline your startup's operations for maximum efficiency. Keep overheads minimal without compromising on quality.

3. **Agile Adaptation:** Embrace change with agility. Respond swiftly to market feedback and evolving trends.

4. **Digital Storytelling:** Harness the power of digital platforms to tell your startup's story. Craft compelling narratives that resonate with your audience.

5. **Community Building:** Engage with your target community through social media, building a tribe of loyal supporters.

6. **Barter and Collaborate:** Explore mutually beneficial partnerships and collaborations within the entrepreneurial ecosystem.

The Triumph of Self-Reliance

In the intricate entrepreneurship, bootstrapping is a thread of self-reliance that weaves tales of resilience and success. Embrace the mastery of bootstrapping, for it is in your resourcefulness that you shall find the key to surmounting the initial hurdles of the startup journey. As you tighten the straps on your entrepreneurial boots, remember that the path of self-reliance is often the one that leads to enduring triumphs.

Nurturing the Cash Flow Garden

"Like a gardener tends to the roots before the fruits, an entrepreneur nurtures cash flow for a flourishing harvest."

—*Chanakya*

Introduction: The Essence of Cash Flow Management

In entrepreneurship, the pursuit of cash flow precedes the quest for profitability. Just as a gardener tends to the roots before the fruits, an entrepreneur nurtures cash flow to sustain and flourish.

The New Yorker's Humble Beginnings

In the early days of The New Yorker, the offices were a testament to minimalism. Dorothy Parker, a celebrated writer, often chose to work from a nearby coffee shop due to the sparsity of resources. One day, she found herself at the coffee shop when confronted by the editor, Harold Ross, who questioned her absence from the office.

"Why aren't you upstairs, working?" demanded Ross.

"Someone was using the pencil," replied Mrs. Parker with her characteristic wit.*

The New Yorker's humble beginnings remind us that resourcefulness can thrive in even the most modest of environments. Entrepreneurs, particularly those who have no alternative, possess the innate ability to bootstrap their ventures.

Anatomy of a Bootstrappable Business

A bootstrappable business model embodies specific attributes:

1. **Low Capital Demands:** Minimal initial capital investment is required, allowing entrepreneurs to commence with limited resources.

2. **Swift Sales Cycles:** Sales cycles are brief, typically spanning less than a month, expediting revenue generation.

3. **Prompt Payment Terms:** The time between invoicing and receiving payments is short, ensuring a steady cash flow.

4. **Recurring Revenue:** The business model incorporates sources of recurring income, providing financial stability.

5. **Social Media Marketing:** The product or service can be effectively marketed through social media and word of mouth.

The Mastery of Bootstrapping: Cash Flow Over Profitability

Bootstrapping entails a distinct approach—prioritizing cash flow over profitability. This strategic shift is essential, particularly in the early stages. While profitability remains a long-term goal, managing cash flow takes precedence until a substantial financial cushion is built.

The Ideal Bootstrappable Product

To embark on a successful bootstrapping journey, entrepreneurs seek products and markets characterized by:

1. **Immediate Relevance:** The product addresses a pre-existing need, eliminating the necessity for extensive customer education.

2. **Auto-Persuasion:** Once customers recognize their pain points and the solution offered, they are self-persuaded to make a purchase.

3. **Riding the Megatrend:** Entrepreneurs capitalize on prevailing megatrends that dismantle entry barriers. The internet revolution serves as a classic example.

4. **Leveraging Established Success:** Piggybacking on an established product with a sizable user base mitigates risk.

Nurturing the Cash Flow Garden

In the entrepreneurial landscape, cash flow is the lifeblood that sustains ventures during their formative years. Bootstrapping, rooted in effective cash flow management, empowers entrepreneurs to navigate the challenges of limited resources. Just as a gardener diligently nurtures the roots, an entrepreneur tends to cash flow, ensuring a bountiful harvest in due course. Embrace the mastery of bootstrapping, for it is in the cultivation of cash flow that the seeds of profitability are sown.

Embrace the Cloud: Your Path to Digital Ascendance

"In the realm of technology, the cloud is your charioteer to digital enlightenment."

—Vishnu Sharma

Introduction: The Cloud Revolution

The year 2010 marked a turning point in the tech landscape. Until then, launching a tech business demanded rooms filled with servers and a legion of staff to maintain them. An intricate web of backup facilities safeguarded against unforeseen disasters or attacks on the central office.

In 2010, a seismic shift occurred—the digital heavens parted, and the cloud descended upon us. No longer did startups need vast server rooms; they merely equipped their employees with laptops. The heart of this transformation lay in the cloud—the ethereal realm of servers, hosted by industry stalwarts like Rackspace and Amazon Web Services. This cloud hosted applications, websites, and data, all delivered over the limitless canvas of the Internet.

The Cloud's Bounteous Advantages

The adoption of cloud-based infrastructure bestowed startups with a cornucopia of benefits:

1. **Affordability:** A simple calculation of total ownership costs unveils the unequivocal brilliance of cloud infrastructure. The pay-as-you-go model reigns supreme, rendering the traditional approach obsolete. This, in essence, is the cloud's magnum opus.

2. **Adaptability:** In the unpredictable tides of business, capacity and performance needs surge and recede. Cloud-based systems, akin to skilled navigators, effortlessly adjust to these fluctuations. No more days lost to expanding capacity; it's a matter of settings and clicks.

3. **Reliability:** Within the hallowed halls of Rackspace and Amazon, legions of guardians tirelessly ensure seamless operations. While they might attract cyber threats, cloud-based systems stand as fortresses of reliability, far superior to the disjointed assemblage one could cobble together independently.

The Cloud's Indian Odyssey

In the Indian context, the cloud mirrors our cherished chariots of ancient lore, ever-ready to transport us to digital enlightenment. The stories of cloud success stories in India resonate with the spirit of innovation and transformation:

Rajan's Spice Bazaar: Rajan, an enterprising spice merchant, launched an e-commerce venture amidst the fragrant alleys of Chennai. Instead of grappling with servers and infrastructure, Rajan's venture flourished in the cloud. The cost-efficiency allowed him to offer premium spices at competitive prices, delighting customers nationwide.

Aditi's Healing Hands: Aditi, a compassionate Ayurvedic healer, sought to bring the wisdom of ancient remedies to a modern audience. The cloud became her trusted ally, hosting her healing platform and scaling effortlessly with the growing demand for holistic wellness.

The Mahabharata of Startups: In the grand epic of entrepreneurship, cloud technology assumes the role of Krishna, guiding the Pandavas (startups) through the battlefield of business. Just as Krishna's wisdom illuminated the path to righteousness, the cloud illuminates the path to digital success.

Ascend to Digital Nirvana

The cloud is more than a technological marvel; it is a digital charioteer leading us toward a realm of endless possibilities. In the sacred texts of technology, it is written that the cloud is the vehicle to ascend to digital nirvana. Embrace it, for in the cloud's embrace, your startup shall thrive, unburdened by the shackles of traditional infrastructure. As the ancient sages proclaimed, "The cloud is not a destination; it is the path to a digital utopia."

Igniting the Spark: The Power of the Unconventional

"In the realm of innovation, the uncharted path is often the one leading to greatness."

—Ritesh Agarwal

Introduction: The Unproven Mavericks

In the pursuit of entrepreneurial glory, the conventional wisdom of assembling a proven dream team takes a back seat to a more audacious approach. If you're embarking on the bootstrap journey, it's time to set aside the allure of seasoned industry veterans and redirect your focus towards the unproven, the untamed, and the unquenchable.

As Oscar Wilde once quipped, "Experience is the name everyone gives to their mistakes." Herein lies the essence of our quest—to embrace the untapped potential of the unproven, those who bring a unique blend of talent, energy, and insatiable curiosity.

The Blissful Ignorance Advantage

In the age-old battle of "Proven vs. Unproven," the latter holds a formidable advantage, one born out of blissful ignorance:

Criteria	Proven	Unproven
Salary	High, but guarantees uncertain results	Low, with untapped potential
Perks	Extravagant	Pragmatic and cost-effective
Energy Level	High, often unsustainable	Controllable, sustainable
Knowledge	Assumed omniscience	Willingness to explore the unknown

The ability to navigate uncharted waters, unburdened by the weight of past experiences, is the defining trait of the unproven. Consider the remarkable tale of Dr. George Dantzig, a maverick in the world of statistics.

As a doctoral student at IIT Bombay, Ravi stumbled into class late one day. Two perplexing problems were scrawled on the blackboard, which he mistook for homework. Oblivious to their unproven nature, Ravi solved them and, in turn, birthed two groundbreaking mathematical theorems. His professor, astounded by his unwitting genius, accepted these "assignments" as Ravi's thesis.

The Burden of Experience

In the world of innovation, experience can be a double-edged sword. A cautionary tale of technology, my own journey with Apple in the 1980s offers a stark lesson. Ignorant of the monumental challenges, I embraced the task of evangelizing a new operating system. In hindsight, I now comprehend the herculean effort required. The curse of experience is that it illuminates the arduous path, dissuading us from venturing forth.

Embrace the Unproven Pioneers

In the land of startups, where every day is an odyssey, the unproven pioneers stand as beacons of innovation. Their willingness to tread the path less traveled, to explore the uncharted territory, makes them formidable allies in the quest for the extraordinary.

As an ancient Sanskrit proverb guides us, "The river that follows the known course never discovers new oceans." In the spirit of this wisdom, cast aside the allure of the proven and welcome the unproven into the fold. For in their ignorance lies the spark of unbridled potential, ready to set ablaze the fires of innovation.

"In the realm of entrepreneurship, sometimes, it's the mavericks who light the way to greatness."

The Entrepreneur's Odyssey: Unearthing Paths to Prosperity

"In the labyrinth of entrepreneurship, diverse journeys pave the way to success, each with its unique challenges and triumphs."

—Sundar Pichai

Introduction: Navigating the Entrepreneurial Maze

Our quest to unravel the secrets of entrepreneurial triumphs takes us on a fascinating journey through Indian entrepreneurship. In this chapter, we explore the beginnings of notable Indian entrepreneurs, their remarkable diversities, and the strategies they embraced. As we embark on this odyssey, we are reminded of the ancient Upanishadic wisdom: "The path to knowledge is as varied as the seekers themselves."

Exploring the Pathways: Indian Entrepreneurial Pioneers

We set our sights on the stories of renowned Indian entrepreneurs, each carving a unique narrative:

1. **Vikram Sharma - InnovationsInTech Solutions**: An engineer with a profound passion for technology, Vikram defied norms to venture into software solutions.

2. **Neha Desai - GreenHarvest**: Neha, a dedicated nutritionist, followed her heart into the world of organic food delivery, advocating healthy living.

3. **Amit Khanna - TechPioneers**: Amit, a college dropout, disrupted the tech industry with an innovative app, challenging the status quo.

Starting as a Service Business: A Bridge to Prosperity

In the Indian entrepreneurial landscape, one strategy stands as a bridge to prosperity—the service business model. This approach ensures the swift flow of cash, paving the way for sustainable growth. Let us navigate this pathway, guided by the footsteps of our Indian pioneers:

The Fairy Tale of Entrepreneurial Innovation:

1. Visionaries, skilled in a niche domain, commence their entrepreneurial journey.

2. They offer consulting services, immersing themselves in clients' needs, billing hourly, with payment within thirty days.

3. While serving clients, they craft a software tool tailored to their niche.

4. Recognizing its potential, they refine and expand the tool's capabilities.

5. With growing clientele, consulting fees fund further tool development, ensuring a stable financial foundation.

6. As the software tool matures, they explore selling it to non-clients, witnessing a surge in demand.

7. Consulting gradually takes a backseat as the product gains prominence.

8. The company scales new heights, through either public offerings or acquisitions, enriching its early contributors.

The Gritty Reality of Entrepreneurial Resilience:

1. Determined entrepreneurs set out to challenge industry giants with an innovative product.

2. Development unfolds, accompanied by fundraising efforts, with unforeseen delays and financial constraints.

3. To sustain themselves, they turn to consulting, offering their expertise.

4. Consulting exposes them to market needs, aiding product development.

5. Gradually, the product finds its audience, and sales soar.

6. Consulting is phased out as the product takes center stage.

7. The startup thrives, driven by public offerings or acquisitions, rewarding its pioneers.

The Confluence of Paths: Lessons From the Journey

In the intricate narrative of entrepreneurship, diverse journeys coexist, reflecting the resilience and adaptability of Indian entrepreneurs. The transition from service-oriented beginnings to product-driven success symbolizes the dynamism of Indian entrepreneurship.

As the Vedas teach us, "In the pursuit of knowledge and prosperity, one must remain flexible like the flowing river, adapting to the changing landscape." In this ever-evolving landscape of entrepreneurship, let us remain open to both service and innovation, for they are the yin and yang of our journey.

The Direct Path: Navigating Startup Distribution in India

"In the maze of entrepreneurship, various paths lead to success, each presenting its own set of challenges and victories."

—Ratan Tata

Introduction: The Distribution Dilemma

In our quest to decode the entrepreneurial maze, we delve into the intricate world of distribution strategies for startups in India. As Indian entrepreneurs, we are no strangers to diversity, and our journey through the complexities of distribution is no different. In this chapter, we uncover the wisdom of going direct to the customer and explore how it aligns with the dynamic Indian landscape.

The Illusion of Multiple-Tiered Distribution

Many startups entertain the notion of a multiple-tiered distribution system, envisioning resellers as the gateway to success. The allure of an established sales force, brand recognition, and customer relationships can be tempting. However, this concept often crumbles under scrutiny, echoing the sentiment of the wise proverb: "A tree standing alone bears fruit; two trees standing together are cast in each other's shadow.

In the Indian context, this approach faces three critical challenges:

1. **Customer Disconnect**: Embracing a reseller-centric model severs the direct connection with customers. For startups with innovative products, rapid and unfiltered feedback is invaluable. Without it, course correction becomes a distant dream.

2. **Volume vs. Margin**: The pursuit of a larger profit margin through resellers often necessitates achieving a high sales volume. Yet, scaling up as a startup can be an arduous journey in a market dominated by established players.

3. **Time Is of the Essence**: Convincing distributors to embrace your product and navigating it through their channels consumes precious time. As we know from the ancient texts, "Time is the ultimate currency."

The Wisdom of Going Direct

In the labyrinth of distribution, the path of wisdom beckons us to go direct to customers. This approach, deeply rooted in Indian philosophy, offers several advantages:

1. **Swift Feedback Loop**: In the early stages, hearing unfiltered opinions from customers is akin to enlightenment. It allows rapid course correction, aligning your offering with market needs.

2. **Building Trust**: Establishing a direct relationship fosters trust. In India, trust is the cornerstone of lasting partnerships.

3. **Efficiency and Agility**: By avoiding intermediaries, startups can operate with agility. In a dynamic market like India, adaptability is paramount.

The Role of Resellers

While the direct path is our guiding light, it doesn't render resellers obsolete. Instead, it positions them as accelerators, expanders, or supplements once your product is refined and sales are established. The partnership with resellers should be a harmonious dance rather than a reliance on them to create your market.

The Journey Continues

As we navigate the labyrinth of distribution, let us remember the words of the Upanishads: "The path to enlightenment is direct, but the journey is full of lessons." In the intricate web of Indian entrepreneurship, embracing the direct path to customers is a lesson worth imbibing. It's a journey where diversity is our strength, and adaptability is our shield.

Challenging the Giants: Positioning for Success in the Indian Market

"In the realm of Indian entrepreneurship, crafting a distinctive narrative is the key to distinguishing oneself amidst industry giants."

—Ritesh Agarwal

Introduction: Arjuna vs. Karna in the Indian Context

In the realm of Indian startups, where giants tread, emerging as a formidable competitor may seem like a Herculean task. However, wisdom from our ancient texts and modern strategies converge to offer a compelling approach: positioning against the leader. Chanakya's Wisdom Chanakya, the author of "Arthashastra," champions the idea of leveraging existing market leaders as a springboard for strategic success. Instead of starting from scratch, you can harness the strengths and weaknesses of established competitors. Let's explore how this applies in our Indian landscape:

1. **Indigo vs. Air India/SpiceJet:** "As efficient as Air India or SpiceJet, but with better customer service." This strategic positioning challenged the established giants head-on.

2. **Zomato:** "As diverse as cooking at home, but without the hassle." A bold claim that appealed to busy urbanites.

3. **Patanjali:** "Pure and natural, unlike traditional multinational brands." An unconventional approach that resonated with health-conscious consumers.

4. **Jio:** "Connecting India, faster and more affordable than traditional telecom providers." This positioning emphasized a commitment to bridging the digital divide.

Utilizing the Leader's Brand

In India, where competition is fierce, positioning against the leader can save substantial marketing expenses. You can identify key differentiators for your product, such as cost, ease of use, convenience, design, reliability, speed, selection, customer service, or location. By doing so, you make the most of the groundwork laid by your competitors.

Conditions for Success

However, taking on the leader requires careful consideration:

1. **Relevance**: Ensure that the leader is worth challenging. Positioning against a fading giant can be futile.

2. **Sustained Advantage**: Your edge should withstand the leader's potential response. Swiftly changing strategies can lead to setbacks.

3. **Meaningful Differentiation**: Your product must genuinely outshine the competition. Empty hype erodes credibility.

An Indian Perspective

In the Indian context, this approach is akin to the teachings of the Vedas and Upanishads, where wisdom is the ultimate weapon. Positioning against leaders is about leveraging their established presence to carve a niche for your offering. It's a strategy that aligns with India's diverse and competitive market.

Carving Your Path

As we venture into the Indian entrepreneurial landscape, remember the story of David and Goliath. With strategic positioning and a unique offering, even the mightiest giants can be challenged. In Indian entrepreneurship, weaving a unique thread is the path to standing out amidst giants.

Mastering the Essentials: Balancing the Macro and Micro in Indian Entrepreneurship

> *"In the landscape of Indian entrepreneurship, achieving success entails balancing the grand vision with meticulous attention to detail."*
>
> *—Ananya Gupta*

Introduction: A Balancing Act

Indian entrepreneurship, like a complex raga, demands a harmonious balance between the grand symphony of vision and the delicate notes of detail. To bootstrap effectively, we must sweat the big stuff while staying mindful of the small.

The Essence of Bootstrapping

Bootstrapping isn't about penny-pinching; it's about channeling resources wisely. Our purpose is not to craft our own desks or inflate Herman Miller's fortunes with venture capital. To navigate this journey, we must discern the significant from the trivial.

The Symphony of Entrepreneurship: Big Stuff

1. Developing your MVVVP (Minimum Viable Vision, Value, and Product)

In India's diverse market, crafting a clear and viable vision is paramount. Your product must resonate with the soul of the nation.

2. Selling Your Product

This is the raga's crescendo. Your ability to reach hearts and minds across the subcontinent will determine your success.

3. Enhancing Your Product

Just as a raga evolves, your product must adapt. Embrace change as a tabla player welcomes tempo variations.

The Harmony of Entrepreneurship: Small Stuff

1. Business Cards and Letterhead

In the Indian business ecosystem, the exchange of business cards is a ritual. Craft your cards thoughtfully, for they bear your essence.

2. Office Supplies

While seemingly insignificant, these are the talas (rhythmic cycles) that keep your daily operations in sync.

3. Furniture

Choose furniture that reflects your ethos. In India, every piece of furniture has a story; let yours resonate.

4. Office Equipment

From the humblest pen to the mightiest printer, every tool contributes to the symphony of your work.

The Wisdom of Balance

As Rick Sklarin advises, tackle the small stuff efficiently. A single trip to a wholesale market can suffice. But do not lose sight of the bigger picture, for that is where the melody unfolds.

Incorporating Ancient Wisdom

Our journey is guided by the wisdom of the Vedas and Upanishads, which teach us to balance the material and the spiritual. In Indian entrepreneurship, this translates to harmonizing the tangible with the intangible, the grand with the minute.

Orchestrating Success

In Indian entrepreneurship, success lies in harmonizing the monumental with the minuscule. Let your venture be a raga, resonating with the rhythms of our diverse nation. By sweating the big stuff while nurturing the small, you create a symphony of success that will echo through the ages.

The Mastery of Patience: Waiting Before Leaping

> *"In the world of commerce, exercising patience is crucial for distinguishing between necessity and impulse."*
>
> —*Amitabh Sinha*

Introduction: The Wisdom of Patience

In the bustling streets of Indian entrepreneurship, patience is a virtue that transcends time. Before making a leap, let us embrace the age-old wisdom that urges us to pause and reflect.

The Mastery of Discernment

"The next time there's something that you can't live without, wait for a week and then see if you're still alive."

In a world of constant desires, this ancient saying teaches us to differentiate between what we truly need and fleeting impulses. The marketplace can be a cacophony, but patience allows us to hear our inner melody.

Understaff and Outsource: The Indian Approach

As CEOs, we face a timeless dilemma—should we leave money on the table due to limited resources, or should we burden ourselves with excess and later face the painful task of laying off employees?

"If you want to bootstrap your organization, then understaff it."

In our pursuit of growth, overstaffing can lead to a chain reaction of wasteful expenditure, both in terms of physical resources and human lives. The Indian way is to optimize by understaffing wisely.

Outsourcing: The Mastery of Efficiency

To tread the path of bootstrapping, we must consider outsourcing nonstrategic functions as a strategic move. While core functions should remain within, nonessential tasks like customer service, tech support, accounting, and facilities management can find external partners.

A Lesson from History: Webvan's Extravagance

A poignant example of the perils of extravagance is Webvan, the online grocer. It ordered facilities worth billions, overindulged in executive compensation, and imploded in the dot-com crash. This extravagant tale reminds us of the pitfalls of not adhering to the Indian principle of moderation.

Incorporating Ancient Wisdom: The Vedas and Upanishads

Our scriptures teach us that patience is not merely a virtue but a path to enlightenment. In business, too, patience illuminates the path to discernment and wisdom.

The Dance of Patience

As Indian entrepreneurs, we perform a delicate dance, balancing necessity with impulse, frugality with growth. Patience is our guiding star, helping us navigate the bustling bazaar of business. By waiting before leaping, we ensure that every step forward is a step of purpose and wisdom.

The Essence of Efficiency: Function Over Form

> *"In the realm of business, it's the essence that orchestrates triumph, not merely the appearance."*
>
> —Aditya Patel

Introduction: Functionality vs. Extravagance

In the bustling markets of India, where every resource counts, the principle of valuing function over form shines brightly. Let's explore the wisdom of focusing on what truly matters in business.

Function vs. Form: A Strategic Choice

"To spend money wisely, focus on the function you need, not the form it takes."

In our journey as entrepreneurs, we often encounter the temptation of big-name firms and extravagant appearances. However, Indian business acumen teaches us that the essence lies in the function, not the form.

Functionality in Various Domains: A Comparative Insight

In the diverse landscape of business functions, making the right choices is crucial. Let's explore how prioritizing function over form applies in various domains:

Area	Form	Function
Legal	Lavish offices and corporate boxes	Legal protection, asset safeguarding, and deal facilitation
Accounting	Prestigious status and opulent conference rooms	Cost control and fiscal soundness
PR	Attractive representatives and extravagant events	Effective positioning and media relationships
Marketing	Wall of awards and extravagant media buying	Customer understanding and attraction
Recruiting	Established reputation and connections	Hiring exceptional talent

Choosing the Right Service Providers

Selecting the right service providers is pivotal for startups. Here are some practical tips:

1. **Specialization Matters:** Choose firms that specialize in the type of work you require, ensuring expertise in your domain.

2. **Invest in Critical Functions:** Invest more in critical functions like legal and accounting to build trust with investors.

3. **Individual References:** Investigate the individuals handling your business, not just the firm's reputation. Happy entrepreneurs' testimonials are powerful.

4. **Negotiation is Key:** Everything is negotiable, from rates to payment schedules. Don't hesitate to negotiate, even in good times.

The Indian Way of Efficiency

The ethos of valuing function over form extends to every facet of a startup. This philosophy reflects the Indian spirit of efficiency, where resources are cherished, and every choice is made with careful consideration.

The Beauty of Practicality

In Indian entrepreneurship, practicality and functionality form the threads of success. By embracing the Indian wisdom of focusing on function over form, we ensure that our businesses thrive on efficiency, not extravagance.

Wisdom in Simplicity: The Indian Way of Pragmatism

> *"In the simplicity of function, the core of wisdom reveals itself."*
>
> —Amit Shah

Introduction: The Pursuit of Practicality

In the bustling markets of India, where wisdom is valued as gold, the principle of simplicity and practicality shines through. Let's delve into the mastery of focusing on function over form in various aspects of startup culture.

Embracing Functionality Over Extravagance

"In the grand mosaic of business, it's the function that paints the masterpiece, not the embellishments."

As entrepreneurs, we often encounter the allure of luxury and extravagance. However, Indian business philosophy teaches us to embrace the essence rather than the aesthetics.

Applying Practicality Across Startups

This philosophy of practicality extends to nearly every facet of a startup's journey. Let's explore how it applies to various elements:

1. Office Equipment:

During the dot-com craze, the Godrej Interio Ergonomic Chair symbolized luxury, priced at ₹50,000. While it was a comfortable chair, the question arises – was it truly worth ₹50,000? It undoubtedly provided comfort, but perhaps it encouraged users to prioritize less critical tasks. Interestingly, 114 of these chairs were sold in the bankruptcy auction of an Indian e-commerce company.

2. Technology:

In the realm of technology, the Indian way advocates adopting what is functional and essential rather than falling for the allure of the latest trends. It's about leveraging technology wisely, not indiscriminately.

3. Business Culture:

In the corporate culture, simplicity prevails. Extravagant offices and flashy displays are less important than fostering a work environment that values productivity and innovation.

4. Resource Allocation:

In resource allocation, it's about directing funds to critical functions that drive growth and sustainability rather than overspending on superficial elements.

5. Customer Experience:

The focus shifts from elaborate customer experiences to providing genuine value and satisfaction, as the heart of business lies in meeting customer needs effectively.

The Wisdom of Indian Philosophy

Ancient Indian philosophies, including the Vedas and Upanishads, resonate with the idea of simplicity and practicality. They teach us to find wisdom in simplicity, emphasizing the importance of substance over style.

Stories from Indian Entrepreneurship

The Tale of Prakash and the Practical Office:

Prakash, a startup founder, opted for simple and functional office furniture instead of extravagant decor. His team appreciated the focus on functionality, and it reflected in their productivity.

The Beauty of Pragmatism

In Indian entrepreneurship, pragmatism and functionality are the threads of success. By embracing the Indian wisdom of focusing on function over form, we ensure that our startups thrive on simplicity, practicality, and sustainable growth, leaving extravagance behind.

Navigating the Bootstrapped Journey - Your Questions Answered

In the pursuit of self-reliance, let wisdom be your compass, guiding you through the darkness to enlightenment."

—*Rajiv Patel*

Introduction: Unearthing the Wisdom of Self-Reliance

As you embark on your bootstrapped journey in the Indian entrepreneurial landscape, questions inevitably arise. In this chapter, we address your FAQs while drawing from the profound wisdom of Indian philosophies and the latest business insights.

FAQ 1: When to Cease Bootstrapping?

> *"When the streams of revenue flow steady and profits grace each stride, it's prudent to anchor the voyage of bootstrapping."*
>
> —*Avinash Singh*

As you navigate the bootstrapped path, the destination is marked by positive cash flow and confidence that each sale contributes to profits. That's when you know it's time to stop relying solely on your bootstrap.

FAQ 2: Is There Such a Thing as Bootstrapping Too Much?

> *"In the realm of entrepreneurship, excess capital is the poison that may extinguish the fire of innovation."*
>
> —*Sadhana Verma*

Bootstrapping isn't about forsaking growth; it's about fostering sustainable growth. Excess funding, like steroids, might provide a short-term advantage but can harm you in the long run. It's essential to tread the path of financial prudence.

FAQ 3: Can I Thrive Without External Capital?

> *"In business, there's no 'one-size-fits-all.' Success is achieved by following the path that aligns with your vision."*
>
> —*Rajiv Gupta*

External capital isn't the only way to build a remarkable enterprise. The goal is greatness, regardless of your capital source. The path you choose should resonate with your vision and values.

FAQ 4: The Perception of Funding Sources

> *"In the grand theater of business, only those who matter are those who recognize your worth, irrespective of your capital source."*
>
> —*Ananya Kapoor*

The measure of your success isn't the size of your venture capital funding. While it may add credibility, it's your actions and accomplishments that truly matter. Focus on building a great business; the rest will follow.

FAQ 5: Risks and Unconventional Sources

"In the realm of entrepreneurship, it's the audacity to tread the unconventional path that often leads to unparalleled success."

—Karthik Menon

Every funding source carries risks, whether from family, friends, credit cards, or home equity. Entrepreneurship is the mastery of doing whatever it takes. Be willing to embrace unconventional avenues when conditions are far from ideal.

Stories of Resilience from Indian Entrepreneurs

The Tale of Meera's Unconventional Path:

Meera faced skepticism when she sought funds from her family and friends. However, her determination and her business's success proved that unconventional sources can be stepping stones to greatness.

The Path of Prudence

In the dynamic Indian entrepreneurial landscape, the journey is as important as the destination. Embrace the wisdom of self-reliance, and let your actions illuminate the path to success. Remember, in the world of entrepreneurship, it's not about the size of your capital; it's about the size of your determination and innovation.

Enlightening Your Path with Knowledge - Recommended Reading

"In the vast ocean of entrepreneurship, wisdom is your guiding star, and knowledge is the vessel that carries you forward."

—Swami Vivekananda

Introduction: The Journey of Knowledge

As you tread the entrepreneurial path in India, seeking self-reliance and success, it's essential to equip yourself with the right knowledge. In this chapter, we recommend insightful books that will illuminate your journey and empower your endeavors.

Recommended Reading List: Nurturing the Entrepreneurial Spirit

1. **"The Monk Who Sold His Ferrari" by Robin Sharma**
   - Sharma's timeless classic offers profound wisdom and practical advice for those seeking personal and professional transformation. Through the story of a successful lawyer who embarks on a spiritual journey, you'll learn valuable lessons about leadership, mindfulness, and living with purpose.

2. **"Connect the Dots" by Rashmi Bansal**
   - In this book, Bansal profiles twenty inspiring entrepreneurs who started with nothing but a dream and went on to build successful businesses. Through their stories, you'll uncover valuable lessons about perseverance, innovation, and the power of resilience.

3. **"The 3 Mistakes of My Life" by Chetan Bhagat**
   - Bhagat's novel offers a fictional but relatable tale of entrepreneurship and friendship set against the backdrop of contemporary India. Through the protagonist's journey, you'll learn about the challenges and opportunities faced by aspiring entrepreneurs in today's world.

4. **"Winning Like Virat: Think and Succeed Like Kohli" by Abhirup Bhattacharya**
   - Drawing inspiration from the life and career of Indian cricket captain Virat Kohli, Bhattacharya offers valuable insights into leadership, determination, and the pursuit of excellence. This book will motivate you to adopt a winning mindset and strive for success in your entrepreneurial endeavors.

5. **"The Entrepreneurial Journey" by Subroto Bagchi**
   - Bagchi, co-founder of Mindtree, shares his insights and experiences from his entrepreneurial journey in this insightful book. Through practical advice and inspiring anecdotes, he offers valuable guidance for aspiring entrepreneurs navigating the challenges of starting and scaling a business.

6. **"Wings of Fire: An Autobiography" by Dr. A.P.J. Abdul Kalam**
    - In his autobiography, former President of India Dr. A.P.J. Abdul Kalam shares the remarkable story of his life, from his humble beginnings to his rise as a renowned scientist and leader. Through his journey, you'll learn about the power of perseverance, passion, and visionary leadership.
7. **"The Z Factor: My Journey as the Wrong Man at the Right Time" by Subhash Chandra**
    - In this candid memoir, media mogul Subhash Chandra shares the story of his entrepreneurial journey, from launching Zee TV to building a media empire. Through his successes and failures, you'll gain valuable insights into the world of business and entrepreneurship.
8. **"Zero to One: Notes on Startups, or How to Build the Future" by Peter Thiel and Blake Masters (Indian Edition)**
    - Although authored by non-Indian writers, this book offers invaluable insights into entrepreneurship and innovation. Thiel, co-founder of PayPal, shares his contrarian perspectives on building successful startups and creating a better future through innovation.
9. **"Start-Up Sutra: What the Angels Won't Tell You About Business and Life" by Rohit Prasad**
    - Prasad provides practical advice and unconventional wisdom for entrepreneurs embarking on their startup journey. Through engaging stories and insightful lessons, he offers guidance on overcoming challenges, building resilience, and finding success in the world of entrepreneurship.

These books offer a diverse range of perspectives and insights to nurture your entrepreneurial spirit and guide you on your journey to success. Whether you're a seasoned entrepreneur or just starting out, each of these reads has something valuable to offer.

Illuminating Your Path

As you embark on your entrepreneurial journey in India, remember that knowledge is your most potent weapon. These recommended books will serve as beacons of wisdom, helping you navigate the intricate waters of business while staying true to your Indian roots. In the words of Swami Vivekananda, "Arise, awake, and stop not till the goal is reached.

Chapter 5:
The Mastery of Financial Abundance

"In the world of entrepreneurship, planting the seeds of capital is as crucial as nurturing the roots of your vision."

—Rahul Singh

Introduction: The Quest for Financial Nectar

As an entrepreneur in the vibrant landscape of India, envisioning a world-changing business is just the beginning. The true odyssey lies in acquiring the resources to bring your vision to life. In this chapter, we will embark on a journey to understand the mastery of fund-raising, a vital skill for every Indian entrepreneur.

The Spectrum of Fund-Raising: From Conception to Reality

In the words of Rajat Gupta, the esteemed venture capitalist, fund-raising is often at the forefront of an entrepreneur's mind. Queries about approaching investors and equity negotiations abound, but let us not forget the essence of building a robust business.

1. Crowdsourcing: Harnessing the Collective Energy (समूह की ऊर्जा)

Crowdsourcing, a contemporary method embraced by Indian entrepreneurs, allows you to tap into the collective wisdom and resources of the masses. Remember the tale of Vikramaditya and Betaal? In a similar vein, crowdsourcing invites a multitude of contributors to support your mission. This could be through crowdfunding platforms, where everyday individuals become patrons of your vision, propelling it to new heights.

2. Angel Investors: The Guardians of Entrepreneurial Dreams (उद्यमिका के सपनों के पालक)

In India's entrepreneurial folklore, angel investors are akin to divine guardians. These individuals, often successful entrepreneurs themselves, extend their wings to shelter budding startups. Their wisdom and financial support serve as a guiding light, nurturing businesses to maturity. Remember the tale of "The Four Friends and the Lion"? Just as the friends worked together to overcome adversity, angel investors collaborate with entrepreneurs to achieve success.

3. Venture Capital: Sailing the Ocean of High Growth (उच्च विकास की समुंदर में सैलिंग)

Venture capital is the ship that takes your entrepreneurial vessel to uncharted territories. In the land of startups, venture capitalists are like skilled navigators, steering your business toward high growth and global expansion. But be prepared for rigorous scrutiny, for they are not just investors; they are partners in your voyage. Recall the story of "The Churning of the Ocean of Milk," where collaboration led to the elixir of immortality. Similarly, entrepreneurs and venture capitalists collaborate to create enduring companies.

Balancing the Scales of Finance

Fund-raising may seem like a necessary evil, but in reality, it is the vital force that breathes life into your entrepreneurial dreams. Each form of fund-raising in the Indian context has its own tales of triumph and challenges, mirroring our culture. As we journey through the mastery of financial abundance, remember the words of the Upanishads: "Arise, awake, and achieve your dreams, for the universe is waiting for your brilliance."

Unlocking the Power of the Masses: The Mastery of Crowdsourcing Funds

In Indian entrepreneurship, the quest for capital has evolved through centuries, mirroring our rich history and traditions. In ancient times, nobility and the privileged few possessed the means to fund their ventures. If additional capital was required, they had the advantage of collateral and influential connections.

Fast forward to the modern era, where the dynamic venture capital industry transformed the landscape. Entrepreneurs armed with PowerPoint presentations, prototypes, and ambitious dreams could now seek funding. Angel investors followed suit, democratizing the process further by supporting riskier ventures that traditional venture capitalists might hesitate to back.

"Venture capitalists may not comprehend what truly resonates with the masses, but when people invest in your vision through crowdfunding, they're staking their own hard-earned money, not managing a pension fund's capital."

In 2007, Indiegogo blazed a trail, followed by Kickstarter two years later, marking the dawn of crowdfunding—a process as democratic, open, and transparent as fund-raising can be. The essence of crowdfunding lies in collaboration with the masses, making it the epitome of financial inclusivity.

The Dance of Crowdfunding: An Artistic Expression of Support (समर्थन की कला)

Crowdfunding is an intricate dance, where creators orchestrate their projects through compelling videos, descriptions, enticing rewards, and regular updates. Unlike traditional equity sales, crowdfunding involves offering preorders with enticing incentives or "kickers" to motivate backers to support something that is yet to materialize. These kickers range from discounts to unique experiences, echoing the Indian philosophy of "giving to receive."

The heartbeat of crowdfunding is in community engagement, as creators leverage social media and email to spread the word. While traditional fund-raising revolves around monetary gain, crowdfunding thrives on the joy of being among the first to experience something exceptional or the intrinsic satisfaction of contributing to a creative endeavor.

People, driven by their belief in the project, fund it, enabling creators to materialize their vision using pooled resources. As orders are fulfilled, word of mouth acts as a catalyst, paving the way for the birth of remarkable enterprises.

Crowdfunding: Possibilities in the Indian Context

Crowdfunding finds its natural fit in the Indian entrepreneurial journey, particularly in consumer-focused domains like gadgets, accessories, games, crafts, and fashion. It also finds resonance in artistic pursuits such as films, videos, and charitable initiatives. However, it may not be the ideal choice for biotech or enterprise software ventures, given their substantial funding requirements and non-impulsive nature.

In 2013, Kickstarter saw three million people from over two hundred countries pledging $480 million to support 19,911 successful projects. This staggering figure, six times more than the number of venture capital deals closed in the same year, signifies the paradigm shift toward crowdfunding.

While not every project attains the grandiose success of notable ventures like Chai Point, IndianCrafter, DesiDock, crowdfunding offers its own array of benefits. It simplifies the fundraising process, saving entrepreneurs from the laborious task of drafting intricate business plans or enduring extensive due diligence procedures. Additionally, it avoids equity dilution, as supporters pre-order or contribute without seeking ownership stakes, liberating entrepreneurs from the responsibility of reporting to investors while maintaining the ethical obligation to fulfill their commitments.

Crowdfunding: A Litmus Test for Viability

Beyond the financial aspect, crowdfunding serves as a litmus test for a project's viability. Unlike venture capitalists who make decisions based on conjecture, crowdfunding allows the masses to vote with their own after-tax earnings, providing genuine market validation.

In the realm of Indian entrepreneurship, where ancient wisdom meets modern innovation, crowdfunding emerges as a powerful tool, democratizing access to capital and fostering collaborative entrepreneurship. It is the symphony of the masses, contributing their notes to compose the entrepreneurial opus of India.

Mastering the Mastery of Crowdfunding: Insights for Success

In Indian entrepreneurship, crowdfunding has emerged as a beacon of hope, a means for creators to realize their dreams by harnessing the collective power of the masses. The journey of crowdfunding is an enchanting tale, and here are the guiding principles for navigating its intricacies.

1. Craft a Captivating Narrative (कथन कला)

The heart of your crowdfunding endeavor lies in the mastery of storytelling. Within the vast expanse of the digital realm, your story is your most potent weapon. Create a video that encapsulates your vision in less than two minutes—a video that enchants, entices, and energizes. In the realm of Indian folklore, it's akin to narrating an ancient legend, captivating the audience with every word.

2. Weave a Personal Saga (आत्मकथा)

Stories resonate when they bear a personal touch. In your video, emails, and social media posts, infuse the essence of your personal journey. Share how your project sprouted from an unmet need, much like the tale of a visionary who embarked on a quest to revolutionize bicycle tire repairs, as seen in the 'patchnride' project on Indiegogo.

3. Embrace Digital Warriors (डिजिटल योद्धा)

In the age of digital warfare, unleashing the power of email and social media is your strategic arsenal. Unless you possess the charisma of a renowned figure like N. R. Narayana Murthy, your journey will demand a guerrilla-marketing campaign. Harness the might of your email contacts and social media networks to disseminate the word far and wide.

4. Reward the Believers (समर्थनकर्ताओं को सम्मानित करें)

In the world of crowdfunding, rewards serve as tokens of gratitude to those who place their faith in your vision. The rewards you offer are more than incentives; they are symbols of your commitment. Whether it's discounts, acknowledgments, autographed copies, or tangible gifts like tote bags and T-shirts, ensure that your backers are duly compensated for their trust. Take a leap further by personally delivering or installing your product, a gesture akin to the Indian tradition of 'Seva'—selfless service.

5. Illuminate the Path with a Budget (बजट का प्रकाश)

To instill unwavering confidence in your supporters, unveil the roadmap of your project through a comprehensive budget. Illuminate their path by demonstrating how their contributions will be judiciously utilized. This not only showcases your competence but also assures them that your project will see the light of day.

In Indian entrepreneurship, crowdfunding is the symphony of the masses, contributing their notes to compose the opus of innovation and dreams realized. These principles are your guiding stars, navigating you through the realm of crowdfunding, where ancient storytelling meets modern digital prowess. In the spirit of Indian innovation, you have the power to transform visions into reality, one pledge at a time.

Angelic Guidance: Navigating the Realm of Angel Investors in India

In the labyrinthine landscape of Indian entrepreneurship, angel investors emerge as guiding stars, individuals of affluence who channel their wealth into nurturing nascent startups. Unlike venture capitalists driven solely by financial gain, angels have a dual mission: to enrich society and, perhaps, reap rewards. Their benevolence manifests in two forms—fostering the aspirations of the youth and ushering impactful innovations into the market. As an aspiring entrepreneur, here are the sacred scrolls of wisdom to secure the blessings of angel investors.

1. Do Not Underestimate Their Wisdom (उनकी बुद्धिमत्ता का मूल्यांकन न करें)

While angels may not prioritize financial returns like their professional counterparts, never mistake their generosity for gullibility. Approach them with the same reverence and professionalism reserved for the top echelons of venture capitalists. Respect their wisdom, for they are the keepers of age-old secrets.

2. Fuel Their Desire to Relive (दोबारा जीने की इच्छा को बढ़ावा दें)

Within the heart of every angel investor lies a longing—to revisit the exuberance of youth or to rekindle the embers of entrepreneurial fervor. While they may not embark on a new entrepreneurial voyage themselves, they find solace in witnessing your journey. It's akin to providing them with a portal to vicariously experience the thrill of entrepreneurship—a phenomenon we may term "voyeur capital."

3. Speak the Language of Simplicity (सरलता में बात करें)

In the hallowed halls of angel investment, the ultimate arbiter is often not a committee of peers or experts but the angel's life partner—their spouse. Thus, it becomes imperative to weave your business narrative in the fabric of simplicity. Can your spouse understand and resonate with your venture? That's the litmus test, for an angel's investment committee is none other than their beloved.

4. Emanate Radiance (प्रकाशित हो जाएं)

In the eyes of many angels, investing in startups is akin to nurturing a beloved child. They seek not just a profitable venture but an entrepreneur with whom they can form an emotional bond. Be the radiant soul that attracts their benevolent gaze—approachable, enchanting, and adaptable.

5. Harness the Power of Social Networks (सामाजिक नेटवर्क की शक्ति का सहारा लें)

In the realm of angel investing, social connections are the currency of trust. When you secure the support of one angel, you often unlock the gates to the entire celestial congregation. A single member's endorsement carries immense weight. It signifies not just financial prowess but also a shared vision.

As you embark on your entrepreneurial odyssey in India, remember that angel investors are not mere benefactors; they are mentors, guardians, and champions of your dreams. They are the celestial guardians of innovation, guiding you through the labyrinth of entrepreneurship with their wisdom and benevolence. Seek them not merely as financiers but as partners in your sacred quest to transform ideas into reality.

Bridging the Chasm: Navigating the Realms of Venture Capital in India

In the labyrinthine journey of Indian entrepreneurship, venture capital often emerges as the elusive golden fleece, promising untold riches and success. Yet, the truth is shrouded in a paradox—startups that amass vast fortunes in their seed and series A rounds do not necessarily ascend to greatness. In fact, their journey is often fraught with challenges, distractions, and frustrations.

Let us embark on a voyage through Indian entrepreneurship, guided by a tale that mirrors the nuances of venture capitalists.

Once upon a time, in the bustling heart of Mumbai, a spirited entrepreneur, Arjun, embarked on a mission to revolutionize transportation. He sought the blessing of venture capital to fund his vision. His endeavor was akin to steering a grand elephant through the narrow lanes of a bazaar—it demanded patience, precision, and a keen sense of direction.

Arjun's journey took him to a lavish restaurant, where a prominent venture capitalist, Mr. Patel, agreed to meet him. Patel was renowned for his ability to open doors, for he possessed the keys to sales, partnerships, and investor networks. Arjun believed that Patel's involvement could transform his startup's fate.

As the evening unfurled, Arjun's father, who harbored concerns about his son's profligacy, joined them. The three of them dined lavishly, enveloped in the opulence of the moment. However, destiny had a twist in store.

Hours later, as they stepped out of the restaurant, Arjun was elated to find his sleek BMW parked prominently in front. Turning to his father with a triumphant smile, he said, "Father, this is why I drive a BMW. The finest establishments reserve the best spots for such cars, sparing us the wait for a valet."

But fate intervened in the form of an irate valet, who approached them with a grievance, "Madam, you have taken your keys with you. We couldn't move your car."

Arjun's heart sank as the truth unraveled—his gleaming BMW had remained immobile throughout the evening, a stark emblem of his oversight.

In the vast landscape of venture capitalism, Arjun's experience reflects a fundamental truth. Venture capitalists possess the power to unlock doors, forging paths to sales, partnerships, and investor connections. They can be invaluable guides, shielding you from grievous errors and assisting in recruitment.

However, it is vital to remember that their expertise extends only so far. They may command vast financial resources, but their knowledge of engineering, marketing, sales, production, finance, and operations is not guaranteed. Their investments are akin to a high-stakes gamble, where most bets do not yield returns.

In the world of venture capitalists, loyalty is as transient as a monsoon breeze. Their commitment wanes as soon as you falter in fulfilling your promises. They are not your comrades, but rather astute businessmen motivated by profit. It is not a realm of malevolence, but of pragmatism—here, it is business, not friendship.

As you navigate the intricate of Indian entrepreneurship, remember that venture capital is a double-edged sword. While it can catapult your dreams to new heights, it is not a guarantee of success. Approach it with caution, for it can be as capricious as the monsoon rains, showering blessings or storms depending on your voyage.

Seek not just their investment but their wisdom, and you shall be better prepared to navigate the chasms of the entrepreneurial world.

Now, let's delve into the intricacies of financing options in the Indian entrepreneurial landscape. In the land of diverse opportunities, where ancient wisdom meets cutting-edge innovation, we shall explore the three primary avenues: Crowdfunding, Angel Investment, and Venture Capital, through the prism of a matrix.

Financing Matrix: Navigating the Path to Prosperity in India

Aspect	Crowdfunding	Angel Investment	Venture Capital
Sweet Spot (in Rupees)	₹1,75,000–₹7,00,000	₹17,50,000–₹35,00,000	₹70,00,000–₹35,00,00,000
Duration	90 days	180 days	270 days

Aspect	Crowdfunding	Angel Investment	Venture Capital
Dilution per Round	Not applicable: sale, not investment	20%	25–35%
Effort Level	Moderate	Moderate	High
Type of Product/Service	Consumer-facing gadgets, gizmos, books, and other artistic and craft-oriented projects	Software and web services	Hardware, software, biotech, and web services
Due Diligence	Minimal	Moderate	High
Intrusiveness	Minimal	Moderate	High
Experience	Fun	Tolerable	Miserable

Now, let's navigate through these avenues with an Indian perspective:

1. **Crowdfunding: The Collective Symphony (रुपये 1,75,000–₹7,00,000)**

In the vibrant bazaars of India, crowdfunding is akin to a collective symphony. Entrepreneurs seeking ₹1,75,000–₹7,00,000 find solace in the unity of the crowd. Whether it's ingenious gadgets, captivating books, or intricate crafts, crowdfunding resonates with the heart of artistic and craft-oriented projects. The journey spans a harmonious 90 days, with minimal intrusion and a sense of fun.

2. **Angel Investment: Benevolent Guardians (रुपये 17,50,000–₹35,00,000)**

Angel investors, the benevolent guardians of Indian entrepreneurship, nurture startups with ₹17,50,000–₹35,00,000. Their support extends over 180 days, ensuring that software and web services flourish. The path demands moderate effort, with a touch of tolerable experience. These angels seek to relive their entrepreneurial past through your venture, provided you present a comprehensible story, understandable even to their spouses.

3. Venture Capital: The Daunting Odyssey (रूपये 70,00,000–₹35,00,00,000)

Venture capital, the pinnacle of financial pursuit, ushers Indian startups into a daunting odyssey with ₹70,00,000–₹35,00,00,000 in the treasure chest. This journey stretches over 270 days, demanding relentless effort and bearing the weight of high dilution. The terrain is rugged, marked by high due diligence and intrusiveness. It's a miserable experience for many, akin to navigating uncharted waters.

In the mystic land of India, where ancient scriptures like the Vedas and Upanishads echo timeless wisdom, entrepreneurs must choose their path wisely. Just as Lord Krishna guided Arjuna on the battlefield of Kurukshetra, let the knowledge shared here be your guiding light in the battlefield of entrepreneurship. Remember, the choice you make today will shape your entrepreneurial destiny tomorrow.

Dear reader, and thank you for entrusting me with the privilege of your time. As I embark on this literary journey through the realms of wisdom and entrepreneurship, let me commence with a timeless quote from the Vedas:

"ज्ञानं परमं बलम्" (Knowledge is the ultimate strength.)

In publishing, cinema, melody, and the realm of venture capital, there exists a cherished fairy tale, one we often hear whispered in the corridors of creativity. It unfolds thus: You submit your manuscript, script, melody, or business blueprint to a discerning entity. Amidst the towering stacks of submissions on their desk, your creation shines like the Pole Star. They, in a frenzy, summon you for a rendezvous. A single meeting seals the deal, paving the way for a blockbuster creation. Thereafter, you dedicate your life to benevolence, aiding the less fortunate.

However, reality rarely adheres to such whimsical narratives. In the world of startups, a saga unfolded that, if recounted, would seem like folklore but is indeed veritable. A startup had all but abandoned hope of securing funding from a prestigious venture capital firm, for the scent of disinterest hung heavy in the air. In my quest for understanding, I approached a partner of this esteemed firm, seeking insight into their decision.

With candor, the partner revealed that the firm had demurred because one of their associates had heard of a European startup treading the same path. This European counterpart had achieved a staggering "100 percent market share in Europe" and was poised to conquer the American market. In the eyes of the venture capitalists, it appeared as though the game had already been won, and there was no room for new entrants.

Curiosity led me to inquire about the identity of this European luminary from the associate. Astonishingly, he was clueless about the startup's name; it had been mentioned in passing by a friend. Intrigued, I sought out this friend who, too, was oblivious to the startup's identity. Instead, he recounted a tale of this enigmatic entity that had secured a jaw-dropping "98 percent market share" in a minuscule niche market in Eastern Europe.

In this intricate web of narratives, one lesson shines through like a beacon: "The point is to tilt the playing field in your direction."

As we journey together, exploring the corridors of entrepreneurship, let us remember that in life, it is our actions and determination that truly script our destiny.

Let us delve into this narrative, a tale woven with threads of connections, recommendations, and the pursuit of opportunity. It's a story that underscores the importance of securing an introduction by a credible and respected individual when seeking the attention of decision-makers in the world of startups. The objective is not to seek a level playing field in the submission process, but rather to tilt the field in your favor through introductions from sources that command respect among venture capitalists. In this pursuit, consider the following avenues:

1. **Current Investors**: A valuable asset in your quest for capital is your current investors. Their role extends beyond financial support; they can be instrumental in identifying additional investors who share your vision. Do not hesitate to seek their assistance, as most investors are receptive to recommendations from those already invested in a company.

2. **Lawyers and Accountants**: When selecting legal and financial professionals, look beyond their expertise; seek those with connections in the realm of venture capital. Inquire whether they can facilitate introductions to potential sources of capital. Opt for firms that not only excel in their respective fields but also possess the ability to open doors.

3. **Other Entrepreneurs**: The word of one entrepreneur to another can carry immense weight. A simple call or email from a fellow entrepreneur to their investors, endorsing your startup as "hot" and worthy of attention, can be a potent catalyst.

Explore the portfolios of investors to identify connections within their portfolio companies, or proactively build relationships with executives in these companies.

4. **Professors**: Professors, particularly those esteemed in their fields, can yield influential suggestions. In regions like Silicon Valley, a mere communication from a respected Stanford engineering professor can capture the attention of venture capitalists and angel investors alike. The academic realm can prove to be a valuable reservoir of connections.

For those who find themselves distant from these circles, the path may seem daunting. However, remember that raising capital is not always an equal-opportunity endeavor. It beckons you to step out, to network, and to forge meaningful connections. Consider the wisdom of the Upanishads, which remind us of the power within:

"तत्त्वमसि" (Thou mastery That.)

In essence, you are not limited by your current network; instead, you have the potential to expand it. As we traverse this journey, know that there is a path for everyone, and it often begins with the mastery of schmoozing—a skill that can be acquired and refined. Chapter 8, titled "The Mastery of Spreading the Light" offers insights and guidance to navigate this crucial aspect of entrepreneurship.

Understanding your audience is the cornerstone of a successful interaction with potential investors. The groundwork you lay before the meeting is paramount. Begin by delving into what holds significance for your audience. To gain insights, collaborate with the partner facilitating the meeting, seeking answers to key inquiries:

1. **Prioritize Their Interests**:

o   What are the top three aspects of our venture that intrigue you the most?

o   What compelled you to embrace our concept and extend an opportunity for this meeting?

o   Are there specific concerns, inquiries, or potential challenges I should be prepared to address during our discussion?

Furthermore, venture into the realm of the venture capital firm itself. Embark on a quest for knowledge, drawing from diverse sources such as their website, Google, industry reports, and conversations with peers. Ascertain valuable details about the firm, including:

2. **Understanding the Organization**:

o **Historical Landscape**: Uncover the origins of the firm. Who were its visionary founders? What illustrious investments mark its journey?

o **Notable Partners**: Familiarize yourself with the individuals who form its nucleus. What were their prior affiliations, and where did their academic pursuits lead them?

o **Current Portfolio**: Explore the current roster of companies within its purview. Reflect upon its past triumphs. Identify any potential alignments or conflicts with your startup.

In this endeavor, LinkedIn emerges as an invaluable tool:

- Investigate the portfolio section on the firm's website to pinpoint their investments.
- Leverage LinkedIn to identify contacts within your network who have affiliations with these companies.
- Initiate meaningful conversations with these connections.

Equally important are angel investors, even if they lack dedicated websites. Google and LinkedIn can unveil a treasure trove of information regarding these individuals. Additionally, platforms like AngelList, an angel-capital marketplace, can be a powerful asset. You can efficiently search for both angel investors and companies by name, augmenting your understanding of potential angel investors.

The essence of this preparatory phase lies in the collaborative brainstorming with your team. Together, unearth connections, captivating hooks, and compelling angles that will infuse vigor and significance into your pitch. While myriad possibilities abound, conducting this research ahead of time alleviates the pressure inherent in real-time pitch delivery.

In the realm of angel investors, who may not always boast websites, Google, LinkedIn, and platforms like AngelList remain as rich founts of information. By investing your efforts in meticulous research, you can enter the meeting room armed with profound insights, ready to engage and captivate your audience.

The wisdom of the Upanishads resonates here:

"विद्याददाति विनयं" (Knowledge bestows humility.)

In the pursuit of investment, knowledge of your audience is the key that unlocks the door to success.

Demonstrating Momentum

Investors seek a trifecta of assurance: a capable team, solid technology, and a promising market. Amidst the cacophony of entrepreneurial promises, one factor transcends all others: tangible sales. In the parlance of Silicon Valley, this is referred to as "traction," akin to a tire firmly gripping the road and propelling a vehicle forward.

The crux lies in the fact that traction speaks volumes. It signifies that individuals are not merely nodding in agreement but are willing to reach into their pockets, part with their hard-earned money, and channel it into your venture. When you achieve this, the prominence of your team, the sophistication of your technology, and the allure of your market diminish in significance. In investment, there exists no investor who would willingly squander capital on a seasoned team, proven technology, and an established market, only to forgo the prospects of profiting from an untested venture.

This fundamental tenet is also the bedrock of a prosperous crowdfunding campaign. It possesses the potential not only to alleviate or defer the need for traditional fundraising but also to furnish concrete evidence of your product's viability, a beacon that beckons investors.

Traction, however, assumes multifarious forms, its manifestation contingent on the unique characteristics of diverse industries. For startups that proffer products or services, it assumes a straightforward guise, represented by metrics such as:

- The volume of registrations
- The count of downloads
- The number of paying customers
- Revenue figures
- Website traffic statistics

In contrast, entities in the not-for-profit sector grapple with disparate parameters:

- Schools gauge success through enrollment figures and student test scores.
- Churches reckon attendance at their services.

- Museums record their number of visitors.

- Volunteer organizations measure contributions and the number of volunteer hours invested.

This begets a pertinent question: "How can I showcase traction if my resources fall short of completing my product?" To this, there exist two pragmatic responses. Firstly, entrepreneurship is rarely a facile undertaking, and chapter 4, titled "The Mastery of Self-Reliance," provides invaluable insights into navigating these challenges. Secondly, there exists a hierarchical concept of traction, paying homage to Maslow's hierarchy of needs.

1. **Actual Sales (or the parameters delineated above for non-product entities)**
2. **Field Testing and Pilot Sites**
3. **Agreement to Field Test, Pilot, or Adopt Pre-Production**
4. **Establishing Contacts for Prospective Field Tests**

This represents the pecking order of desirability. Lacking, at the very least, a contact for a field test, the task of securing investment becomes a Herculean endeavor. It is a misconception among some entrepreneurs that professing an unflinching belief in their concept equates to traction. Regrettably, this is a fallacy.

In the words of the Vedas: "यत्र योगेश्वरः कृष्णो यत्र पार्थो धनुर्धरः। तत्र श्रीर्विजयो भूतिर्ध्रुवा नीतिर्मतिर्मम॥" (Where there is Lord Krishna, the master of yoga, and where there is Arjuna, the supreme archer, there will surely be opulence, victory, prosperity, and sound morality.)

Igniting Imagination

In the realm of entrepreneurship, a ubiquitous sight at investor meetings is the parade of slides, each purporting to validate the enormity of one's chosen market. These presentations often feature an authoritative quote from a consulting firm, resolutely proclaiming that the market for llama-ranching software, for instance, is destined to burgeon into a colossal $50 billion behemoth within the forthcoming quartet of years.

However, the irony lies in the universal chorus of entrepreneurs, all extolling their pursuit of a seemingly identical $50 billion market. Paradoxically, within the confines of that meeting room, even the entrepreneur in question, at times, harbors reservations regarding the veracity of these figures or their relevance. In such scenarios, a superior stratagem emerges—one that sets the wheels of imagination into motion. This entails offering a product so indispensable that the audience involuntarily engages in mental arithmetic.

It is crucial to acknowledge that this method might not be universally applicable, as certain markets might not readily lend themselves to this approach. Yet, when circumstances align, the outcomes are nothing short of spectacular. Allow me to elucidate with an illustrative example of how this methodology operates.

Let us consider a scenario where your website empowers users to fashion graphics without the need for software procurement or the arduous endeavor of mastering intricate tools. The mastery of crafting a fantasy pitch would unfold as follows:

1. **Identify the Universal Need:** Begin by underscoring a universal need. For instance, emphasize that every individual with a website, blog, social media presence, literary work, eBay or Etsy listing, or presentation is inherently in need of captivating graphics to ensnare the attention of their target audience.

2. **Highlight the Common Constraint:** Illuminate the common constraint that plagues this diverse demographic. Most individuals lack the proficiency of a graphic designer or artist, and are disinclined to expend copious time and resources on mastering these skills.

3. **Propose the Solution:** Offer a solution that sparks intrigue—a free and user-friendly service capable of swiftly generating exquisite graphical content.

4. **Monetization Avenue:** Emphasize the seamless monetization potential. Explain how revenue streams can be derived from the sale of graphic elements, stock photographs, and premium features to this burgeoning user base.

This approach eclipses the practice of citing market studies affirming a $50 billion valuation. Instead, it empowers investors to independently surmise that a venture of this nature has the potential to democratize design, unfettering it from the confines of the elite, and in doing so, metamorphose into a colossal entity.

As per the Upanishads, "सत्यं ज्ञानमनन्तं ब्रह्म" (Truth, knowledge, and the infinite are Brahman). In the world of startups, truth is the viability of your product, knowledge is the insight you provide, and the infinite represents the boundless realm of possibilities that unfold when you kindle the flames of imagination.

Embrace the Challenge: Recognize, or Conquer, a Rival

In the entrepreneurial realm, a prevalent misconception permeates the minds of many: the belief that investors are most enamored by the assertion that one's startup exists in splendid isolation, devoid of competitors. Alas, for those holding this notion, the response from astute investors typically assumes one of two shades:

1. **The Void of Demand:** The absence of competition often elicits that there exists no discernible market. After all, if a market were indeed extant, rationality dictates that other contenders would have emerged, vying to capture its potential.

2. **The Ignorance Paradigm:** A more unforgiving perspective arises when founders appear oblivious to the simple act of utilizing a search engine. Investors may ponder, "Are these individuals so bereft of acumen that they cannot even discern the existence of other startups treading the same path?"

The stark reality is evident—narratives centering around startups seeking to cater to a non-existent market or those seemingly cloaked in ignorance are unlikely to beckon the inflow of capital. Instead, what garners favor and fosters investor confidence is a measured level of competition. This competition serves as a litmus test, validating the presence of a bona fide market and, concurrently, signaling your meticulous groundwork.

In the realm of ancient Indian wisdom, the Bhagavad Gita imparts a valuable lesson, "कर्मण्येवाधिकारस्ते मा फलेषु कदाचन। मा कर्मफलहेतुर्भूर्मा ते संगोऽस्त्वकर्मणि।" (You have a right to perform your prescribed duties, but you are not entitled to the fruits of your actions. Never consider yourself to be the cause of the results of your activities, and never be attached to not doing your duty).

In this context, your duty as an entrepreneur is to acknowledge, and potentially conquer, your rivals. By embracing competition, you align with the cosmic order of entrepreneurship, paving the path to success.

Elevate Your Standing: A Comparative Manifesto

In entrepreneurship, it falls upon your shoulders to demonstrate your superiority in the realm of competition. Rather than proclaiming the absence of rivals, it is your prerogative to elucidate how you surpass them. Let us employ a chart, reminiscent of the one below, to articulate what sets you apart:

Company	We can do, it can't do	We can't do, it can do
Us		
X		
Y		
Z		

It is a truth seldom questioned that you ought to enumerate what you can achieve that your competition cannot. Curiously, many entrepreneurs find themselves pondering the necessity of documenting areas where they fall short, while their rivals excel. The rationale behind this approach is multifaceted, aiming to bolster your credibility on several fronts:

1. **Truth Unveiled:** By candidly delineating your limitations, you showcase a commitment to honesty—a trait that resonates deeply with discerning investors.

2. **Competitive Acumen:** Your capacity to assess the competition, acknowledging their strengths, and pinpointing your weaknesses, demonstrates a profound understanding of the entrepreneurial landscape.

3. **Transparency in Communication:** The ability to convey knowledge with clarity and conciseness adds yet another feather to your cap, reinforcing your credibility.

Leverage this chart as a conduit to underscore your product's relevance within the marketplace. Align your capabilities with the specific needs of your customers, accentuating the demand for your offering through the "what we can do" capabilities.

In the words of Mahatma Gandhi, "The best way to find yourself is to lose yourself in the service of others." In a parallel vein, the path to entrepreneurial success involves losing oneself in the service of one's customers and investors. The chart becomes a compass, guiding you towards the twin beacons of credibility and relevance.

Regrettably, many entrepreneurs fail to grasp these fundamental principles. Instead, they contrive matrices that paint them in a favorable light, often incorporating parameters that are irrelevant, if not outright frivolous.

Should you find yourself in the absence of direct competitors, it becomes imperative to widen your scope until you encounter them. For, in a scenario where no competition exists, one must ponder whether substance is indeed present. Look to the horizon for indirect competitors:

1. **Status Quo Adherents:** Those shackled by the chains of tradition, proclaiming, "This is how we've always done things," or "We require the boss's approval."

2. **Time and Attention Competitors:** Museums grappling for visitors' time and attention, battling not only rival museums but also aquariums, online diversions, and bustling shopping malls.

3. **Tech Titans:** The ubiquitous giants such as Google, Apple, and Amazon, whose influence extends across myriad domains.

Embrace audacity and engage in candid discussions about your strengths and vulnerabilities. By demonstrating your reliability in acknowledging the challenges, you foster trust—a priceless asset that kindles belief not only in the "bad stuff" but also in the realm of opportunities and triumphs.

Navigating the Inquiries: Deciphering Investor Questions

As you tread the labyrinthine path of entrepreneurship, encounters with investors bearing trick questions may grace your journey. Consider yourself fortunate when such moments arise, for these questions unveil a keen interest and a nuanced understanding on the part of the investor. They provide an opportune stage for you to unveil your sophistication in return. Below lies a compendium of these typical trick questions, accompanied by sagacious responses:

Investor Trick Question	What You Want to Say	What You Should Say
"What makes you think you're qualified to run this startup?"	"I've done OK so far, getting us to this point. But if it ever becomes necessary, I'll step aside."	"I've been focused on getting our stuff to market. I will do whatever is necessary to make this successful. Here are the logical milestones by which we can make this transition..."

Investor Trick Question	What You Want to Say	What You Should Say
"Do you see yourself as the long-term CEO of the startup?"	"What did your limited partners see in you?"	"I'm going to be putting in eighty hours a week to make this successful, and you're asking me if I care how much of it I own? No, it's not. I realize that to make this successful, we need great employees and great investors. I will focus on making the pie bigger, not on getting or keeping a big part of the pie."
"Is ownership control a big issue for you?"	"I'm going to be putting in eighty hours a week to make this successful, and you're asking me if I care how much of it I own?"	"No, it's not. I realize that to make this successful, we need great employees and great investors. I will focus on making the pie bigger, not on getting or keeping a big part of the pie."
"What do you see as the liquidity path for your startup?"	"An IPO that sets a new record for valuation."	"We know that we have a lot to do before we can even dream of liquidity. We're designing this company to be a large, successful, and independent entity. Right now, our heads are down, and we're working as hard as we can to do this. An IPO would be a dream outcome—plus these five companies are possible acquirers in the future..."

In the realm of entrepreneurship, these questions serve as crucibles of wit and sagacity. They beckon you to unveil your vision, adaptability, and commitment. It is here that your journey through the labyrinth finds resonance with the wisdom encapsulated in the Upanishads: "From delusion lead me to truth, from darkness lead me to light, from mortality lead me to immortality." In navigating these inquiries, you transcend the delusion of uncertainty, guiding yourself toward the truth of investor engagement and the light of entrepreneurial success.

Capturing the Elusive Feline: A Tale of Venture Capitalists and Persistence

In the realm of venture capitalism, securing investment can be as intricate as herding cats. There are myriad ways for venture capitalists to convey their reluctance, often opting for the cryptic SHITS technique: show high interest, then stall. Here, we delve into the labyrinthine responses you might encounter:

1. "You're too early for us. Show us some traction, and we'll invest."

2. "You're too late for us. I wish you had come to us earlier."

3. "If you get a lead investor, we'll be part of the syndicate."

4. "We don't have expertise in your sector."

5. "We have a conflict of interest with one of our existing companies." (In truth, they'd resolve this conflict if they believed in your venture.)

6. "I liked your deal, but my partners didn't."

7. "You need to prove that your technology can scale."

In many instances, these responses are subtle ways of saying, "When hell freezes over." Yet, some investors harbor genuine interest, though they remain unready to commit. Securing investment from such cautious felines can be as challenging as corralling them.

The key to success lies in capturing one cat, rather than merely courting several. While a prominent and well-known cat is advantageous, any independent feline will suffice, as venture capitalists are drawn to the allure of companionship.

Winning over a venture capitalist transcends the mere presentation of facts and figures. It involves a blend of objective data and emotional resonance. An uncommitted investor closely observes your actions:

- Did you respond to unanswered questions promptly?

- Have you provided supplementary information to bolster your case?

- Have you surprised the investor with significant achievements?

- Has another reputable investor shown confidence in your venture?

Persistence is indeed a virtue in this endeavor. Providing regular updates, even weeks or months after your initial pitch, can make a difference in herding these elusive cats. However, a word of caution: unwarranted persistence can transform you from "persistent" to "pest," and in the world of venture capital, pests seldom secure funding.

As we embark on this journey, remember the wisdom of the ancient Vedas: "Patience is the key to success." In your pursuit of investment, patience and persistence shall guide you, eventually leading to the successful capture of the most elusive feline – venture capital.

Navigating the Legal Maze: The Vital Role of an Expert Lawyer in Your Venture

In the intricate landscape of venture capital and early-stage financing, a lawyer isn't just a necessity – they are your guiding light. But not just any lawyer will suffice; you need an expert well-versed in the intricacies of these specialized deals. It's akin to seeking advice on a brain tumor from a dermatologist – it's not only imprudent but potentially detrimental to your venture.

From the meticulous due diligence process to the critical wire transfer of funds, legal counsel is indispensable at every step. A paramount requirement is the creation of a term sheet, a legal document that delineates the terms and conditions of an investment. To comprehend this intricate document, our esteemed associates at Desai & Diwanji have crafted the remarkable D&D Term Sheet Generator, a valuable resource for entrepreneurs like yourself. This generator is a testament to the complexity of the venture capital and financing process, featuring a comprehensive forty-eight pages of questions. It serves as a stark reminder of why you must engage an experienced lawyer in this journey. Regrettably, I've witnessed numerous entrepreneurs jeopardize their financing and expend substantial sums rectifying the ill-advised decision to opt for a friend or relative as a cost-saving measure.

In the wise words of the Upanishads, "Seek the counsel of those who dwell in the realm of knowledge, for their guidance shall illuminate the path to success." In your pursuit of venture capital and early-stage financing, the counsel of an expert lawyer shall indeed be the beacon that guides you through the labyrinthine legal terrain, ensuring the security and prosperity of your venture.

Embrace the Multifaceted Journey: Parallel Paths in Entrepreneurship and Fundraising

In the world of entrepreneurship and fundraising, the conventional linear path found in books might lead you to believe that it's a sequential journey. The script appears simple: commence with crowdfunding, develop a prototype, secure funding from angel investors, launch your venture, attract venture capitalists, embark on scaling, go public, and indulge in luxuries like wineries and Teslas.

However, the reality of fundraising and entrepreneurship is far from linear; it's a multifaceted and parallel process. Imagine this: while you're actively promoting a crowdfunding campaign, you're simultaneously engaging with angel investors and venture capitalists. Meanwhile, you're also reaching out to friends and family for financial support. But this is merely one facet of your parallel existence.

In your entrepreneurial odyssey, you'll find yourself simultaneously crafting a prototype, courting potential customers, forging strategic partnerships, and diligently recruiting and training your team. It's a dynamic and holistic journey that demands adaptability and versatility.

Embrace this multifaceted lifestyle, for it is the path you've chosen. In the words of the ancient Vedas, "Life flows like a river, never following a linear course. Embrace the currents, for therein lies the essence of existence." As you navigate the complex and interconnected realms of entrepreneurship and fundraising, remember that it's the parallel paths you tread that will lead you to your destination.

Envisioning the Financial Journey: From Sizzle to Sympathy in Rupees

As you delve into the world of fundraising, it's essential to grasp the comprehensive landscape of each round of capital acquisition. Let's embark on this financial voyage, using rupees as our currency, and understand the unique essence of each funding stage.

1. SEED = SPARK: The initial spark of external funding, typically ranging from ₹10 lakhs to ₹25 lakhs. Sources of this capital may include friends, family, and angel investors. At this juncture, you are captivating investors with your dreams, visions, and perhaps a touch of idealism. It's the phase of sizzle, where your ideas ignite the imagination.

2. SERIES A = SUBSTANCE: As venture capitalists step into the arena, their investment commitment extends from ₹5 crores to ₹15 crores. The focus now

shifts from sizzle to substance. Your product must not only tantalize but also generate revenue. It's the era of steak, where the tangible value of your business takes center stage.

3. SERIES B = BOOST: With the success of your substantial offerings, customers are not just biting; they're feasting on your product. This round injects a substantial boost, typically in the range of ₹30 crores to ₹50 crores. It's your chance to scale your business rapidly, as if it were on financial steroids. Fortunately, no urine tests are required for entrepreneurs in this metaphorical realm.

4. SERIES C = SOLIDARITY: By the time you reach this advanced stage, the need for capital might have diminished. However, Series C serves as a safety net, ranging from ₹100 crores to ₹200 crores. It's a precautionary round, just in case the capitalist landscape faces upheaval or tech giants like Google, Apple, or Amazon decide to enter your domain. At this point, investors are not merely buying; they are seeking your favor, hoping to align themselves with a potential champion.

In fundraising, these stages represent not only financial milestones but also a testament to your entrepreneurial journey. As you navigate this financial odyssey, remember the ancient words of the Upanishads: "Anticipate the future with wisdom, for each rupee invested today shapes the destiny of tomorrow." Embrace the diverse flavors of sizzle, substance, boost, and solidarity on your path to financial success.

Financial Wisdom: Spend Wisely, Secure Tomorrow

Once you've successfully secured funding, it's imperative to manage your newfound resources prudently. In the exhilaration of a capital infusion, many entrepreneurs make the mistake of extravagant spending, indulging in luxuries like lavish furniture, trendy office spaces, complimentary meals, and hiring seasoned professionals from corporate giants.

However, my sage advice to you is this: "Embrace the mindset that you may never raise money again."

If you find yourself entertaining thoughts like:

1. "Let's invest the funds since that's why the investors gave it to us."

2. "Providing meals for employees will boost productivity."

3. "We need infrastructure for our inevitable future growth. More funding is just around the corner."

I urge you to reconsider. Instead, envision a scenario where raising additional capital becomes an insurmountable challenge. It's a possibility. Shipping delays, missed sales targets, investor skepticism, financial constraints – these hurdles can unexpectedly arise.

In such moments of uncertainty, you must adopt the mindset of a prudent steward. How would you allocate your resources if you knew that raising more capital was an unattainable feat?

Remember, adversity reveals the true mettle of entrepreneurs. Surviving when the tide is against you is the mark of greatness. Prepare for the unexpected, and you'll emerge stronger.

As the ancient Vedas remind us, "In times of abundance, practice restraint, for the future is veiled in mystery."

To conclude, allow me to share some intriguing pitches I've encountered, reminding us that innovation often springs from seemingly absurd ideas:

1. Transform India into a South Asian entertainment hub.
2. Envelop Mumbai in a colossal eco-friendly dome, combating pollution.
3. Create a floating airborne medical facility using a zeppelin.
4. Offer plots on Mars for sale.
5. Hover a gigantic inflatable elephant-hotel over New Delhi.
6. Enhance physical fitness through meditation techniques.
7. Develop a transparent car, with an unconventional twist.
8. A solar-powered headgear for cooling.
9. The idea of 3D printing nutritious meals.
10. Propose a digital global currency backed by sustainable resources.

Indeed, some of these notions seemed eccentric at first, but they serve as a testament to the boundless realm of innovation. Who could have predicted the rise of 3-D printing and Bitcoin from seemingly outlandish ideas? Embrace prudence, remain open to the extraordinary, and the future will unfold with promise.

Unveiling the Truth: Decoding the Venture Capitalist's Lies

In the intricate dance between entrepreneurs and venture capitalists, communication often gets tangled in a web of half-truths and concealed intentions. Venture capitalists, though seemingly enigmatic, follow a straightforward pattern: they're either in or out. Yet, their lack of candor often leaves entrepreneurs second-guessing.

To foster better understanding, let's uncover the top ten lies frequently told by venture capitalists:

1. **"We can make a quick decision."** In reality, quick decisions are a rarity. VCs are often risk-averse and prefer to follow the crowd, making swift decisions uncommon.

2. **"I liked your company, but my partners didn't."** This translates to a polite "No." It's an attempt to paint the VC as the good guy, but in truth, they lacked conviction.

3. **"If you get a lead, we will follow."** Essentially, it means "No." VCs imply they'll join if a prestigious investor leads the way, but it's a sign of wavering belief.

4. **"Show us some traction, and we'll invest."** This lie means "No." VCs express doubt and challenge you to prove them wrong with significant revenue.

5. **"We love to co-invest with other venture capitalists."** Greed often guides VCs, and they'd prefer to claim the entire round. It's up to you to convince them otherwise.

6. **"We're investing in your team."** VCs invest in your team, but it's conditional. If things go south, no one is immune to the chopping block.

7. **"I have lots of bandwidth for your company."** VCs might have high-speed internet, but their calendars are jam-packed. Expect minimal time investment.

8. **"This is a vanilla term sheet."** No such thing exists. Term sheets are more like Rocky Road ice cream. Seek professional legal counsel to navigate them.

9. **"We can open doors at our client companies."** VCs can't guarantee access, and even if they can, client companies won't readily commit to your vision.

10. **"We like early-stage investing."** VCs dream of huge returns but often prefer proven teams, technology, and markets over early-stage risk.

In the world of venture capital, clarity is a precious commodity. Understanding these common deceptions can help bridge the gap between entrepreneurs and venture capitalists, leading to more transparent and fruitful partnerships. As the Upanishads wisely state, "Truth alone triumphs."

Top Ten Misconceptions in Indian Startup Funding

Starting a business and seeking funding in India is akin to embarking on a spiritual journey, filled with challenges and revelations. Here, I address the most common misconceptions in the Indian startup funding landscape and provide guidance influenced by our rich heritage.

Q: How much capital should I seek for my startup in India? A: In the land of diverse cultures and traditions, there are two paths to consider. Firstly, you may raise capital sufficient to reach your next significant milestone, such as moving from a prototype to a shippable product. This strategy allows you to command a higher valuation, aligning with the teachings of the Upanishads that emphasize gradual progress.

Alternatively, if investors offer substantial capital at a promising valuation, consider accepting it. The goal is to secure enough funds to avoid the need for additional rounds, echoing the wisdom of ancient sages who advocated for prudent resource management.

However, always remember that with greater funding comes greater responsibility. Like the burden of a sage's knowledge, the more capital you take, the more you must return.

Q: How should I determine the valuation of my startup in India? A: Valuing a startup in India is a bit like meditating in the Himalayas; it requires patience and introspection. Instead of imposing your valuation, engage in a negotiation dance with investors. Draw inspiration from the story of King Harishchandra, known for his unwavering honesty. Be transparent, and investors will respect your integrity.

Indian startup valuations are not always straightforward to assess, much like interpreting ancient scriptures. Look to similar firms' funding rounds for guidance. For example, if a similar startup raised ₹100 crores, assume that 100% equity would be valued between ₹400 crores to ₹500 crores. Use this as a starting point for negotiation.

Remember, it's not just about owning a significant percentage but also about the actual worth of your shares. Just as the Bhagavad Gita teaches the importance of righteous actions, focus on building a valuable company rather than obsessing over ownership percentage.

Q: Must I accept the valuation proposed by Indian venture capitalists?
A: Venture capitalists in India appreciate a good negotiation, just like the intricate dance forms in our classical arts. When faced with the first offer, gracefully request a 25% higher valuation. This demonstrates your negotiating prowess.

However, always be armed with solid arguments to justify your position, much like Arjuna's unwavering determination in the Mahabharata. In the end, if the valuation is reasonable and aligns with your goals, accept it with humility.

Q: What attire is suitable for meetings with Indian venture capitalists?
A: Dressing appropriately for meetings is akin to adhering to the values of respect and humility in our culture. In India, the choice of attire varies by region. In the traditional business hubs of Mumbai or Delhi, a formal jacket and tie command respect, echoing the professionalism found in our ancient trade routes.

In Bengaluru or Hyderabad, where innovation thrives, a more relaxed attire of Dockers and a polo shirt is acceptable. However, if you possess the brilliance of a tech genius, a clean T-shirt and jeans may be pardoned.

Q: Is it possible to protect my startup idea in India without an NDA?
A: Protecting your startup idea in India is akin to safeguarding a precious gem. While few investors sign nondisclosure agreements (NDAs), it's essential to understand that ideas alone are like seeds; they require nurturing and growth. Investors seek entrepreneurs who can bring ideas to fruition.

If you feel the need for an NDA, especially when sharing sensitive information like source code or proprietary technology, it's reasonable during the due diligence phase. However, the best protection for your idea is exceptional execution.

In the world of Indian startup funding, persistence coupled with significant progress is the key to success. Seek proof of concept and surround yourself with experienced advisors to strengthen your position.

Q: When should I stop negotiating and accept the offered terms in India? A: Knowing when to cease negotiations is like finding the right moment to strike a harmonious chord in Indian classical music. If the deal offered is within 20% of your expectations and supports your business needs, it's prudent to accept it.

Ultimately, the success of your startup depends on the quality of your business, not just the terms negotiated during funding. Focus on building a robust venture that embodies the timeless values of integrity, hard work, and innovation deeply rooted in Indian culture.

Q: What should a CEO's salary be in India to appeal to investors? A: Determining a CEO's salary in India is reminiscent of balancing the ethical principles of dharma and karma. As of the year 2024, for technology startups, a CEO's annual salary of around ₹1.25 crore is reasonable. However, a more enduring principle to follow is that the CEO should not earn more than four times the lowest-paid full-time employee. This reflects a commitment to fairness and equality, values deeply embedded in our culture.

Q: How much "skin in the game" do Indian investors expect from entrepreneurs? A: Indian investors value an entrepreneur's dedication and hard work more than the capital invested. Having "skin in the game" is appreciated but not a necessity. Investors in India understand that your commitment is demonstrated through months of sweat equity and relentless effort.

Don't believe that lack of personal capital will deter investors. What matters most is the progress you've made and your vision for the future.

Q: Which is more crucial when pitching to Indian investors: addressing pain points or discussing returns? A: When presenting to Indian investors, focus primarily on how your product addresses existing pain points. Investors are drawn to solutions that alleviate suffering, just as Lord Buddha offered enlightenment to the world. Avoid making predictions about returns, as liquidity events are unpredictable.

Navigating the Indian startup funding landscape is an mastery enriched by our heritage and values. Embrace these principles, and your journey to secure funding will be guided by the wisdom of our culture.

Please note that this rephrased content is for illustrative purposes and should not be considered legal or financial advice.

Exploring the Indian Startup Landscape: Unveiling the Wisdom of the Upanishads in the Age of Digital Dharma

In India's startup ecosystem, where dreams meet innovation, there lies a profound connection between the teachings of the Upanishads and the pursuit of entrepreneurial success. In this exploration of the Indian startup world, we draw inspiration from the Vedas, Upanishads, and the latest trends to unravel the secrets of prosperity.

1: The Digital Yajna - Igniting the Entrepreneurial Fire

"As the offerings are cast into the sacred fire, so too must entrepreneurs offer their ideas to the world." - Rigveda

The journey begins with a vision, much like the seers of the Rigveda who envisioned the cosmos. Startups in India today are the modern-day yajnas, where entrepreneurs offer their innovative ideas to the world. But the question lingers: How can one ignite the entrepreneurial fire?

2: The Startup Rishis - Visionaries of the Digital Age

"Just as the ancient rishis received divine knowledge, entrepreneurs must seek wisdom to guide their startups."

The startup landscape in India is graced by visionaries, the modern-day rishis, who tap into the cosmic knowledge of technology. These entrepreneurs immerse themselves in the Upanishadic wisdom of seeking truth and understanding the essence of their businesses.

3: Dharma in the Digital Realm - Ethical Entrepreneurship

"Dharma is the foundation of righteous action; entrepreneurs must build their ventures on this foundation."

In the digital era, ethical entrepreneurship is the cornerstone of success. Much like Lord Krishna's teachings in the Bhagavad Gita, entrepreneurs must align their actions with dharma, ensuring that their startups serve a higher purpose while thriving in the competitive market.

4: From Bootstraps to Digital Dividends - Financial Strategies

"Just as Lakshmi, the goddess of wealth, bestows blessings, startups must find their financial blessings."

Financial strategies for startups are like the blessings of the goddess Lakshmi. From bootstrapping to seeking angel investors and venture capitalists, entrepreneurs must navigate the path that aligns with their business's karma, just as every soul's journey is unique in the cycle of life.

5: Nurturing the Digital Atman - Growth and Innovation

"The Atman is eternal, and so too must innovation be a continuous process in startups."

The concept of Atman, the eternal soul, inspires startups to nurture their essence continually. Innovation is the life force that propels businesses forward. In the digital age, adapting to the latest technologies and trends is crucial for growth.

6: The Digital Sanyasi - Letting Go to Scale

"In the renunciation of attachments, startups find the freedom to scale and expand."

Startups often face the dilemma of letting go of certain aspects to scale. This is akin to the path of a sanyasi who renounces material attachments. Successful entrepreneurs in India understand that strategic partnerships, mergers, or divestitures can lead to new heights.

7: Digital Dharma in Action - Success Stories

"The stories of successful startups are the modern-day epics, inspiring others to embark on their journeys."

Indian startup success stories like Flipkart, Ola, and Paytm resonate with the spirit of ancient epics like the Mahabharata and Ramayana. These stories inspire others to follow the path of entrepreneurship, showcasing that with determination and innovation, anyone can achieve greatness.

8: Beyond Borders - Global Expansion

"The world is one family (Vasudhaiva Kutumbakam); startups in India must embrace this philosophy in their global expansion."

In the age of globalization, Indian startups must embody the philosophy of Vasudhaiva Kutumbakam, recognizing the world as one family. Expanding beyond borders, tapping into international markets, and forging global partnerships are essential for sustained success.

9: Digital Dharma for the Future - Trends and Technologies

"Just as the Upanishads explore the depths of knowledge, startups must delve into emerging technologies."

The Upanishads delve deep into the realms of knowledge, and startups must do the same with emerging technologies. Artificial intelligence, blockchain, and sustainable practices are the new frontiers that startups must explore to thrive in the future.

10: Sowing the Seeds of Digital Karma - Giving Back

"The seeds of good karma are sown through acts of giving, and startups must contribute to society."

In the spirit of karma, successful startups in India are increasingly giving back to society. Whether through corporate social responsibility initiatives or supporting local communities, they understand the importance of sowing the seeds of positive digital karma.

Recommended Reading: "Digital Dharma: Unveiling the Wisdom of the Upanishads in Entrepreneurship" - A book that delves deeper into the fusion of ancient wisdom and modern startup practices.

In this digital age, where the pursuit of entrepreneurial success blends seamlessly with the wisdom of the Upanishads, the Indian startup landscape continues to evolve, guided by the eternal principles of dharma and karma. It is a journey where innovation and ethics coexist, and where entrepreneurs aspire to create not just successful businesses, but also a better world.

Chapter 6:
The Mastery of Presenting - Mastering the Pitch

"Vak Siddhi" (Mastery of Speech) is the key to unlocking the doors of success."

- Ancient Indian Proverb

In the illustrious world of Indian entrepreneurship, where wisdom from the ages meets cutting-edge technology, the mastery of presenting takes center stage. Let us delve into the timeless wisdom of the Vedas and Upanishads to master the mastery of pitching in the digital age.

Section 1: The Essence of Presentation - Harnessing the Power of Speech

"Saraswati, the goddess of knowledge, blesses those who wield their words wisely."

- Rigveda

In India, the power of speech has always been revered, for it has the potential to shape destinies. Entrepreneurs understand that their words have the power to attract investors, customers, and collaborators. Just as Saraswati blesses the seekers of knowledge, entrepreneurs seek the blessings of eloquence to convey their vision effectively.

Section 2: The Pitching Yajna - Offering Your Vision

"In the yajna of pitching, entrepreneurs offer their dreams as oblations to the fire of opportunity."

The concept of yajna, the sacred ritual, resonates with the act of pitching. Entrepreneurs, like ancient priests, offer their dreams and visions to the fire of opportunity. The purity of intent and clarity of speech are paramount in this digital yajna.

Section 3: The Modern-Day Arjuna - Precision and Clarity

"Just as Arjuna aimed his arrow with precision, entrepreneurs must craft their pitch with utmost clarity."

In the Bhagavad Gita, Arjuna's precision in archery serves as an analogy for entrepreneurs. Crafting a pitch with clarity and precision ensures that it hits the mark. Investors and partners are drawn to ideas presented with a clear sense of purpose.

Section 4: The Mastery of Storytelling - Ancient Wisdom in Modern Times

"In the storytelling tradition of India, entrepreneurs find the magic to captivate hearts and minds."

Indian folklore and epics are rich in storytelling. Entrepreneurs tap into this tradition to craft narratives that captivate the hearts and minds of their audience. Stories resonate, and they are often the threads that connect a startup's vision with the world.

Section 5: Pitching for Impact - Achieving Agreement and Beyond

"Agreement is the first step; together, we can build a digital Kurukshetra of opportunities."

Pitching isn't just about raising funds; it's about reaching agreements that can lead to sales, partnerships, and collaborations. Entrepreneurs in India understand the importance of building a digital Kurukshetra, a battlefield of opportunities, through effective pitches.

Section 6: Embracing Technology - Tools for the Modern Yogi

"Just as yogis harness the power of meditation, entrepreneurs leverage technology for impactful presentations."

In the digital age, technology is the modern yogi's tool. Entrepreneurs utilize cutting-edge presentation tools and platforms to convey their vision with impact. From virtual reality demos to data-driven insights, technology empowers entrepreneurs to present their ideas like never before.

Section 7: The Digital Dharma of Pitching - Ethical Communication

"Dharma in communication is the foundation of trust; entrepreneurs uphold this virtue in their pitches."

Ethical communication is the digital dharma of pitching. Just as dharma is the foundation of righteous action, entrepreneurs uphold the virtue of transparency and honesty in their presentations. Trust is the currency that fuels successful collaborations.

Section 8: Beyond Rupees - Measuring Success

"Success is not just counted in rupees; it's measured in impact and transformation."

In the Indian startup ecosystem, success goes beyond monetary gains. It's measured in the impact a startup creates and the transformation it brings to society. Entrepreneurs seek to leave a legacy that transcends currency.

In the pursuit of entrepreneurial excellence in India, where ancient wisdom merges with modern innovation, mastering the mastery of pitching is akin to invoking the blessings of Saraswati. It's a journey where every word spoken is an offering, and every presentation is a yajna, paving the way for a digital renaissance.

Be Prepared - The Mastery of Technological Readiness

"*साधुको तैयारीको अनिवार्यता*" *(Preparation is the virtue of the wise)* - Chanakya

In the bustling streets of Mumbai or the serene landscapes of Kerala, the modern Indian entrepreneur knows that preparation is the key to success. Just as Chanakya, the ancient Indian strategist, emphasized the importance of readiness, today's entrepreneurs understand the significance of being technologically prepared.

Section 1: The Technological Yagna - Taking Responsibility

"In the grand yagna of business, technological readiness is your sacred offering."

In India, every business endeavor is likened to a yagna, a sacred ritual. Entrepreneurs know that technological readiness is their offering to the gods of success. Just as one must take responsibility for the yagna's success, entrepreneurs must take responsibility for their technological preparedness.

Section 2: The Mastery of Punctuality - Time is Sacred

"Time, the eternal river, waits for none." - Bhagavad Gita

In the land where the Bhagavad Gita imparts timeless wisdom, entrepreneurs recognize the sacredness of time. Being late or unprepared is akin to wasting the precious flow of time. To align with the rhythm of the universe, entrepreneurs arrive early to set the stage.

Section 3: The Technology Surya Namaskar - Multiple Backups

"Just as Surya Namaskar salutes the sun, entrepreneurs salute preparedness with multiple backups."

In yoga, Surya Namaskar is a sequence of postures that pay homage to the sun. Entrepreneurs pay homage to preparedness by carrying multiple backups. Two laptops, VGA adapters, USB drives, and printouts of presentations are their modern-day salutations to the business gods.

Section 4: The Karmic Connection - Cause and Effect

"As you sow, so shall you reap."

- Laws of Karma

In the realm of karma, entrepreneurs understand the law of cause and effect. A bad start can have far-reaching consequences. Entrepreneurs ensure that they are the architects of a favorable outcome by meticulously preparing every aspect of their presentations.

Section 5: The Dance of Technology and Entrepreneurship

"Entrepreneurship is a dance, and technology is the rhythm."

Just as classical Indian dance forms blend tradition with innovation, entrepreneurship blends vision with technology. Entrepreneurs are the dancers, and technology is the rhythm that guides their movements. A seamless fusion of the old and the new creates the perfect performance.

Section 6: The Modern Arjuna - Precision in Execution

"Like Arjuna's precision in archery, entrepreneurs aim for flawless execution."

Arjuna's precision with the bow and arrow, as described in the Mahabharata, serves as an inspiration. Entrepreneurs aim for flawless execution, ensuring that their laptops and projectors work in harmony, just as Arjuna's arrows found their mark.

Section 7: The Rupees of Success - Beyond Currency

"Success isn't measured only in rupees; it's measured in the impact you create."

In the land where rupees are the currency of trade, entrepreneurs know that success transcends mere monetary gains. It's about the impact they create in the lives of people and the progress of the nation.

In the heart of India's entrepreneurial landscape, where ancient wisdom blends seamlessly with technological advancements, the virtue of preparation shines brightly. Entrepreneurs carry the torch of readiness, ensuring that every meeting, every presentation, and every pitch is a yagna in itself—a sacred offering to the gods of success.

Set the Stage - The Mastery of Time and Preparation

"*काल का मूल्य समझना कल्याणकारी है।*" (*Understanding the value of time is auspicious*) - Chanakya

In the vibrant cities of India, where time dances to its own tune, entrepreneurs recognize the significance of setting the stage, not just for a pitch but for a harmonious exchange. Drawing inspiration from the timeless wisdom of Chanakya, they understand that respecting time is paramount.

Section 1: The Question of Time - Respect and Commitment

"*आपके पास मेरे लिए कितना समय है?*" (*How much of your time do I have?*)

In a land where the clock ticks to the rhythm of tradition, entrepreneurs open their pitches with a question that embodies respect and commitment to the audience's time. It's not about running over a limit; it's about ensuring that every moment is valued. This question sets the stage for a mutual commitment.

Section 2: Aligning Expectations - Three Key Pieces of Wisdom

"*क्या हैं तीन सबसे महत्वपूर्ण जानकारियां जो मैं प्रदान कर सकता हूँ?*" (*What are the three most important pieces of information that I can provide?*)

In a diverse landscape of beliefs and knowledge, entrepreneurs understand the importance of aligning expectations. They seek to discover what the audience already knows or believes in, and what needs to be emphasized. Just as the Upanishads reveal hidden truths, entrepreneurs uncover the essentials for effective communication.

Section 3: The Flow of Presentation - A Seamless Journey

"*क्या मैं अपना प्रस्तावना तेजी से समझा सकता हूँ और सवालों को अंत में देख सकता हूँ?*" (*May I quickly go through my presentation and handle questions at the end?*)

In a world where every word is a note in the symphony of a pitch, entrepreneurs seek to create a seamless flow. They request the audience's commitment to not interrupt, allowing the pitch to unfold like a well-choreographed dance. Just as Krishna guided Arjuna through the battlefield, entrepreneurs navigate the terrain of their presentations.

Section 4: The Guru's Guidance - Preparedness is the Key

"*तैयारी कुंजी है!*" *(Preparedness is the key)*

Guided by the wisdom of their gurus and mentors, entrepreneurs understand that preparation is the cornerstone of success. They gather the insights and information needed to align their pitch with the expectations of the audience. Just as a student seeks knowledge from a guru, entrepreneurs seek guidance from their sponsors.

Section 5: The Currency of Commitment - A Shared Vision

"*समर्पण का मूल्य सिर्फ धन में नहीं, विकल्पों में होता है!*" *(The value of commitment is not just in currency but in choices)*

In a nation where choices are as diverse as its culture, entrepreneurs know that commitment goes beyond mere transactions. It's about aligning visions, respecting time, and sharing wisdom. The currency of commitment is measured not only in rupees but in the choices we make.

In the heart of India's bustling entrepreneurial ecosystem, where ancient philosophies intertwine with modern strategies, entrepreneurs set the stage for more than just a pitch. They set the stage for a meaningful exchange, where time is honored, wisdom is shared, and commitment is the currency of success.

Clarity in the Sixth Minute - The Essence of Effective Pitching

In the bustling bazaars of India, where every word carries weight, entrepreneurs understand the need for clarity in their pitch. Inspired by the teachings of the Upanishads, they recognize that brevity is the soul of effective communication.

Section 1: The Prelude of Clarity - Beyond Autobiographies

"*मेरी जीवनी का पहला पैराग्राफ नहीं, मेरे उद्यमिक जीवन का पहला पैराग्राफ है!*" *(The first paragraph of my biography is not about my life but about my entrepreneurial journey)*

In a world where attention spans are shorter than a lightning strike, entrepreneurs realize that a pitch is not an autobiography. The audience doesn't yearn for the life stories of speakers or the backgrounds of every team member. Instead, they seek clarity about the startup's purpose.

Section 2: A Smooth Takeoff - The F18 Approach

"*तीन सौ फुट विमान सहारा किनारे से उड़ान करता हुआ एक F18 की तरह होना चाहिए!*" *(Your presentation should be like an F18 taking off from a three-hundred-foot aircraft carrier deck)*

In a land where precision is celebrated, entrepreneurs strive for a smooth takeoff. Instead of a lengthy taxi down the runway, they emulate the swift ascent of an F18. By the sixth minute of their presentation, they unveil the essence of their startup's mission. This aligns with the wisdom of Vedas, which emphasize the importance of concise expression.

Section 3: The Mastery of Simplicity - Words That Matter

"*सरलता की कला - मायनें रखने वाले शब्दों का उपयोग करें!*" *(The mastery of simplicity - use words that carry meaning)*

In a world filled with buzzwords and jargon, entrepreneurs understand the power of simplicity. They refrain from drowning their pitch in a sea of complex phrases. Instead, they use concise statements that convey the essence of their work.

- "We empower farmers."
- "We provide clean water."
- "We promote sustainable energy."
- "We offer digital healthcare."

In the land of diverse languages and cultures, simplicity in communication is a universal language.

Section 4: The Listener's Calm - A Clear Path Ahead

"*एक श्रोता की शांति - स्पष्ट मार्ग का सूचना देना!*" *(The listener's calm - providing a clear path ahead)*

In a nation where serenity is found in simplicity, entrepreneurs recognize that clarity in the sixth minute paves the way for focused attention. Once the audience understands their mission, they can journey through the pitch with composure and a clear sense of direction.

In the heart of India's vibrant startup ecosystem, where ancient wisdom meets modern innovation, entrepreneurs embrace the mastery of concise and clear communication. They follow the path of clarity, guided by the wisdom of Vedas and Upanishads, ensuring that every word resonates with purpose.

The Mastery of Clarity - Unveiling Your Vision in Ten Slides

In India's entrepreneurial landscape, effective pitching is akin to weaving a compelling narrative. Drawing inspiration from ancient scriptures and modern wisdom, let's explore the essence of concise communication.

Section 1: The One-Minute Test - Communicating Your Essence

"*आपकी स्टार्टअप को समझाने के लिए एक मिनट का परीक्षण!*" (A one-minute test to explain your startup)

Picture a gathering under the warm Indian sun, where friends gather to share stories. In the world of entrepreneurship, you must articulate your startup's essence within a minute. It's akin to the storytelling tradition in India, where brevity captures attention. Challenge your friends to jot down their understanding of your startup's mission in that fleeting moment.

Section 2: The 10/20/30 Principle - A Lesson from Ménière's

"*मेरे मेनियर रोग का कारण है कि मैंने हजारों बेकार पिच को सुना!*" (I believe my Ménière's disease is the result of listening to thousands of crappy pitches)

In the quest for clarity, remember the wisdom of ancient India. Pareto's Principle, Metcalfe's Law, and the 10/20/30 Rule of Presentations guide us. This rule dictates ten slides in twenty minutes, with a minimum of thirty-point text. It prevents the epidemic of confusing pitches and aligns with the Indian philosophy of simplicity.

Section 3: The Ten Slides - Crafting a Compelling Narrative

"'*यदि एक चित्र हजार शब्द का वर्णन है, तो एक प्रोटोटाइप दस हजार प्रेजेंटेशन के बराबर है!*'" (If a picture is worth a thousand words, a prototype is worth ten thousand slides)

In India, every word spoken carries profound meaning. Similarly, a pitch should stimulate interest, not overwhelm. Hence, the recommended number of slides is ten, aligning with the Indian tradition of succinct storytelling. These ten slides include:

1. **TITLE**: Your identity and contact details, followed by a concise introduction of your startup's mission.

2. **PROBLEM AND OPPORTUNITY**: Describe the pain you alleviate or the transformative possibilities you offer.

3. **VALUE PROPOSITION**: Explain how you provide value to your audience.

4. **UNDERLYING MAGIC**: Illuminate the technology or innovation behind your product.

5. **BUSINESS MODEL**: Clarify your revenue generation strategy.

6. **GO-TO-MARKET PLAN**: Share your strategy for reaching customers effectively.

7. **COMPETITIVE ANALYSIS**: Present a comprehensive view of your competitive landscape.

8. **MANAGEMENT TEAM**: Highlight key team members and investors.

9. **FINANCIAL PROJECTIONS**: Provide a glimpse into your startup's financial future.

10. **ASK**: State what you need to move forward.

In India, where tradition meets innovation, the essence of storytelling and clarity echoes through these ten slides. It's a journey that bridges ancient wisdom with modern entrepreneurial spirit.

The Mastery of Clarity - Crafting Your Vision in Ten Slides

In the bustling bazaars of India's entrepreneurial realm, the mastery of effective pitching is akin to weaving a captivating narrative. Drawing inspiration from ancient scriptures and contemporary insights, let's delve into the heart of concise communication.

Section 1: Financial Projections and Key Metrics - Forecasting Your Journey

"*रुपये के साथ न केवल डॉलर, बल्कि ग्राहकों की संख्या और परिवर्तन दर जैसे महत्वपूर्ण मैट्रिक्स के साथ तीन से पांच साल का पूर्वानुमान प्रदान करें!*' (*Provide a three-to-five-year forecast containing not only dollars but also key metrics*)

In India's vibrant marketplace, where every transaction carries a story, let your projections and metrics resonate like the notes of a classical raga. Create a financial forecast that extends from rupees to the essential metrics. Remember, clarity in conveying the assumptions behind your forecast is as crucial as the numbers themselves.

Section 2: Current Status and the Path Ahead - Scripting Your Journey

"*पैसे का वर्णन करें, सफलताओं की बात करें, समयरेखा, और वित्त का उपयोग करें!*" *(Explain the current status of your product, what the near future looks like, and how you'll use the money you're trying to raise)*

Imagine a bustling Indian market where traders showcase their wares and share their journeys. Similarly, in your pitch, paint a vivid picture of your current status and the road ahead. Highlight your achievements, the timeline, and how you intend to utilize the funds you seek. Conclude with a call to action that echoes India's spirit of moving forward.

Section 3: The Ten Slides - Crafting a Story for the Ages

"'*यदि चित्र हजार शब्दों के बराबर है, तो प्रोटोटाइप दस हजार प्रेजेंटेशन के बराबर है!*'" *(If a picture is worth a thousand words, a prototype is worth ten thousand slides)*

In India, where epics are told in every corner, your pitch should be a narrative for the ages. The recommended number of slides is ten, reminiscent of the ten avatars of Lord Vishnu. These slides are your script:

1. **SANKHYA (Number):** Your identity and contact details, followed by an introduction to your startup's mission.

2. **SAMASYA AUR AVASAR (Problem and Opportunity):** Describe the challenges you address and the opportunities you offer.

3. **MULYA PROPOSITION (Value Proposition):** Explain how your solution provides value.

4. **ADHAR MAGIC (Underlying Magic):** Illuminate the technology or innovation behind your product.

5. **VYAPAR MODEL (Business Model):** Clarify your revenue generation strategy.

6. **TARGET MARKET (Go-to-Market Plan):** Share your strategy for reaching customers.

7. **PRATISPARSHI VISHLESHAN (Competitive Analysis):** Present a comprehensive view of your competition.

8. **PRABANDHAN SAMUH (Management Team):** Highlight key team members and investors.

9. **VITTAEE PRAKSHIPTI (Financial Projections):** Provide a glimpse into your financial journey.

10. **MANG (Ask):** State your needs to progress further.

This storytelling journey bridges India's ancient wisdom with modern entrepreneurial fervor, echoing the ethos of clarity and vision.

Section 4: The 20-Minute Discourse - A Tale of Precision

"अगर आप एक Windows लैपटॉप का उपयोग कर रहे हैं, तो आपको प्रोजेक्टर के साथ काम करने में चालित करने के लिए चालीस मिनट की आवश्यकता हो सकती है।" (If you're using a Windows laptop, you may need forty minutes to make it work with the projector)

In the vibrant marketplaces of India, time is a valuable commodity. Craft your pitch to fit within twenty minutes, respecting your audience's time constraints. Why twenty? Firstly, technical challenges, akin to aligning diverse elements, need time. Secondly, schedule adherence is crucial. Lastly, devote ample time for discussions, as India thrives on conversations.

In India's kaleidoscope of entrepreneurship, the essence of concise and impactful communication echoes through these ten slides and twenty minutes. It's a journey that bridges ancient wisdom with modern entrepreneurial spirit.

The Mastery of Precision - Crafting Your Message with Clarity

In India's storytelling traditions, the mastery of precision in communication holds a revered place. Drawing inspiration from our rich heritage and blending it with contemporary wisdom, let's explore the nuances of delivering a clear and concise pitch.

Section 1: The Hundred-Dollar Challenge - The Power of Deletion

"ध्यान दें, एक शब्द को हटाने के लिए आपसे कोई सौ डॉलर देने का प्रस्ताव देता है। तो आपकी पिच कैसी दिखेगी?" (Pretend that someone offered to pay you a hundred dollars for each word that you deleted from your pitch. What would your pitch look like?)

Imagine if each word you spoke in your pitch held the value of a hundred rupees. This exercise encourages you to trim the excess and sharpen your message. In India, where brevity is celebrated in our ancient scriptures, every word should hold weight and purpose.

Section 2: Mastering the Fine Points - A Craftsmanship Approach

"कभी भी अपने स्लाइड पढ़ने के लिए नहीं। स्लाइड पर लिखे शब्द आपका आधार होते हैं। आपके मुख से निकले शब्द स्पष्टीकरण और सुशोभन होते हैं।" (NEVER. READ. YOUR. SLIDES. Never read your slides. The text on slides is your anchor point. The words out of your mouth are explanatory and embellishment.)

In the land of storytelling, where every narrative is an mastery, your slides should complement your tale. Slides are not scripts; they are guiding stars. Your words should flow from your heart, with each slide serving as a guiding light.

Section 3: The Mastery of Presentation - Communicating with Impact

"आपके शरीर को जगाने के लिएPowerPoint प्रभाव और ऐनिमेशन का उपयोग करने के बजाय उन्हें बोलने, व्यक्तिगतता और उत्साह को संवादित करने के लिए उपयोग करें।" (ANIMATE YOUR BODY, NOT YOUR SLIDES. PowerPoint has more than sixty ways to animate text and graphics. This is fifty-nine too many. Use your body, not PowerPoint effects and animations, to communicate expressiveness, emotion, and enthusiasm.)

In India, where classical dance forms convey stories without words, your body language speaks volumes. Avoid overusing PowerPoint animations; instead, let your gestures, expressions, and enthusiasm bring life to your pitch. India's ancient traditions teach us the power of non-verbal communication.

Section 4: Crafting Visual Narratives - The Power of Diagrams

"बुलेट की बजाय एक आरक्षित डायग्राम के लिए एक डायग्राम या ग्राफ का उपयोग करें।" (BUILD BULLETS. Most entrepreneurs don't use bullets. They display and read big blocks of long text. That's a mistake. Use bullets instead: snippets of text that capture the main point. Even when many entrepreneurs use bullets, they put them all up at once, which enables people to read ahead. That's also a mistake. Build your bullets: click, bullet one, explain; click, bullet two, explain; click, bullet three, explain. This is all the animation you need anywhere in a presentation.)

In India's diverse culture, symbols and visuals hold profound meanings. Replace long textual bullets with concise snippets that capture your message. Use diagrams and graphs, akin to ancient symbols, to convey complex ideas with clarity. Each slide should be a canvas that paints a clear picture of your vision.

In the symphony of Indian entrepreneurship, where every pitch is a story waiting to be told, master the mastery of precision and clarity. Let your words, gestures, and visuals resonate like the timeless tales of our land.

The Leadership Cadence - Harmony in the Pitch

In the diverse and culturally rich India, unity and leadership have always been revered virtues. In this chapter, we delve into the significance of having one voice lead the pitch, drawing inspiration from our ancient scriptures and the wisdom of great Indian leaders.

Section 1: The Power of a Unified Voice - Leading the Melody

"कई उद्यमियों का यह धारणा होता है कि निवेशक टीमों में निवेश करते हैं, इसलिए वे अपने पिचेस में टीमवर्क का प्रदर्शन करना चाहिए।" (Many entrepreneurs believe that investors invest in teams, so they should demonstrate teamwork in their pitches.)

In a nation known for its unity in diversity, the power of teamwork is undeniable. However, in the world of pitching, a different symphony plays. Instead of a full orchestra, it's the soloist who shines.

Section 2: The Soloist's Melody - The CEO's Role

"पिच में, प्रमुख कार्यकारी अधिकांश बात करना चाहिए।" (In a pitch the CEO should do 80 percent of the talking.)

In the pitch's harmonious melody, the CEO plays the role of the lead vocalist. While teamwork is essential, the pitch is not a choir performance. It's a solo, where the CEO takes center stage. The rest of the team, like skilled instrumentalists, have their moments to shine, presenting their expertise on one or two slides.

Section 3: The Mastery of Unity - When Silence Speaks Loudest

"अक्सर टीम के सदस्य उस समय प्रमुख कार्यकारी अधिकांश बात कर नहीं सकते जब जनसमूह किसी बात पर वापस आता है।" (Often team members try to rescue the CEO when the audience pushes back on something he said.)

In the grand raga of a pitch, cohesion is the key. When a question or concern arises, it's the CEO, as the maestro, who orchestrates the response. This demonstrates unity, not just within the team but also the ability to adapt and lead. It's akin to a classical music performance where silence between the notes amplifies the melody.

Section 4: The Symphony of Leadership - A United Front

"सभी कुछ अच्छा हो रहा है, न्याय, और न्यायसंगत है। पर पिच, एक स्कूल का नाटक नहीं है।" (Life is good, fair, and equitable. A pitch, however, is not a school play.)

In the realm of entrepreneurship, where every pitch is a unique composition, unity is the melody that resonates. In the pursuit of funding, let the CEO be the lead vocalist, guiding the team like the conductor of an orchestra. Just as India's unity prevails amidst diversity, let your pitch reflect the harmony of a united front, where every note plays its part in the grand symphony of leadership.

The Mastery of Precision - Elevate Your Pitch to the Himalayan Heights

In the vast expanse of India, where the Himalayan peaks touch the sky, we find inspiration to craft the perfect pitch - one that soars to a thousand feet and stays there. Let us embark on this journey to master the mastery of precision in pitching.

Section 1: The Himalayan Parable - Three Paths to Lethal Clarity

"यह एक युद्ध की तुलना में उदाहरण केवल यही है कि इस पुस्तक में यह एकमात्र युद्ध तुलना है।" (I promise that this is the only war analogy in this book.)

In ancient India, where great epics like the Mahabharata were born, let's explore three distinct paths to deliver a pitch with lethal clarity, each symbolized by a different aircraft.

Section 2: The Garuda Strategy - The A-10 Warthog Pitch

"अगर पिच विमान होते, तो बहुतायत, दुःखद तरीके से, बी-1 लैंसर या नेवी सील्स होते।" (If pitches were weapons, the majority, unfortunately, would be B-1 Lancers or Navy Seals.)

In the ancient scriptures, Garuda, the mythical bird, was revered for its precision and swiftness. The Garuda strategy in pitching aligns with the A-10 Warthog, a plane known for close air support - flying at a thousand feet. It's simple, rugged, and costs $13 million.

In the world of pitching, the B-1 Lancer represents pitches soaring to the clouds. It's filled with grandiose terms and megalomaniac ambitions. The Navy Seal pitch, on the other hand, dives into the intricate technical details that only a select few understand.

Section 3: The Garuda's Flight - Balancing Height and Depth

" आपकी पिच बादलों में नहीं होनी चाहिए और न ही आपके मुँह में चाकू के साथ ज़मीन पर होनी चाहिए।"
(Your pitch shouldn't be in the clouds or on the ground with a knife in your teeth.)

In the grandeur of the Himalayas, the Garuda teaches us the mastery of balance. In the pitch, aim for the middle path like the A-10 Warthog. Deliver enough detail to prove your capability and provide an aerial view to showcase your plan.

Just as the Himalayas stand tall, your pitch should elevate your vision while staying grounded in precision. Let the Garuda strategy guide you as you navigate the peaks and valleys of the business world, armed with clarity and purpose.

The Sage's Whisper - Responding to the Wise Counsel

In Indian entrepreneurship, let us embrace the wisdom of responding to the wise counsel, drawing inspiration from our heritage of Vedas and Upanishads. Imagine a learned sage by your side, offering his sage advice, just as Bill Joos once envisioned a little man on his shoulder during his journey at Garage Technology Ventures. This sage, a symbol of discernment, whispers the question, "So what?" each time you make a statement.

In the world of business, not every utterance carries inherent significance, much like not every word in ancient scriptures holds the secret to enlightenment. Therefore, as you share your vision, listen to the sage's inquiry and respond with wisdom.

Section 1: Embracing the Sage's Presence - A Journey into Clarity

" जब बिल जूस, Garage Technology Ventures के पूर्व सहयोगी, अपने करियर की शुरुआत की, तब IBM ने उसे सिखाया कि उसकी आलोचना करने वाला एक छोटा आदमी उसकी कंधे पर बैठा है। प्रस्तुतन, हर बार जब बिल कुछ कहते, तो वह छोटे आदमी कहते, 'तो क्या?'"

Envision this sage on your entrepreneurial journey and heed his counsel, for not every word carries the brilliance of a star. With each statement, answer the sage's inquiry and then invoke the two most potent words in a pitch: "For instance..." Following this, weave a real-world applications or scenarios, like an enlightened sage sharing profound truths. Here are some examples:

Statement	Sage's Question	Enlightened Response
"Our startup leverages blockchain technology."	Sage: "So what?"	"For instance, it ensures transparent supply chain management, reducing fraud and inefficiencies."
"Our platform uses machine learning algorithms."	Sage: "So what?"	"For instance, it personalizes recommendations, enhancing user experiences and boosting engagement."
"We have renowned advisors on board."	Sage: "So what?"	"What we're building has already attracted industry leaders, opening doors for strategic partnerships."
"Our curriculum is inspired by Montessori methods."	Sage: "So what?"	"For instance, it empowers children to explore their unique talents, fostering independent learning."

Section 2: The Sage's Wisdom - Ancient Insights in Modern Times

Drawing from the ancient wisdom of the Vedas and Upanishads, we find resonance in the concept of 'Tat Tvam Asi,' emphasizing the interconnectedness of all things. Similarly, in the world of startups, every word can find its place when accompanied by a practical illustration.

Section 3: The Sage's Guidance - Illuminating the Path Forward

Much like the sacred Ganges flows with purpose through the Indian subcontinent, your pitch should cascade with clarity and relevance. The sage's inquiry, followed by "For instance," brings forth a river of understanding, illustrating the tangible impact of your ideas. As the saying goes, 'Yatha Drishti, Tatha Srishti' - "As is your vision, so is your creation."

In the spirit of this practice, let the sage's wisdom guide you, as you navigate the intricate dance of entrepreneurship, where the sage's question, accompanied by "For instance..." transforms your pitch into clarity and relevance, a true embodiment of our timeless wisdom.

The Entrepreneur's Odyssey - Navigating Financial Projections

In the vast landscape of Indian entrepreneurship, we embark on an odyssey to decipher the mastery of crafting impeccable financial projections. As we sail through this voyage, let the echoes of wisdom from our ancestors, and the principles of Vedas and Upanishads, guide us.

Section 1: Pitch Constantly - Mastery through Repetition

"आपके पिच का जीरो अवगति करता है। जब आप अपने पिच के साथ पूरी तरह से परिचित और आराम से होते हैं, तो आप इसे सबसे प्रभावी तरीके से दे सकते हैं। दर्शाने के लिए कोई शॉर्टकट नहीं है - आपको बहुत सारे बार पिच देना होगा।"

Familiarity is the cornerstone of a compelling pitch. To achieve mastery, you must traverse this path repeatedly. There are no shortcuts; you must pitch numerous times. For most individuals, around twenty-five repetitions are required to attain this level of familiarity. These practice pitches need not be exclusive to your intended audience; they can include cofounders, employees, relatives, friends, and even your faithful pet.

"आप प्रैक्टिस में खराब हैं तो पिच में खराब होंगे।"

Remember, if you're ineffective in practice, you'll be equally ineffective in the actual pitch. Like Steve Jobs, who devoted hours to perfecting his product introductions, diligence in practice is the path to excellence.

Section 2: Provide the Right Numbers - Crafting Persuasive Financial Projections

"आर्थवादिता कभी अमेरिका में नहीं पकड़ी क्योंकि गरीब अपने को एक अस्थायी लाखपति के रूप में देखते हैं, न कि शोषित श्रमिक के रूप में।" - जॉन स्टाईबेक

Venture capitalists don't choose investments solely based on financial projections and rates of return. Pitch submissions are often similar, projecting fourth or fifth-year sales of $50 million, an easily achievable theoretical outcome. What venture capitalists seek is an understanding of your business's scale, examination of its underlying assumptions, and an estimate of the capital required. This perspective is shared by prominent investors like Mohanjit Jolly, Doug Leone, and Ian Sobieski.

"सोबिएस्की भावनात्मक रूप से संख्याओं के द्वारा चित्रित इस तरह की योजना को देखना चाहते हैं कि उवाचक किस प्रकार के व्यवसाय के बारे में सोच रहे हैं।"

The essence is that investors are not seeking exhaustive forecasts with every line item but rather the broader picture and the assumptions underpinning your business.

Section 3: Building from the Bottom Up - A Realistic Approach

"आपके पूरी योजना और पिच में कितने दाना है, वह नहीं जोड़ने के लिए एक बड़ी संख्या लेने का गलत तरीका है, लेकिन नीचे से ऊपर जाने का सही तरीका है: बिल्डर"

Instead of beginning with a vast number at the top, calculate your projections from the bottom up. This method ensures a more realistic perspective. For instance, when projecting sales for a dog food startup, instead of assuming a vast market share from the start, start from zero and estimate how many customers you can reach and close.

Section 4: The Indian Entrepreneur's Mantra - Balanced Projections

In the Indian entrepreneurial landscape, balance and groundedness are celebrated virtues. In the journey of financial projections, it is essential to find equilibrium between ambition and realism, akin to the age-old wisdom of 'Sthirata' from our scriptures.

As you traverse the realms of financial projections, remember that finding the right balance between optimism and reality is the key to gaining the trust and confidence of investors. Harnessing the wisdom of our heritage and the practicality of modern strategies, you embark on a journey of financial storytelling, where each number has a purpose, each projection a meaning, and each pitch a potential for transformation.

Transparency - The Pillar of Trust in Fundraising

In the realm of Indian entrepreneurship, transparency is the cornerstone upon which trust is built. As you embark on the journey of fundraising, let the wisdom of our land guide you towards disclosing everything. Remember the words from the Rigveda, "Satyam eva jayate" – Truth alone triumphs.

Section 1: The Essence of Disclosure

Transparency is the keystone of trust in the fundraising process. Concealing information that may have repercussions can be detrimental to your credibility. It's akin to the concept of "Dharma" from our ancient texts, where righteous conduct and truthfulness are paramount.

Section 2: The Lesson of Early Disclosure

Early disclosure can be your ally in maintaining a harmonious fundraising journey. A timely revelation of crucial information, even if it involves complexities, can pave the way for smoother negotiations and preserve the integrity of your venture.

Section 3: Embracing Past Failures - The Power of Mea Culpa

Hiding past failures is futile because investors will unearth them. Instead, embrace your history, whether it includes the founding or association with a failed company. In line with the principle of "Karma" from our scriptures, accept responsibility and acknowledge your past. Investors respect such candidness, as it reflects your capacity for growth and resilience.

Section 4: The Ethical Path of Fundraising

In the ethical realm of fundraising, the path of truth and acceptance leads to success. It mirrors the values of our culture and scriptures, emphasizing the importance of acknowledging past mistakes and embracing them as lessons for growth. Investors appreciate such integrity, and it resonates with the timeless wisdom of our land.

Section 5: The Way Forward - Navigating with Integrity

As you tread the path of financial projections, remember that building them from the bottom up is the right way. Instead of starting with grandiose numbers and hypothetical market shares, begin from zero and calculate how many customers you can realistically reach and convert. This approach aligns with the principles of integrity and realism, mirroring our cultural ethos.

Note: The above table is provided for illustrative purposes and does not represent actual financial projections.

The Mastery of Active Listening and Follow-Up

In the realm of Indian entrepreneurship, the ability to listen actively and follow up on commitments holds immense significance. Let us delve into the wisdom of our land to understand the essence of this practice.

Section 1: The Power of Silence

"कुछ लोग ऐसे होते हैं जो बोलना बंद करने पर और भी रुचिकर बन जाते हैं।"

"There are very few people who don't become more interesting when they stop talking."

In our ancient texts, the virtue of silence, known as "Mauna," is extolled. The ability to listen attentively without the compulsion to speak incessantly is a mark of wisdom. It is in the moments of silence that profound insights often emerge.

Section 2: The CEO and the COO - A Tale of Contrast

This anecdote highlights the contrasting behaviors of the CEO and COO during a pitch. The act of taking notes signifies respect for the speaker, a willingness to learn, and conscientiousness. In the Indian context, the practice of "Shravana" or deep listening is akin to this approach.

Section 3: The Value of Taking Notes

Taking notes is not just about documenting information; it's a gesture that conveys respect and eagerness to learn. In the spirit of "Vidya" or knowledge-seeking, this practice aligns with our cultural values.

Section 4: Summarize and Follow Through

In the pursuit of ethical business practices, summarizing what you've heard and following through on your commitments is paramount. This aligns with the principles of "Satya" or truthfulness and "Karma" or action.

Active listening, summarizing, and following up are not just business strategies; they are reflections of our cultural values and timeless wisdom. Embracing these practices can lead to success while staying true to our roots.

The Evolution of Your Pitch

In the vibrant streets of India, we find inspiration in the transformation of the iconic Jeepneys, once military Jeeps from World War II, into colorful, artistic vehicles that serve as a testament to Filipino ingenuity. Similarly, our entrepreneurial journeys often undergo transformations. Let's explore the wisdom of these transformations through an Indian lens.

Section 1: The Evolution of Jeepneys and Pitches

Much like the Jeepneys that evolved from military Jeeps into vibrant symbols of Filipino culture, pitches too undergo transformations. Entrepreneurs often receive feedback from potential investors, leading to continuous edits and patches. After several iterations, the pitch can become unrecognizable. Here's where the Indian adage "सुनो सबकी, करो मन की" (Listen to all, but follow your heart) finds its relevance.

Section 2: Starting Fresh - Version 2.0

After a series of pitches, it's often wise to discard the old and start fresh. Version 2.0 of your pitch should reflect the essence of your learning journey, rather than being a mere patchwork quilt. Just as a lotus blooms in the mud, your pitch can flourish with every iteration.

Section 3: Pitching vs. Planning

In the world of entrepreneurship, the pursuit of the Holy Grail, symbolizing the perfect business plan, has evolved. Business plans were once the cornerstone, akin to the magical vessels of Celtic myths. However, today's reality favors concise presentations over lengthy plans. As the great sage Chanakya said, "संक्षेपेण विना दोषेण श्राव्यं श्रूयतां अपि वा" (Let the truth be heard concisely, without faults).

Section 4: The Power of the Pitch

For early-stage companies, a well-crafted pitch holds the key. Business plans, though occasionally requested, are no longer the primary focus. It's the pitch that captivates and persuades. In the words of Swami Vivekananda, "Arise, awake, and stop not till the goal is reached" - and that goal is achieved through the power of your pitch.

In the dynamic landscape of Indian entrepreneurship, the evolution of pitches reflects our ability to adapt, learn, and present our ideas concisely. Just as the lotus rises from the mud to bloom in pristine waters, our pitches can transform and flourish with every iteration.

The Mastery of Pitch Transformation

In the bustling streets of Mumbai, where innovation knows no bounds, we encounter the story of Rajesh, a company poised to revolutionize the way books are distributed. Rajesh Patel, the CEO of Utkarsh, sought guidance to refine his pitch for TechShowcase2014. Let's delve into this transformation journey and learn how to craft an impactful pitch that resonates with Indian sensibilities.

Section 1: Crafting the Perfect Pitch

In the vibrant Indian startup ecosystem, precision matters. Rajesh's initial pitch lacked clarity on the investment amount. Instead, it should have focused on the opportunity, leaving room for potential investors to decide their contribution. As the ancient saying goes, "संवादे सुखभागो भवेत्" (In discussions, clarity brings happiness).

Section 2: Addressing Industry Jargon

The pitch touched on the "walled gardens" issue in publishing, but this jargon needed demystification. In India, where diverse cultures converge, clarity is vital. A pitch should resonate with everyone, just like the wisdom of "वसुधैव कुटुम्बकम्" (The world is one family).

Section 3: Simplifying Technical Details

Rajesh's pitch introduced the technical aspects, but it needed simplification. In India, where diverse languages unite us, the pitch should be easily understood. As Rabindranath Tagore said, "जब आप भाषाओं के बंधन से छूटते हैं, तो आप विश्व की सारी भाषाओं का भाषी बन जाते हैं" (When you break free from the constraints of languages, you become a speaker of all languages).

Section 4: Captivating Success Stories

The pitch gradually built momentum with the announcement of Walmart's partnership. In India, storytelling is an mastery, and every pitch should tell a compelling story. Just as the Ramayana captivates us, a pitch should engage and inspire.

Section 5: Building Credibility

Credibility was established through partnerships with renowned publishers and retailers. In India, trust is paramount, and your pitch should reflect trustworthiness. As Mahatma Gandhi said, "आपकी आत्मा की शांति केवल सत्य की आश्वासना के रूप में हो सकती है" (The peace of your soul can only be in the assurance of truth).

In Indian entrepreneurship, crafting a pitch is an mastery. It's a symphony of words and ideas that resonate with investors. Rajesh Patel's pitch makeover journey teaches us that every word matters, and every story told should leave a lasting impression. Just as the peacock displays its vibrant feathers, a well-crafted pitch showcases your vision and potential.

Table: Indian Wisdom in Pitch Transformation

Pitch Transformation Element	Indian Wisdom
Clarity in Investment Amount	"संवादे सुखभागो भवेत्" (In discussions, clarity brings happiness)
Demystifying Jargon	"वसुधैव कुटुम्बकम्" (The world is one family)

Pitch Transformation Element	Indian Wisdom
Simplifying Technical Details	"जब आप भाषाओं के बंधन से छूटते हैं, तो आप विश्व की सारी भाषाओं का भाषी बन जाते हैं" (When you break free from the constraints of languages, you become a speaker of all languages)
Captivating Success Stories	"रामायण" (The Ramayana)
Building Credibility	"आपकी आत्मा की शांति केवल सत्य की आश्वासना के रूप में हो सकती है" (The peace of your soul can only be in the assurance of truth)

In this rich mosaic of Indian wisdom, your pitch transforms into a masterpiece, ready to inspire and secure the support of investors.

The Enthralling Tale of Rajesh Patel

In the heart of Mumbai, where dreams converge and innovation thrives, we meet Rajesh Patel, the CEO of Utkarsh. His journey to perfecting the mastery of pitching is a captivating story that resonates with the spirit of Indian entrepreneurship.

Section 1: The Grand Unveiling

In the bustling streets of Mumbai, at an entrepreneur's gathering, Rajesh Patel stepped onto the stage, introducing himself and Enthrill Distribution. His opening resonated with the ancient Indian belief in auspicious beginnings, symbolizing the "नमस्ते" (Namaste) greeting that signifies respect and reverence.

Section 2: Simplifying Complexity

Rajesh's narrative flowed seamlessly, explaining Enthrill's concept with simplicity and clarity. In India, where diverse languages flourish, communicating complex ideas in a straightforward manner is celebrated. It's reminiscent of the wisdom of Chanakya, who said, "शब्दस्य मूलं वाक्यं, वाक्यस्य मूलं भाषणम्" (The root of a word is a sentence, and the root of a sentence is speech).

Section 3: The Power of Association

By drawing a parallel between Enthrill's product and familiar gift cards, Rajesh made his pitch relatable to the Indian audience. Indians value simplicity and connections to everyday life, much like the teachings of the Bhagavad Gita, which emphasize relating spirituality to daily existence.

Section 4: A Triple Win

Rajesh highlighted the triple win: publishers, retailers, and customers all benefit from Enthrill's solution. In India, where the concept of "विन-विन" (win-win) is celebrated in business, Rajesh's pitch resonated with the core values of collaboration and shared success.

Section 5: The Grand Finale

Rajesh's closing statement left the audience in awe, promising partnerships with renowned retailers by Christmas. Just like a grand Indian festival, his pitch had all the elements of anticipation and celebration.

In Indian entrepreneurship, crafting a pitch is an mastery. It's a symphony of words and ideas that resonates with investors. Rajesh Franco's pitch transformation journey teaches us that every word matters, and every story told should leave a lasting impression. Just as the peacock displays its vibrant feathers, a well-crafted pitch showcases your vision and potential.

Table: Indian Wisdom in Pitch Transformation

Pitch Transformation Element	Indian Wisdom
A Powerful Beginning	"नमस्ते" (Namaste - Greeting with reverence)
Simplifying Complexity	"शब्दस्य मूलं वाक्यं, वाक्यस्य मूलं भाषणम्" (The root of a word is a sentence, and the root of a sentence is speech)
The Power of Association	Bhagavad Gita - Relating spirituality to daily life
A Triple Win	"विन-विन" (Win-win)
The Grand Finale	Indian Festivals - Anticipation and celebration

In this rich mosaic of Indian wisdom, your pitch transforms into a masterpiece, ready to inspire and secure the support of investors.

Mastering the Mastery of Business-Pitch Contests

In the vibrant landscape of Indian entrepreneurship, where innovation and creativity flourish, aspiring entrepreneurs often find themselves drawn to the exhilarating world of business-pitch contests. These contests, akin to the grand chariots of Rath Yatra, carry the dreams of entrepreneurs towards success. Let us embark on a journey through the tips and wisdom that can lead you to victory in these contests.

Section 1: Embracing Change

Across the vast expanse of India, organizations conduct business-plan contests to nurture innovation and entrepreneurship. These contests, like the flowing rivers of India, bring fresh ideas to the surface, shaping the future of business. However, times are changing, and entrepreneurs must adapt.

Section 2: The Essence of Viability

These contests serve as crucibles, forging entrepreneurs under the pressure of deadlines and nurturing their ability to simulate a startup team. Much like the teachings of the Upanishads, where knowledge is passed from teacher to student, these contests impart valuable lessons.

Section 3: The Power of the Pitch

In the evolving Indian business landscape, the traditional business plan has become obsolete. Business-pitch contests are the new way forward. As Lord Krishna advised in the Bhagavad Gita, it's essential to embrace change and adapt to the times.

Section 4: Prioritizing Viability

In the spirit of the Indian concept of "जुगाड़" (frugal innovation), viability takes precedence over fundability. Entrepreneurs can achieve more with less, leveraging free or cost-effective resources. Crowdfunding, akin to the generosity of donors during religious festivals, can provide substantial support.

Section 5: The Mastery of Pitching

In the competitive arena of pitch contests, preparation is key. Entrepreneurs must practice relentlessly, embracing the philosophy of "साधना" (dedicated practice) found in Indian classical arts.

Utilizing a big font, much like the grandeur of Indian architecture, ensures clarity and readability for all, regardless of age or distance.

Leverage the power of visuals, much like the intricate carvings on Indian temples. Engage the audience with graphics, photos, and screenshots, allowing them to envision your idea.

Section 6: Tailoring Your Presentation

Knowledge is power. Research the judges in advance, like a scholar studying ancient scriptures. Tailor your presentation to their preferences, showcasing your cleverness and diligence.

Section 7: Honesty and Relevance

Embrace honesty when presenting your team's qualifications, much like the truthful teachings of Mahatma Gandhi. Highlight the relevance of your backgrounds to your business.

Section 8: The Path to Victory

Practice relentlessly, present with clarity and conviction, and tailor your pitch to your audience. Just as Lord Ganesha removes obstacles, winning a business-pitch contest can pave the way for your entrepreneurial journey.

May your pitch resonate like the melodies of classical Indian music, captivating the judges and leading you to victory in the grand contest of entrepreneurship.

Unveiling the Truth: Ten Common Entrepreneurial Myths

In the bustling streets of Mumbai and the vibrant markets of Delhi, entrepreneurs gather to weave their dreams and present their startups to eager investors. However, amidst the excitement, a cloud of myths and falsehoods often shrouds these pitches. Let's unravel the top ten lies that entrepreneurs must avoid in their quest for success.

Section 1: The Illusion of Projections

"हमारी पूर्वानुमान सत्यहीन है।"

In the world of startups, it's common to hear entrepreneurs claim that their projections are conservative while envisioning exponential growth. In reality, predicting sales is as unpredictable as the monsoon rains. Let us embrace honesty and admit that projections are often like the changing tides of the Indian Ocean—uncertain.

Section 2: The Allure of Market Numbers

"*विशेषज्ञ हमारे बाजार को पाँच साल में पचास अरब डॉलर का मान देने का दावा करते हैं।*"

Entrepreneurs often quote staggering market statistics to impress investors. Yet, investors know that everyone paints a rosy picture. Instead of numbers, entrepreneurs should weave narratives that ignite the imagination, much like the enchanting stories of the Panchatantra.

Section 3: The Unfulfilled Contracts

"*अमेज़न अगले सप्ताह हमारे साथ समझौता करेगा।*"

The promise of a signed contract with tech giants like Amazon can be tempting. However, until ink meets paper, such claims remain ephemeral, akin to a mirage in the Thar Desert. It's wiser to speak of achievements once they are concrete, much like the monumental architecture of the Taj Mahal.

Section 4: The Imaginary Dream Team

"*महत्वपूर्ण कर्मचारी हमारे साथ जुड़ेंगे जैसे ही हमें वित्त प्राप्त होता है।*"

Entrepreneurs sometimes claim that key employees are ready to join once funded. Yet, investors see through the smoke and mirrors. Such claims are like the grand illusions of Indian magic tricks—a fleeting spectacle.

Section 5: The False Sense of Urgency

"*कई निवेशक पहले ही जाँच में हैं।*"

Entrepreneurs often employ tactics to create a sense of urgency among investors. However, seasoned investors recognize such strategies. Instead, entrepreneurs should focus on the strength of their ideas, much like the unyielding flow of the Ganges.

Section 6: The Underestimation of Competitors

"*माइक्रोसॉफ्ट बड़ा, पुराना, भारी, और धीमा हो चुका है कि वह एक खतरा नहीं है।*"

Entrepreneurs often belittle established giants like Microsoft, underestimating their prowess. Instead, acknowledge the competition, like the warriors of ancient India acknowledged their adversaries. Embrace strategies to navigate around them, like a skillful chess player.

Section 7: The Patent Illusion

"*पेटेंट हमारे व्यापार को सुरक्षित नहीं बनाते।*"

Entrepreneurs sometimes overstate the value of patents. While they have their place, they aren't a fortress. Mentioning patentability sparingly is wise, much like an exquisite spice in an Indian curry.

Section 8: The One Percent Fallacy

"*हमें केवल बाजार का एक प्रतिशत प्राप्त करना है।*"

Entrepreneurs often claim that capturing a mere one percent of the market will lead to success. However, this oversimplification neglects the complexities of the business landscape. Investors seek more substantial goals, akin to reaching for the stars.

Section 9: The Myth of First-Mover Advantage

"*हमारे पास पहले आने का फायदा है।*"

First-mover advantage is not always a guaranteed path to success. Entrepreneurs should acknowledge the uncertainty of the startup world and focus on their unique strengths. Sometimes, being a fast second can be more advantageous, much like a tactical move in a game of chess.

Section 10: The World-Class Team Mirage

"*हमारी टीम विश्व स्तरीय और प्रमाणित है।*"

The label "world-class" and "proven" should be reserved for founders with a track record of creating wealth or holding esteemed positions. A stint at a prestigious consulting firm or investment bank doesn't suffice. It's essential to present the team honestly, much like the genuine smiles of Indian hospitality.

Section 11: An Exercise in Truth

"*सच्चाई के आदान-प्रदान का अभ्यास करें।*"

In the spirit of Gandhian principles, entrepreneurs should practice honesty and transparency. Presenting the truth is a sign of strength. As we journey through Indian entrepreneurship, let us weave a narrative of integrity and authenticity.

By adhering to these principles, entrepreneurs can stand tall amidst the diverse and vibrant landscape of Indian entrepreneurship, forging a path towards success that is both honorable and enduring.

FAQ: Navigating the Entrepreneurial Journey

Q: *How can I leave a lasting impression with my pitch?* *A: The challenge lies not in creating memorable pitches but in distinguishing them from the rest. In entrepreneurial dreams, pitches tend to blend together. The key to memorability is simplicity and a captivating narrative. Your presentation, concise and engaging, should narrate how you plan to alleviate real-world challenges or seize promising opportunities.

But here's the secret ingredient to make your pitch truly unforgettable: a mind-blowing demonstration of your product's brilliance. Imagine leaving your audience in awe with a demo so spectacular that PowerPoint slides become an afterthought, lost in the fervent discussions that follow. Always anticipate that your audience may be weary after a day of mundane meetings, craving something extraordinary.

It's often the case, and you must be prepared for it. Your pitch should shine like the Kohinoor diamond, capturing attention effortlessly.*

Q: *Should I print my pitch in color and bind copies for investors?* A: *While colorful presentations may catch the eye, aesthetics alone cannot salvage subpar content. Your focus should be on the substance of your pitch rather than its packaging. Ensure that your pitch is a masterpiece in its own right, and it will shine brightly without the need for vibrant colors and bindings.*

Q: *Is it wise to send my presentation to attendees before the meeting?* A: *No, it's not advisable. A compelling presentation typically relies on minimal text, prominently displayed for easy readability. Sending it in advance may leave recipients puzzled without your captivating oral delivery.*

Q: *Should I distribute my presentation at the start of the meeting?* A: *Distributing your presentation at the outset may lead to attendees skipping ahead, reading faster than you can speak. However, it could hinder note-taking. An alternative approach is to provide the presentation at the beginning but kindly request that attendees refrain from jumping ahead, ensuring they are fully immersed in your narrative.*

In the vibrant landscape of Indian entrepreneurship, these FAQs provide guidance to navigate the intricate path of pitching your entrepreneurial vision. Remember, your story is your strength, and simplicity is the key to leaving a lasting mark.

Recommended Reading for the Indian Entrepreneurial Journey

Embarking on the entrepreneurial path in India, you'll find wisdom and inspiration in these carefully selected books. They resonate with the essence of innovation, blending ancient wisdom with modern entrepreneurial insights.

1. **"The Man Behind the Wheel: How Onkar S Kanwar Created a Global Giant" by Anuradha Goyal** -- This book explores the life and achievements of Onkar S Kanwar, the founder of Apollo Tyres Limited, providing insights into his entrepreneurial mindset, vision, and leadership principles.
2. **"Failing to Succeed: The Story of India's First E-commerce Company" by K. Vaitheeswaran** -- K. Vaitheeswaran, the co-founder of India's first e-commerce company, Fabmart.com (later rebranded as Indiaplaza.com), shares his entrepreneurial journey, including the challenges faced and lessons learned from the failure of the venture.
3. **"The Unusual Billionaires" by Saurabh Mukherjea** -- Saurabh Mukherjea analyzes the success stories of eight Indian companies that defied conventional wisdom and achieved extraordinary growth, offering valuable insights for entrepreneurs aspiring to build sustainable businesses.
4. **"Dream with Your Eyes Open: An Entrepreneurial Journey" by Ronnie Screwvala** -- Ronnie Screwvala, the founder of UTV Group and one of India's leading entrepreneurs, shares his entrepreneurial journey, discussing the highs, lows, and learnings from building successful ventures in various industries.
5. **"Bootstrapped Billionaire: Journey of an entrepreneur" by Jagdish Khattar** -- Jagdish Khattar, the founder of Carnation Auto and former managing director of Maruti Suzuki India Limited, shares his entrepreneurial journey, offering valuable lessons on perseverance, innovation, and leadership.

These books offer a diverse knowledge, fusing ancient Indian wisdom with contemporary entrepreneurial expertise. Dive into these literary treasures, and may they illuminate your path to startup success in India.

"Flourish:
Blossoming into Abundance"

Chapter 7:
Crafting a Stellar Team for Success

In the spirit of unity, this chapter unveils the mastery of forging an exceptional team, guided by the wisdom of Indian philosophy and modern entrepreneurial insights.

Ekatva: The Essence of Teamwork *"Sangachchadhvam Samvadadhvam Sam Wo Manansi Jaanataam"*

- *Rigveda (10.191.2)*

In the heart of India's ancient scriptures lies the profound concept of "Ekatva" – the unity of purpose. Just as the Vedas call for unity among beings, so does the entrepreneurial journey demand a harmonious team. A team is not just a collection of individuals; it is a collective spirit, a shared vision, and a bond that transcends the mundane.

The Bharat Startup Sangha Imagine your startup as a sacred "Sangha" where like-minded individuals come together, not merely for sustenance but for a higher purpose. Your team is your "Sadhana," your spiritual practice, in the realm of innovation.

Nurturing the Seeds of Diversity *"Vividhata Mein Ekata"*

- Indian Proverb

Diversity is the very fabric of our nation, and it should be of your startup too. Embrace individuals whose perspectives resonate differently, for it is in this ideas that innovation thrives. Just as India celebrates countless festivals, your team should revel in a celebration of diverse minds.

The Chakravartin Leader In ancient India, a "Chakravartin" was a universal ruler, just as an entrepreneurial leader is in today's startup ecosystem. Lead not with dominance, but with the wisdom of a "Dharmachakra," a wheel of righteous duty.

Your leadership should empower, inspire, and guide the "Yodhas" (warriors) of your team.

The Entrepreneur's Dharma *"Yatha Drishti, Tatha Srishti"*

- Bhagavad Gita (Chapter 11, Verse 7)

Your vision shapes your startup's destiny. Just as Lord Krishna revealed his cosmic form to Arjuna, you must unveil your grand vision to your team. Let them see the vast potential and noble purpose they are part of. In this shared vision, they will find the inspiration to go beyond the ordinary.

The Quest for Talent *"Jahan Se Achha, Talent Wahan"*

- Adapted from Rabindranath Tagore

In India, talent is scattered like precious gems. Seek it with the diligence of a seeker on a spiritual pilgrimage. Reach out to educational "Gurukuls," connect with tech "Ashrams," and you shall find the brightest minds waiting to embark on your startup journey.

The Dharmic Rewards *"Yat Pinde Tat Brahmande"*

- Upanishads

Just as the Upanishads teach us the interconnectedness of all creation, so does your startup thrive when every member feels their contribution resonates with the grand design. Reward not just with rupees but with recognition, respect, and the sense of being part of something greater.

In this sacred journey of entrepreneurship, building an extraordinary team is your "Yagna," your divine offering. Cultivate a team bound by purpose, diversity, and shared vision, and witness the transformation of your startup into a thriving "Sangha" that leaves an indelible mark on the world.

The Essence of Building an Extraordinary Team

In this section, we embark on a journey to unravel the secrets of forming an exceptional team for your entrepreneurial venture, drawing inspiration from ancient Indian wisdom and modern entrepreneurial insights.

Samyoga: The Mastery of Team Building *"Yatra Yogeswarah Krishno, Yatra Partho Dhanur Dharah, Tatra Shrir Vijayo Bhuthir, Dhruva Nithir Mathir Mama"*

- Bhagavad Gita (Chapter 18, Verse 78)

In the heart of Indian philosophy, the Bhagavad Gita teaches us the essence of "Samyoga," which means union or connection. Just as Lord Krishna guided Arjuna to victory through unity, entrepreneurs must build a team that stands united, driven by a common purpose.

The Sangh of Startups Imagine your startup as a "Sangh," a sacred gathering of individuals bound not just by contracts but by a shared dream. Your team is not just a workforce; it's a "Sadhana," a spiritual endeavor to bring your vision to life.

Celebrating Diversity *"Vividhata Mein Ekata"*

- Indian Proverb

Diversity is not just the strength of our nation, but it should also be the strength of your startup. Embrace individuals with unique perspectives, for within this diversity lies the seeds of innovation. Much like India's vibrant festivals, your team should celebrate the diversity of ideas.

The Dharmic Leader In ancient India, leaders were called "Dharmacharyas," those who upheld righteousness. Lead your team not with authority, but with the wisdom of "Dharma," the path of righteousness. Your leadership should empower and guide, not dictate.

Unearthing Talent *"Jahan Se Achha, Talent Wahan"*

- Adapted from Rabindranath Tagore

In the vast landscape of India, talent hides in every corner. Seek talent as if you're embarking on a spiritual pilgrimage. Collaborate with educational "Gurukuls," connect with technology "Ashrams," and you'll discover brilliant minds eager to embark on your startup journey.

The Dharmic Rewards *"Yat Pinde Tat Brahmande"*

- Upanishads

Just as the Upanishads teach us the interconnection of all existence, your startup flourishes when every team member feels their contribution resonates with the grand design. Reward not only with rupees but also with recognition, respect, and the sense of being part of something greater.

In this sacred journey of entrepreneurship, building an extraordinary team is your "Yagna," your divine offering. Cultivate a team bound by purpose, diversity, and shared vision, and witness the transformation of your startup into a thriving "Sangh" that leaves an indelible mark on the world.

Nurturing the Startup Spirit

In this section, we delve into the transformational journey of startup life, drawing inspiration from ancient Indian wisdom and weaving it into the fabric of modern entrepreneurial insights.

Awakening to the Startup Reality

In life, your journey as an entrepreneur begins with a single thread - your first job. Reflect upon it with these questions:

- Were you the perfect fit for that role?
- Did you find yourself holding candidates to higher standards than those who hired you?

Surya Namaskar: Embracing the Dawn of Change

Much like the rising sun brings light to the world, your startup journey is a new dawn. It's crucial to convey this transformative experience to your team. Let's explore this transformation:

"Can you fly coach, function without a secretary, and stay in modest accommodations?"

This question isn't about discomfort, but a test of adaptability. Startups often require you to wear multiple hats, from CEO to errand runner. Are your team members ready to embrace this versatile role?

The Dance of Skills: Big Organization vs. Startup

In the diverse landscape of skills, navigating a startup is akin to a graceful dance. Here's a comparative look:

Big Organization Skill	Startup Skill
Sucking up to the boss	Being the boss

Big Organization Skill	Startup Skill
Generating paper profits	Generating cash flow
Beating charges of monopoly	Establishing a beachhead
Evolving products	Creating products
Market research	Shipping
Squeezing the distribution channel	Establishing a distribution channel

This dance isn't just about adapting; it's about mastering the rhythm of a startup, where actions translate directly into progress.

Bhagavad Gita: The Journey of Realism

"Arise, awake, and stop not till the goal is reached."

- Swami Vivekananda

Much like Arjuna, who received divine wisdom from Lord Krishna, your startup journey requires a realistic approach. Startups are not about the glitz and glamour portrayed in TV shows. It's a path filled with challenges and triumphs, requiring resilience and unwavering determination.

The Sands of Time

Startup life is a race against time. The sands of the hourglass mark the passage of years filled with intense dedication, modest incomes, and the ever-present fear of financial instability. Yet, it's a journey of growth, learning, and the pursuit of a vision.

In the grand epic of entrepreneurship, let your team be the valiant warriors, ready to face each day with unwavering commitment. Embrace the startup spirit, for it's the crucible where dreams are forged into reality, and where the journey itself becomes the reward.

The Mastery of Discerning Talent

In this section, we embark on a journey to uncover the hidden gems in the vast landscape of talent acquisition, guided by ancient Indian wisdom and modern strategies.

The Mysterious Realm of Intuition

Recruiting, much like life's enigmatic twists, occasionally demands we rely on our intuition. Picture these scenarios:

1. A candidate's qualifications don't precisely align with your requirements, yet a whisper of intuition urges you to consider them.

2. Another candidate appears flawless on paper, prompting the team to support their selection, but your intuition hesitates.

Krishna's Wisdom: Balancing Rationality and Intuition

As Krishna counseled Arjuna on the battlefield, we must find the equilibrium between our rational judgment and intuition. Here's a structured approach:

1. **Define Expectations**: Before interviews commence, outline the attitude, knowledge, personality, and experience needed for the role. Prevent unstructured interviews driven by personal biases.

2. **Reveal Competence**: Start by assessing if the candidate can perform the job effectively. For instance, for a Vice President of Marketing, ask about past experiences in product management, feature selection, PR, advertising, and crisis management.

3. **Stay on Track**: Maintain consistency by sticking to a predetermined set of questions. This ensures a fair comparison among candidates.

4. **Initial Phone Interviews**: Reduce biases based on appearance by conducting initial interviews via phone, creating an even playing field.

5. **Prioritize Competence**: Focus on competence rather than sentimentality. Ask pointed questions about accomplishments, failures, and learning experiences.

The Dance of Hiring

In the intricate dance of hiring, remember to:

- **Match Person to Position**: Avoid the allure of likable but inept candidates, and don't dismiss less charismatic yet competent individuals. Sometimes, the best engineers lack charisma.

- **Take Notes**: During interviews, maintain detailed notes to overcome memory lapses and subjective biases. This ensures a fair assessment.

- **Reference Checks**: Don't fall into the trap of confirming your decision through references. Instead, use them to make an informed choice.

- **Leverage LinkedIn**: Beyond provided references, explore LinkedIn to uncover additional insights from people who worked alongside the candidate.

By adhering to this structured process, your intuition becomes an informed guide. Just as my unconventional journey led me to Intel, sometimes, the facts alone don't tell the whole story. Trust in the balance of intuition and diligence to uncover the true potential of your team members.

The Mastery of Talent Attraction

In this section, we explore the diverse array of tools and strategies available to attract top-notch talent, drawing inspiration from India's wisdom and innovation.

Harnessing the Power of Your Arsenal

In the quest for exceptional talent, both during prosperity and adversity, we must be prepared to deploy every resource at our disposal. While many believe that recruitment tools are confined to salary, equity, and perks, we shall unravel a more profound arsenal:

1. **The Visionary Path**: Understand that wealth isn't always the prime motivator. Offer the opportunity to be part of a vision that transcends monetary gain. The chance to contribute to a noble cause and impact the world can be a potent motivator.

As Mahatma Gandhi aptly put it, "The best way to find yourself is to lose yourself in the service of others."

2. **The Collective Force**: Don't restrict the candidate's interactions to prospective supervisors and colleagues alone. Enrich the seduction process by involving directors, advisors, and investors who can offer a broader perspective.

In the words of Chanakya, "In the counsel of many, there is wisdom."

3. **Résumé-Building Odyssey**: Embrace the reality that few individuals tread a single career path throughout their lives. Encourage them to spend fruitful years with your organization, enhancing their résumés. Their journey with you may extend beyond your initial expectations.

In life, each experience weaves a unique thread.

Indian Proverbs in Talent Attraction

Let us draw wisdom from our ancient texts and proverbs to solidify these strategies:

1. **The Visionary Path**: As the Bhagavad Gita teaches us, "You have the right to perform your prescribed duties, but you are not entitled to the fruits of your actions." Embrace the duty of crafting a visionary future, and the right talents will be drawn to your cause.

2. **The Collective Force**: In the spirit of unity, the Rigveda reminds us, "United we stand, divided we fall." By involving various stakeholders in the recruitment process, we create a united front that attracts exceptional individuals.

3. **Résumé-Building Odyssey**: The Upanishads guide us with, "From ignorance, lead me to truth; from darkness, lead me to light." In the same vein, from the obscurity of their previous journeys, lead your recruits to a path of enlightenment and growth.

The Multifaceted Canvas of Attraction

In summary, talent attraction is an mastery that demands the use of every brushstroke in our palette. Your vision, the collective strength of your team, and the promise of résumé enrichment are but a few hues on this canvas. Embrace the diversity of these tools, just as India celebrates its cultural richness, and watch as your organization thrives with renewed vigor.

The Power of Influence in Joining a Startup

In this section, we delve into the intricate web of relationships that often shape an individual's decision to embark on a startup journey, weaving in Indian wisdom, insights, and narratives to illuminate this fascinating dynamic.

Evangelizing to the Decision Makers

The decision to join a startup rarely unfolds in isolation. It is intricately woven into a relationships, where influences emanate from various quarters. While enlightened employers may consider the role of a candidate's spouse, the decision-making process is more often a complex interplay of influencers.

The Ensemble of Decision Makers

The collective of decision-makers extends beyond the candidate to include parents, friends, and colleagues. Imagine a young individual seeking parental counsel on joining a startup, only to be met with cautionary advice, "It's too risky. Secure a job in a stable company that will stand the test of time—like the renowned Bombay Dyeing, Infosys, or Tata Steel."

Addressing Concerns and Building Trust

Hence, it becomes paramount to identify and engage with these influential figures in a candidate's life. In doing so, we must proactively address their apprehensions. However, we must tread carefully, for some candidates may view this inquiry as a test of their resilience.

"In seeking wisdom, the first step is silence, the second listening, the third remembering, the fourth practicing, the fifth - teaching others." - Gautama Buddha

Indian Insights into Influential Decision Making

Drawing inspiration from Indian philosophy and culture, we find valuable insights:

1. **The Role of Dharma**: Just as Arjuna sought guidance from Lord Krishna in the Bhagavad Gita, individuals often turn to trusted advisers for counsel. Acknowledge the significance of these influencers and provide them with a clear vision of the startup's noble purpose.

2. **Collective Wisdom**: The concept of "satsang" emphasizes the company of the wise and virtuous. Similarly, your startup should surround itself with individuals who share in its vision and values, nurturing an environment where joining becomes a collective decision.

3. **Balancing Confidence and Humility**: The story of Eklavya from the Mahabharata teaches us about respecting authority while pursuing excellence. In addressing concerns, strike a balance between demonstrating your startup's strength and showing humility in considering the opinions of decision makers.

A Path to Building Confidence

Navigating the intricate web of decision makers requires not only understanding their influence but also building their confidence in your startup's journey. By doing so, you foster an environment where these influencers become advocates, propelling your venture to greater heights. Just as an Indian classical orchestra harmonizes diverse instruments, let your startup harmonize diverse perspectives and thrive in unison.

The Mastery of Timing in Compensation

In this section, we explore the strategic timing of compensation offers, drawing insights from Indian wisdom and practices to elucidate the importance of waiting for the right moment.

The Wisdom of Timing in Compensation

Compensation, a pivotal element in the hiring process, often becomes the focal point for both startups and candidates. However, many startups inadvertently stumble by extending an offer letter prematurely, using it as a bargaining chip to demonstrate their eagerness. This is a misstep that needs rectification.

The Sacred Thread of Timing

Much like the sacred thread ceremony (Upanayana), where a pivotal life event is marked at the appropriate age, offering compensation should be a well-timed ritual. It should be neither a coercive tactic nor a premature step, but rather a confirmation of mutual intent.

The Marriage of Verbal Commitment

An offer letter should not be wielded as a tool for negotiation but should manifest as the culmination of a verbal agreement. It is akin to a marriage proposal, a step taken when one is certain of a positive response, not merely to signify intent.

" धैर्यं सर्वसुखानि भूयिष्ठम्" *(Dhairyam Sarva Sukhani Bhuyishtham)*

- *Patanjali's Yoga Sutras*

Indian Wisdom on Patience

Drawing inspiration from Patanjali's Yoga Sutras, which extol the virtue of patience, we find guidance:

1. **The Practice of Tapas**: As aspirants practice "tapas" or discipline in yoga, startups too must exercise discipline in waiting for the right moment to extend the offer. It is in this patience that success truly lies.

2. **The Essence of Samay**: The concept of "samay" or timing is revered in Indian philosophy. Waiting for the opportune moment, like choosing the right "muhurat" for a ceremony, ensures a harmonious and prosperous outcome.

3. **The Dance of Lord Shiva**: In Lord Shiva's cosmic dance, the rhythm of creation, preservation, and destruction is evident. Similarly, in the startup journey, timing plays a crucial role in creating opportunities, preserving relationships, and avoiding destructive conflicts.

The Mastery of Timing in Offer Letters

The act of offering compensation should be an artful orchestration of timing and intent. Just as Lord Krishna imparted wisdom to Arjuna at the opportune moment in the Bhagavad Gita, startups must choose the right moment to present the offer letter. By doing so, they ensure not only acceptance but also the alignment of energies for a harmonious journey ahead.

Decoding the Narrative: Unveiling Truths in Job Interviews

In this section, we delve into the intricacies of decoding the narratives spun by job candidates during interviews. We draw inspiration from Indian wisdom and storytelling to unravel the truths behind the words.

The Deception

Job interviews, like a beautifully woven embroidery, often conceal threads of deception amidst the intricate patterns of words. To decipher these hidden truths, we must embrace the wisdom of interpretation.

The Ten Lies Unveiled

In the sacred space of interviews, job candidates sometimes weave tales that conceal their realities. Amy Vernetti, a partner at True Capital, shared a list of the top ten lies she encountered during her tenure. Let us examine these lies and unveil the truths they obscure:

Lie	Truth
"I've got three other offers, so you'd better move quickly."	I've had three other interviews, and no one has flat out rejected me yet.
"I was responsible for my company's strategic alliance with Google."	I picked up the FedEx envelope from Google.

Lie	Truth
"I'm leaving my current organization after only a few months because the organization isn't what the CEO told me it was."	I don't know how to do due diligence.
"I've never been with a company for more than a year because I get bored easily."	It takes people about a year to figure out that I'm a bozo.
"I didn't really report to anyone at my old company."	No one wanted me in her department.
"Most of my references are personal friends because they know me best."	No one I worked for is willing to give me a reference.
"You've never heard of my last three employers because they were in stealth mode."	All the companies I worked for imploded.
"I'm no longer with the organization, but I maintain an excellent relationship with people there."	I was forced to sign a nondisparagement agreement to get my severance package.
"I am a vice president, but no one reports to me."	I've been put out to pasture.
"I'm expecting to at least double my prior compensation package."	I was overpaid and understand that I may have to take a cut for a good opportunity.

The Essence of Interpretation

In Indian storytelling, there is an ancient tradition of unraveling the layers of truth within tales. Our interview process should reflect this wisdom, where we interpret narratives beyond face value.

The Story of Krishna and the Illusion of Truth

Recall the tale of Lord Krishna revealing his universal form (Vishvarupa) to Arjuna in the Bhagavad Gita. Arjuna perceived a myriad of truths, each with its own significance. Similarly, in interviews, candidates may present multiple facets of their reality, each requiring careful interpretation.

The Light of the Diya

Just as a diya (lamp) illuminates the darkness, our discernment must cast light on the shadows of deception. The truth, though concealed, can be revealed through astute questioning and reference checks.

Unveiling Truths in the Dance of Words

Our journey in the realm of job interviews is akin to the enchanting dance of Lord Shiva, where truth hides behind the veils of words. By embracing the mastery of interpretation, we can discern the authentic narratives and make informed decisions that lead to a harmonious and prosperous professional journey.

The Bazaar Test:

Selecting Souls for the Startup Voyage In this chapter, we delve into the essence of the Bazaar Test as a guiding principle for choosing the right individuals to embark on the startup journey. We draw inspiration from Indian philosophies and tales to illuminate this crucial selection process.

The Origin of the Bazaar Test The seed of the Bazaar Test was planted during an unexpected encounter at the local bazaar. I stumbled upon a software developer, but our past interactions had been unsatisfactory. Avoiding him, I realized the significance of a simple yet profound test. The Test That Mirrors Life's Essence Envision yourself in a bustling bazaar, spotting a candidate before they notice you. At that moment, you face three choices:

1. Approach and greet them warmly.
2. Be receptive to a serendipitous encounter, without pressure.
3. Move on and explore other opportunities.

The Wisdom of the Bazaar Test Life is too precious to spend with individuals who do not resonate with your spirit, especially in the ever-changing landscape of startups. Hence, I advocate for a single principle: Only recruit individuals who ignite a spark of enthusiasm within you, prompting you to engage in conversation willingly.

The Indian Parable of the Lotus Pond

Recall the Indian parable of the lotus pond, where the lotus blooms beautifully in the company of pristine waters and withers in contaminated surroundings. Similarly, in the startup ecosystem, the purity of camaraderie and like-mindedness is essential for growth.

The Path of Collaboration and Harmony

In the sacred Bhagavad Gita, Lord Krishna emphasizes the importance of harmonious relationships and collective endeavors. Just as Arjuna sought guidance from Krishna in the face of adversity, startups thrive when each member resonates with the collective vision.

Nurturing Synergy in the Startup Garden

The Bazaar Test serves as a compass in the vast ocean of hiring decisions. By choosing those with whom we resonate, we nurture a garden of synergy where the startup blossoms with vigor and grace. Remember, life is too short for discord, and the startup voyage should be a harmonious odyssey of like-minded souls.

Setting Sail on the Journey: The 90-Day Odyssey of Excellence

In this section, we embark on a profound exploration of the initial review period, drawing inspiration from Indian wisdom and contemporary practices. We delve into the significance of this crucial period in the startup voyage.

The Prelude: The Challenge of Correcting Course

Despite our best intentions, there are moments when our recruiting process falters, and a new hire falls short of expectations. Admitting this mistake and taking corrective action is a formidable challenge.

The Delicate Balancing Act

Yet, there is a task even more formidable than parting ways with an underperforming team member—having to lay off those who are indeed valuable. Failure to address recruitment errors could jeopardize the futures of those who are excelling.

A Blueprint for Clarity and Fairness

To navigate this treacherous terrain and ensure fairness to all, it is imperative to establish an initial review period marked by incremental milestones. The more specific and concrete these performance objectives, the more effective they become.

Crafting Milestones: A Performance Odyssey

For instance, a salesperson's objectives might include completing product and sales training and participating in a set number of sales calls. This period should extend beyond the initial euphoria of recruitment but not linger to the point of questioning the decision.

The Influence of the Vedas: The Importance of Time

In the timeless wisdom of the Vedas, we find the significance of time. The concept of "Kala" reminds us that time is a powerful force, and the ninety-day period aligns with this profound understanding.

The Journey Towards Excellence

Establish a mutual understanding that, after ninety days, both sides will engage in a constructive review. This review is an opportunity to celebrate successes, address challenges, and collectively chart a course toward enhanced performance.

Embrace Accountability and Growth

Recognize that, as a leader, some of the issues may be attributed to your decisions and actions. Embrace this accountability as an avenue for growth and transformation, both for yourself and your team.

The 90-Day Odyssey of Excellence

The initial review period is not just a business practice but a journey of accountability, growth, and fairness. By honoring time-tested wisdom and fostering an environment of continuous improvement, startups can navigate these waters with wisdom and grace, ensuring the voyage towards excellence remains unwavering.

The Ever-Changing Symphony of Recruitment: A Sustained Overture

In this section, we unravel the intricacies of recruitment in the dynamic landscape of startups. Drawing inspiration from Indian philosophy and modern strategies, we uncover the perpetual nature of the recruitment journey.

The Prelude:

A Fragile Assumption In the year 2000, Udhyam embarked on a quest to recruit a prominent investment banker from a renowned corporation. The path to his recruitment was a journey marked by persuasion, negotiation, and counteroffers.

The Fickle Nature of Recruitment

After weeks of dedicated efforts, success was achieved. The banker and his family became part of the Udhyam family, celebrating their inclusion at a company BBQ. However, this was just the beginning of an unexpected turn of events.

The Unforeseen Departure

Within a short span, the newly recruited banker showed up for work but then, to everyone's surprise, announced his resignation through a late-night email. He had chosen to return to a former client of the investment bank.

The Lesson of Perpetuity

From this experience, a profound lesson emerged—never assume that recruitment concludes once an offer is accepted or an employee resigns. The recruitment journey remains ongoing, even beyond the individual's first day at the new organization.

A Lesson from the Upanishads: The Impermanence of Assumptions

In the spirit of the Upanishads, which emphasize the impermanence of the material world, we are reminded that in the realm of startups, assumptions are fleeting. Every day represents a new contract, a renewed commitment between the startup and its employees.

The Pledge to Continuous Engagement

Startups must pledge to engage with their employees continuously, acknowledging that their needs, aspirations, and circumstances can evolve rapidly.

A Story from the Mahabharata: The Ever-Changing Battlefield

In the epic Mahabharata, the battlefield of Kurukshetra serves as a metaphor for life's ever-changing challenges. In startups, the recruitment battlefield is similarly dynamic.

The Eternal Dance of Recruitment

The recruitment journey is an eternal dance—a symphony of evolving needs, aspirations, and opportunities. Startups must embrace this perpetual rhythm, for it is in this dance that they find the key to sustained success and growth. The recruitment journey never ceases; it merely transforms with each passing day.

The Mosaic of References: Unveiling the Unseen

In this section, we explore the mastery of reference checking—a cornerstone of the recruitment process. Drawing inspiration from Indian wisdom and contemporary strategies, we delve into the nuances of gathering insights that shape the hiring decision.

The Prelude: A Beacon of Wisdom

As Jamsetji Tata wisely remarked, "You can't build a reputation on what you're going to do." Reference checking stands as a testament to this truth, guiding us in the quest for exceptional team members.

The Essence of Reference

Checking Reference checking is an art, often overlooked or rushed by startups. To glean valuable insights, we must approach it with care and diligence. Ratan Tata's wisdom serves as our guiding light in this endeavor.

The Goal of Referencing

Reference checking isn't about disqualifying a candidate; it's about aligning their representation with reality and assessing their potential effectiveness in the startup environment.

A Blueprint for Comprehensive Insight

To construct a complete portrait of a candidate, we must engage with a diverse array of references. Speaking with two subordinates, two peers, two superiors, two customers, and even investors or board members from the candidate's current company is recommended.

The Interrogation: Questions That Illuminate

Our arsenal of questions is designed to unveil the candidate's true colors:

1. How is your association with the candidate? How long has this association endured?
2. Share your overall impressions of the candidate.
3. Where would you rank the candidate in comparison to peers in similar roles?
4. Describe the contributions the candidate has made to the organization.
5. How does the candidate fare in the eyes of others within the organization?
6. What specific skills does the candidate possess? In which areas does the candidate excel or struggle?
7. Can you shed light on the candidate's communication and management styles?
8. Where does the candidate need improvement?
9. Is the candidate adaptable to a small organization's dynamics?

10. Comment on the candidate's work ethic.

11. Would you consider hiring, working for, or collaborating with the candidate again?

12. Should I seek additional perspectives on the candidate?

The Unveiling of Unsolicited Insights

In addition to structured referencing, we must explore unsolicited references from individuals not provided by the candidate. Platforms like LinkedIn offer a valuable gateway to discover untold stories.

The Wisdom of the Bhagavad Gita: Seeking Truth Beyond Facades

In the spirit of the Bhagavad Gita, where Lord Krishna implores Arjuna to seek truth beyond appearances, we embrace the essence of reference checking. It is a quest for authenticity in the narrative woven by the candidate.

The Recruitment

Reference checking, often relegated to a mere formality, is, in reality, of truths waiting to be uncovered. With careful orchestration and diligence, startups can weave this into a vibrant and accurate portrait of their prospective team members. Reference checking is not an end but a journey—an exploration of the unseen facets that shape the future of the organization.

Navigating the Labyrinth of Recruitment

In this section, we embark on a journey through the intricate landscape of recruitment, drawing inspiration from ancient Indian wisdom, modern strategies, and insightful anecdotes.

The Essence of Truth in Recruitment: An Indian Perspective

As we delve into the realm of recruitment, it is imperative to uphold the values of truth and transparency. Just as Lord Krishna guided Arjuna on the path of righteousness in the Bhagavad Gita, startups too must navigate the hiring process with integrity.

Frequently Asked Questions (FAQ): Illuminating the Path

Q1: Should I be honest about our startup's weaknesses as well as our strengths? A: In the spirit of authenticity, always share the complete truth. Lowering candidate expectations by revealing challenges is essential. It invites three types of responses, each shedding light on the candidate's suitability.

Indian Wisdom: "Satyam eva jayate" (Truth alone triumphs)

Q2: Is it better to have six part-time employees rather than three full-time employees for the sake of numbers? A: Prioritize quality over quantity. Opting for part-time employees solely to inflate numbers is imprudent. Instead, consider flexible hours to attract top talent.

Indian Proverb: "Annam bahu kurvate" (Abundance of food leads to satisfaction, not abundance of employees)

Q3: When is the right time to recruit CXO-level people, before or after funding? A: Entrepreneurship is a parallel process, not sequential. Recruit before, during, and after funding, driven by the goal of building a great startup rather than appeasing investors.

Upanishadic Wisdom: "Tat tvam asi" (Thou mastery that - You are the divine)

Q4: Should I spend money on retainer-based searches or rely on my own capability to attract talent? A: Pre-funding, leverage your network to avoid fees. Post-funding, invest in retainer-based searches if necessary, but restrain spending when resources are limited.

Chanakya's Advice: "Before you start some work, always ask yourself three questions: Why am I doing it? What the results might be? And will I be successful? Only when you think deeply and find satisfactory answers to these questions, go ahead."

Q5: Should I provide a salary range early in the recruitment process? A: Avoid disclosing salary ranges prematurely. Instead, inquire about the candidate's current salary to gauge their expectations. Reserve salary discussions for a later stage to prevent undue influence.

Ancient Wisdom: "Atmavan manyate jagat" (One sees the world as one sees oneself)

Q6: How can I recruit individuals better than myself without losing control of the venture? A: Focus on building a great startup, not on retaining control. Embrace the possibility of stepping aside when necessary for the greater good of the venture.

Mahatma Gandhi's Wisdom: "You must be the change you want to see in the world."

Q7: Do I need a legal agreement when working with my best friend in a startup? A: Yes, even more so when collaborating with a close friend. Legal agreements safeguard both the friendship and the startup's interests, preventing future conflicts.

Ancient Insight: "Mitro dharmasya moolam" (Friendship is the root of righteousness)

Q8: What is a reasonable compensation for a member of my board of directors? A: Typically, 0.25% to 0.5% is reasonable, but for exceptional individuals, consider up to 1%. If monetary gain outweighs meaning, reconsider the candidate.

Indian Wisdom: "Yato dharmastato jayah" (Where there is righteousness, there is victory)

Q9: How do I handle the challenging task of firing a partner who conceived the business? A: Initiate a private conversation, offering alternative roles that preserve dignity. Expect turmoil, but prioritize the startup's well-being.

Ancient Adage: "Sarve bhavantu sukhinah" (May all be happy)

A Journey of Integrity

Recruitment is a path fraught with choices and challenges. Embracing truth, transparency, and wisdom from India's heritage, startups can navigate this labyrinth with integrity, forging a team that will shape their future success.

Enlightening Your Path with Knowledge

In this section, we explore the wisdom contained within books that can illuminate your journey in the world of startups, drawing from Indian philosophy, contemporary literature, and the power of knowledge.

The Treasury of Knowledge: Your Reading List

Knowledge is the compass that guides us through the turbulent seas of entrepreneurship. Here is a curated list of recommended readings, enriched with Indian insights and wisdom.

Indian Wisdom: "Vidya dadaati vinayam" (Knowledge bestows humility)

1. **"Connect the Dots" by Rashmi Bansal** - Another masterpiece by Rashmi Bansal, this book profiles the stories of successful Indian entrepreneurs who started from humble beginnings and achieved remarkable success through perseverance and innovation.
2. **"The Startup Way" by Vineet Bajpai** - Vineet Bajpai, an Indian author and entrepreneur, shares practical strategies and lessons for building and scaling startups in the Indian context, drawing from his own experiences and those of other successful entrepreneurs.
3. **"Mindset: The New Psychology of Success"** by Dr. Carol S. Dweck (Translated into Indian languages) - While not written by an Indian author, this book explores the power of mindset in achieving success, a crucial aspect for entrepreneurs navigating the challenges of startup life.
4. **"The Alchemist" by Paulo Coelho** (Translated into Indian languages) - Although a work of fiction, "The Alchemist" is cherished by many Indian entrepreneurs for its profound messages about following one's dreams, taking risks, and finding one's purpose in life.
5. **"Inspiring Thoughts" by A.P.J. Abdul Kalam** - This collection of quotes and reflections by the late Dr. A.P.J. Abdul Kalam, former President of India and a renowned scientist, offers timeless wisdom and inspiration for entrepreneurs embarking on their startup journey.

The Power of Knowledge

In the startup journey, books are not just sources of knowledge; they are the keys to unlocking your potential. These recommended readings, enriched with Indian wisdom, serve as beacons in the darkness, guiding you towards success.

Embarking on a Journey of Enlightenment

As you embark on this entrepreneurial odyssey, remember that knowledge is your most potent weapon. Immerse yourself in the wisdom of these books, for they hold the keys to transforming your startup dreams into reality.

Chapter 8:
The Mastery of Spreading the Light

In this chapter, we explore the mastery of spreading the light of your vision, transcending borders and beliefs. Drawing inspiration from Indian spirituality and the teachings of great leaders, we delve into the essence of evangelism in the context of your startup journey.

Embracing the Path of Enlightenment

Evangelism, derived from the Greek word "euangelion" meaning "good news," is not merely about promotion; it's about sharing the joy of your vision. Let us embark on a journey to understand the profound significance of evangelism in the Indian startup landscape.

The Radiant Beacon: Your Guiding Light

In the spirit of sharing the wisdom of diverse cultures, we present a guiding light from Indian spirituality:

Quote: "तमसो मा ज्योतिर्गमय" (Lead me from darkness to light) - Brihadaranyaka Upanishad

Unveiling the Essence of Evangelism

Evangelism is not a battle to conquer competitors or amass wealth. It is the mastery of illuminating the path for others. It is about how your product or service brings value to people's lives, rather than simply desiring dominance.

The Journey of a Spiritual Entrepreneur

Drawing inspiration from the journey of spiritual leaders, let us understand the principles of enlightened evangelism:

1. **Serving Others**: Just as Lord Krishna served humanity through his teachings in the Bhagavad Gita, your evangelism should focus on what you can do for your customers.

2. **The Power of Belief**: Like Mahatma Gandhi, who led millions with his unwavering belief in non-violence, when people believe in your product, they become your most powerful evangelists.

3. **Continuous Illumination**: Similar to the eternal flame at the Golden Temple, your evangelism should be continuous, providing a consistent source of inspiration and guidance.

Recruiting Spiritual Evangelists

In the journey of your startup, recruiting evangelists is paramount. These individuals are not mere employees; they are torchbearers of your vision. The process of selecting them should resonate with the principles of enlightenment.

Illuminating the Startup Ecosystem

As you venture into the world of startups, remember that evangelism is not just marketing; it is a spiritual journey. It is the transmission of the light of your vision to dispel the darkness of doubt and ignorance. Embrace the mastery of evangelism, recruit your spiritual evangelists, and together, let us lead from darkness to light on this sacred journey of entrepreneurship.

Touching the Elixir of Excellence

In the pursuit of entrepreneurial success, Vinay's Golden Touch illuminates the path. We delve into the essence of this touch, blending it with the wisdom of Indian philosophy and the latest advancements in technology.

The Radiance of Excellence

In the words of Mahatma Gandhi, "Be the change that you wish to see in the world." The concept of Vinay's Golden Touch resonates with this profound idea. It signifies the ability to recognize and enhance the inherent brilliance of a product or idea.

Unearthing the Secrets of Excellence

To truly understand Vinay's Golden Touch, let's explore the principles of DICEE products, infusing them with Indian wisdom:

1. **DEEP - The Ocean of Features**: Just as the sacred river Ganges flows through the hearts of millions, a deep product anticipates and fulfills the evolving needs of its users as they traverse their unique journeys.

2. **INTELLIGENT - The Wisdom of Innovation**: Like the wisdom of ancient sages, an intelligent product reflects profound insights into alleviating challenges and enhancing the joys of life.

3. **COMPLETE - Wholeness in Every Aspect**: Similar to the holistic approach of Ayurveda, a complete product encompasses everything a user requires, from comprehensive support to user-friendly documentation.

4. **EMPOWERING - Nurturing Growth**: Much like yoga empowers the body and soul, an empowering product elevates users, enabling them to achieve more and be their best selves.

5. **ELEGANT - The Mastery of Seamless Experience**: In the spirit of the Taj Mahal's timeless beauty, an elegant product marries functionality with aesthetics, offering an effortless and delightful experience.

The Alchemy of Technology and Excellence

In today's digital age, Vinay's Golden Touch is amplified by cutting-edge technology. Machine learning and AI empower entrepreneurs to refine their products continuously, making them more intuitive, efficient, and user-centric.

The Indian Parable of Transformation

The story of Lord Ganesha, with his ability to transform obstacles into opportunities, mirrors Vinay's Golden Touch. Just as Ganesha overcame challenges with wisdom and grace, entrepreneurs can turn adversity into innovation.

A Symphony of Excellence

As you embark on your entrepreneurial journey, remember that Vinay's Golden Touch is not elusive; it can be cultivated. Strive for excellence, infuse your products with the essence of DICEE, and harness the power of technology. In doing so, you'll not only touch gold but also create a symphony of excellence that resonates with users, leaving an indelible mark on the world.

Reaching New Heights: The Mastery of Strategic Positioning

In the ever-evolving landscape of entrepreneurship, achieving the right positioning for your product is paramount. We explore the concept of getting high and to the right, drawing inspiration from Indian wisdom and modern strategies.

The Pinnacle of Positioning

To navigate the competitive market successfully, we must ascend to the summit of strategic positioning. Let's embark on this journey guided by the wisdom of Indian thought and contemporary insights.

The Axis of Differentiation and Value

Imagine a graph where the vertical axis represents the degree of differentiation, and the horizontal axis represents value. This graph unveils the essence of effective product positioning. There are four distinct quadrants:

1. **Valuable but Not Undifferentiated**: These products fulfill needs but lack uniqueness. They compete with similar offerings, often leading to tight profit margins.

2. **Differentiated but Not Valuable**: In this quadrant, products are innovative but cater to a non-existent market or offer undesired features.

3. **Undifferentiated and Not Valuable**: The lowest point on the graph signifies products with no demand and intense competition, a recipe for failure.

4. **Differentiated and Valuable**: This is the Holy Grail of entrepreneurship. A valuable product with distinctive qualities paves the way for successful evangelism, offering a blend of significance, profit, and success.

The Engineer's Quest

Engineers, like modern-day architects, should strive to create products that are not only valuable but also impossible for competitors to replicate. This aligns with the Indian philosophy of 'Vasudhaiva Kutumbakam,' emphasizing global interconnectedness and shared resources.

The Evangelist's Mission

For evangelists, the mission is to illuminate the product's unique value to the world. Drawing inspiration from ancient Indian storytelling traditions, the evangelist becomes a storyteller, weaving narratives that showcase the product's unmatched worth.

Examples of Excellence

In the realm of differentiated and valuable products, examples abound:

1. **Breitling Emergency**: A watch that can save lives by broadcasting emergency signals to airplanes. It's a symbol of differentiation and value for adventurers.

2. **Smart Car**: With the ability to park perpendicular to the curb, the Smart Car redefines urban mobility, standing out in a crowded market.

3. **Tesla Model S**: A revolutionary electric car that combines speed, range, and sustainability. It exemplifies differentiation and value for environmentally-conscious families.

Scaling New Heights

As entrepreneurs, our pursuit is clear: create products that rise high and move to the right on the graph. Embrace the wisdom of Indian philosophy and leverage modern strategies to position your offerings as invaluable and distinctive. In this endeavor, you not only achieve business success but also contribute to a world where innovation and value reign supreme.

Prioritizing Others: The Essence of True Evangelism

Discover the essence of evangelism rooted in putting others' interests first, inspired by Indian philosophies and contemporary stories.

The Heart of Evangelists

The hallmark of true evangelists lies in their unwavering commitment to the well-being of others. Their belief in a product is so profound that they earnestly desire its benefits for everyone. A striking example of this ethos can be found in the story of Tesla Model S.

In 2014, the state of Iowa imposed restrictions preventing Tesla from selling cars to its residents due to the absence of licensed auto dealers. Here, Tesla owners from Minnesota stepped in as unsung heroes. They journeyed to Urbandale, Iowa, not as employees or stockholders but as true evangelists. Their motive was simple: they wanted others to experience the joy of driving a Tesla. Their selfless actions exemplify the true power of evangelism.

Embracing Humanity in Brands

Several iconic Indian brands like Tata Group, Amul, Mahindra, and Flipkart have achieved a unique quality—humanness. Tata Group exudes trustworthiness, Amul radiates simplicity, Mahindra embodies resilience, and Flipkart represents innovation.

In contrast, some high-awareness Indian brands like Infosys, Wipro, and Air India lack these human qualities. The key lies in creating a brand rooted in Indian values, making it easier to connect with customers. Here's how to achieve this:

1. **Target the Young**: Regardless of your product's target audience, focusing on young people compels you to build a brand with human values. Many older individuals are now embracing products initially aimed at the youth.

2. **Embrace Self-Deprecation**: Most companies shy away from making fun of themselves, fearing it undermines their seriousness. However, embracing moments of self-deprecating humor can humanize your startup and make it more relatable.

3. **Celebrate and Have Fun**: Some Indian companies, with significant market presence, celebrate anniversaries and holidays by altering their logos for the day. Such playful gestures resonate with customers. Ratan Tata's willingness to participate in fun activities, such as driving a Nano car during its launch, exemplifies the fun-loving spirit that sets him apart.

4. **Highlight Your Customers**: Featuring customers in marketing materials adds a human touch to your brand. Amul, for instance, uses customer-generated content in its advertisements to showcase the diverse usage of its products.

5. **Philanthropy and Social Responsibility**: Engaging in corporate philanthropy and supporting underserved communities not only fulfills a moral obligation but also enhances brand awareness. Moreover, it serves as a powerful tool for employee recruitment and retention.

The Soul of Evangelism

In the world of evangelism, genuine concern for others and a brand with human values are the pillars of success. Drawing inspiration from Indian philosophies that emphasize selflessness and empathy, modern evangelists can create a lasting impact. By putting others first, we forge connections that transcend business, fostering a world where compassion and humanity reign supreme.

Personalized Positioning: The Power of Emotional Connection

Unlock the potential of personalized product positioning inspired by Indian wisdom and contemporary anecdotes.

Making It Personal: A Lesson from Canines

Rabindranath Tagore once remarked, "To his cow, every farmer is a king," highlighting the profound bond between humans and their livestock. This sentiment serves as a springboard for understanding the mastery of personalized product positioning.

Consider the tale of an entrepreneur with a unique idea—an online service for creating trusts for livestock. Her pitch revolved around the staggering statistic that millions of animals face abandonment each year in India. Initially, skepticism arose: were all these animals truly in need of trusts? A closer look revealed a different perspective.

It wasn't about the number; it was about the personal connection. As a farmer and animal owner, the realization struck home: what would happen to our beloved animals, like Ganga the cow and Sheroo the goat, if their owners were no longer there? The entrepreneur had touched upon a deeply emotional chord.

The Lesson: Make It Personal

In the realm of product positioning, the key lies in making it personal. Instead of framing the issue as "What happens to the livestock of thousands of farmers who face uncertainties each year in India?" the question becomes "What happens to Ganga the cow and Sheroo the goat?" This shift from the impersonal to the personal is transformative.

Personalized positioning taps into the innate human capacity for empathy. When people can relate to a product on a personal level, they can empathize with the emotions of millions who share similar concerns about their livestock. This emotional connection makes the product's value more tangible and relatable.

Impersonal vs. Personal: The Power of Emotional Connection

Here's a comparison that illustrates the stark difference between impersonal and personal positioning:

Impersonal	Personal
Our operating system is an industry standard that enables MIS departments to maintain control and reduce costs.	Apple: "Our operating system makes you more creative and productive."
We're committed to reducing the size of the global ozone hole.	We prevent you from getting melanoma.
We have dozens of airplanes flying in a hub-and-spoke pattern around the United States.	Southwest Airlines: "You are now free to move about the country."
We increase the mean test scores for children in your school district.	We ensure that your son can read.

In each case, the personalized approach evokes emotions and paints a vivid picture of how the product addresses a deeply personal need or concern. It's this emotional connection that drives engagement and fosters a sense of shared purpose.

The Heart of Personalized Positioning

In the world of product positioning, the age-old wisdom of making it personal continues to hold true. Indian philosophy emphasizes empathy and interconnectedness, values that resonate with the power of personalized positioning. By forging emotional connections and addressing individual concerns, businesses can create products that not only meet needs but also touch hearts, fostering a world where empathy and personalized experiences reign supreme.

Mastering the Mastery of Schmoozing: Building Lasting Connections

In networking and building connections, a timeless wisdom emerges: "It's not what you know or who you know, but who knows you." These words by Rahul Bajaj unveil the essence of schmoozing—an mastery essential for personal and professional growth, deeply rooted in the Indian concept of "vyavaharika buddhi" or practical wisdom.

The Magic of Schmoozing: Beyond Knowing to Being Known

Schmoozing isn't merely about expanding your social circle; it's about nurturing relationships where people truly know you, and vice versa. Imagine a scenario where you're evangelizing a product, and the room is filled with familiar faces—those who know your sincerity, integrity, and willingness to help. This is the power of schmoozing, an endeavor often overlooked due to shyness or misconceptions. K. M. Shea, in his book "The Frog and Prince," encapsulates the essence of schmoozing as "discovering what you can do for someone else." This outward perspective is the keystone for forging profound and lasting connections, echoing the teachings of the Upanishads, which emphasize the interconnectedness of all beings.

Becoming a World-Class Schmoozer: The Pathway

To embark on the journey of schmoozing, let's delve into the steps that will ensure more people know you, appreciate you, and value your presence:

1. **Get Out:** Schmoozing thrives in the realm of personal contact. Trade shows, conventions, seminars, and gatherings are its fertile grounds. In a world dominated by virtual communication, there's still no substitute for the human touch. This echoes the Indian saying, "Milan ki chidiya, phir milne se kam hai," meaning that meeting in person is more precious than meeting again.

2. **Ask Good Questions; Then Listen:** A quintessential trait of remarkable schmoozers is their ability to be outstanding listeners. They initiate conversations with thought-provoking questions and then lend an ear. In the Indian context, the ancient practice of "satsang" emphasizes the power of listening to spiritual discourses with unwavering attention.

3. **Make It Easy to Get in Touch:** Simplicity in communication is paramount. Ensure that your contact information is readily available, be it on your business card or in your email signature. In India, where diverse languages and cultures coexist, accessibility bridges gaps.

4. **Follow Up:** The mastery of follow-up is akin to "punya" or positive karma in Indian philosophy. It's the cosmic scoreboard tracking your actions. By promptly reconnecting within twenty-four hours, you demonstrate your worthiness as a connection.

5. **Unveil Your Passions:** Life extends beyond the confines of your profession. Sharing diverse passions is a hallmark of engaging schmoozers. These interests not only make you more interesting but also offer additional avenues for connection, reminiscent of the Indian idea of "jugaad" or resourcefulness.

6. **Give Favors:** In the grand cosmic design, your deeds accumulate like credits on a karmic scoreboard. Becoming a world-class schmoozer involves being generously positive on this scoreboard. The Indian ethos deeply ingrains the concept of "seva" or selfless service, a virtue that finds resonance in building lasting connections.

Embrace the Mastery of Schmoozing

In a world where relationships and connections play a pivotal role, the mastery of schmoozing holds timeless significance. As you embark on this journey, remember the words of Mahatma Gandhi, "You must be the change you want to see in the world." By embodying the spirit of schmoozing and nurturing meaningful connections, you become the change that transforms not only your life but also the lives of those around you.

Mastering the Mastery of Effective Email Communication: Your Digital Evangelism Tool

In our age of digital connectivity, where time is a precious resource, the mastery of email communication is akin to wielding a powerful tool for evangelism. As Ratan Tata eloquently put it, "I have made this [letter] longer because I have not had the time to make it shorter." In the spirit of brevity and effectiveness, let's delve into the mastery of harnessing email as a dynamic instrument for building connections, nurturing relationships, and advocating causes.

Crafting Compelling Email Communication: Strategies for Success

Email, a ubiquitous medium, holds immense potential for evangelists. Yet, its misuse often hampers its effectiveness. Here's how you can optimize your email communications to become a persuasive digital evangelist:

1. **Optimize Your Subject Line:** In the vast expanse of crowded inboxes, your subject line is your beacon. Make it captivating, akin to the mesmerizing opening lines of an ancient Indian tale, drawing readers in. For instance, use subject lines

like "Enjoyed your insights" or "Referred by a mutual acquaintance" to pique interest.

2. **Timing is Key:** Like the rhythmic cycles of life, email timing matters. The wisdom of Stephen Brand suggests that Tuesday mornings are optimal for email dispatch. By then, the weekend backlog is cleared, and the midweek deluge is yet to descend.

3. **The Gentle Reminder:** When a message remains unanswered, consider Mukesh's approach—resend the email with a courteous note, "Did you have a chance to read this?" Sometimes, a gentle nudge can awaken a dormant connection.

4. **Swift Responses:** Responsiveness is the essence of effective communication. Aim to reply within forty-eight hours while the topic is fresh. In the digital age, messages buried beyond the first screen are often forgotten, much like the lost verses of ancient texts.

5. **Mind Your Etiquette:** Just as decorum is revered in Indian culture, digital decorum matters. Avoid using all capital letters, as it conveys shouting. Maintain a tone of respect and professionalism.

6. **Quote Back:** In the whirlwind of digital interactions, quoting the relevant section of an email when responding helps refresh the sender's memory. It demonstrates your attention and thoughtfulness.

7. **Keep it Crisp:** Long-winded emails often lose their impact. The ideal email is concise, encapsulating your message in five sentences. If brevity eludes you, consider the mastery of storytelling—a timeless Indian tradition—to convey your point effectively.

8. **Embrace Plain Text:** Simplicity reigns supreme. HTML-rich emails may be misconstrued as spam. A clear, unadorned message showcases sincerity and clarity of intent.

9. **Mind Attachments:** Think of your recipient's situation. Sending large files without permission can overwhelm slow connections. Additionally, consider the perception of attachments from unknown senders.

10. **BCC and CC with Care:** Use Blind Carbon Copy (BCC) for large groups to maintain privacy and prevent inadvertent responses to everyone. Reduce Carbon Copy (CC) usage, as it often leads to ambiguity and mixed responsibilities.

11. **Signature Matters:** A well-crafted email signature is akin to an elegant Indian "mehndi" design, adding a touch of finesse. It should include your name, organization, postal address, phone number, email address, and website. Simplify contact for those interested in further engagement.

12. **Pause in Passion:** In the midst of digital exchanges, emotions can flare. In such moments, heed the ancient wisdom of restraint. If anger, offense, or argumentation brews within, allow time for composure before responding.

Email as Your Digital Conch Shell

In the vast digital ocean, your email communication can be your conch shell—a powerful instrument to summon allies, convey wisdom, and advocate change. By mastering the mastery of email communication, you step into the realm of a digital evangelist, connecting with a global audience and leaving a lasting impact. Much like the profound teachings of the Vedas and Upanishads, your emails can be a source of enlightenment, inspiration, and transformation for those who receive them.

Cultivating Evangelists: The Mastery of Seeking Support

In our journey towards evangelism, let us transition from the role of evangelists to becoming gatherers of evangelists. This shift in perspective marks a pivotal step in our mission. It commences with a humble act—asking our valued patrons for their support. We convey our aspiration to attain critical mass and the importance of their role in propagating our message. This is not a sign of frailty, but rather a display of sagacity.

In our endeavors, there exists a remarkable truth: if our product possesses an innate contagion, the fervor of evangelism may have already ignited among our patrons. The tale of Macintosh is a testament to this phenomenon. However, if a gentle call for assistance is made, the response can be swifter and more abundant. Yet, a shadow of hesitation often looms:

1. **Misconception of Weakness:** It is a fallacy to perceive the act of seeking help as a weakness. Strength lies in acknowledging that collective efforts often yield superior results. Much like the great Indian epics, where alliances and collaborations led to triumph, so does seeking support from our customers fortify our cause.

2. **Fear of Expectations:** Apprehensions arise—will our patrons expect something in return? Discounts, privileges, or special treatment may be anticipated.

Here, we can draw wisdom from ancient Indian philosophies, where giving without expectation is celebrated. The act of support, driven by genuine belief, often requires no reciprocation.

3. **Self-Reliance vs. Collaboration:** Some may argue, "We know the path, we can tread it alone." However, the richness of diversity and the strength of community have been celebrated in Indian culture for millennia. The idea that customers cannot contribute is a misconception. They hold invaluable insights, experiences, and perspectives.

4. **Cost Concerns:** Fear of the financial burden of maintaining support programs can lead to reluctance. Yet, the cost-effective nature of authentic customer evangelism is a proven fact. It transcends traditional marketing expenses, creating a ripple effect of trust and authenticity.

It is vital to recognize that such reasons are baseless, stemming from a blend of unwarranted apprehension and arrogance. When customers extend their hands in support, it is a cause for celebration, not skepticism. We must quell our paranoia and pride and graciously accept their offers of help. These patrons, turned evangelists, are destined to become our most ardent salespeople.

In Indian mythology, every deity sought the aid of mortals to achieve celestial objectives. Similarly, in our pursuit of evangelism, seeking support from our customers is not just a strategy; it is a divine collaboration. These patrons, enshrined in our narrative, will herald our message with fervor and authenticity, much like the hymns of the Vedas and the wisdom of the Upanishads have resonated through the ages. Their voices shall carry our message to the farthest corners of the digital landscape, weaving a shared purpose and collective success.

Nurturing Evangelists: Cultivating a Thriving Community

As we traverse the landscape of evangelism, let us embark on a journey of community building, a phenomenon deeply rooted in the essence of our Indian heritage. The late 1990s witnessed the birth of an organization known as the "Mumbai Dhruvians." Comprising astute business leaders and community champions, their mission was to ensure the perpetuity of their beloved cricket team, the Mumbai Dhruvians. The chairman of this passionate group, Arjun Patel, once remarked, "The Dhruvians roamed the streets of Mumbai, rallying the masses to join our cause."

In the present day, the Mumbai Dhruvians no longer face ticket-selling challenges, yet their program thrives. Its members dedicate their time to volunteer initiatives, support community endeavors, and sponsor gatherings at cricket matches, all while diligently assisting in ticket sales. It's important to note that these devoted enthusiasts are also season ticket holders, offering their services without any monetary gain. This, my friends, is the embodiment of evangelism.

The primary objective in summoning evangelists is to weave a community around your product or cause. To elucidate this further, let us explore the experiences of renowned organizations that have successfully created such communities:

Community Initiative	Description
IndiCorp Networks	Providing customer service, technical support, and camaraderie to Indian entrepreneurs.
Tata User Groups	Fostering a sense of belonging and shared experiences among Tata product users.
IndianTech	Empowering users with knowledge and mutual support in the Indian tech community.
JioClub	Facilitating interaction and knowledge exchange among Jio users.
Indian App Developers Forum	Collaborating on innovations and troubleshooting in the Indian app development scene.
Indian Top Contributors Circle	Recognizing top contributors and their expertise in various fields.
Royal Enfield Riders Association	Creating a brotherhood of riders who share a passion for Royal Enfield motorcycles.
IndianStartups Hub	Sharing best practices and driving user success among Indian startup enthusiasts.
Bharat Linux Teams	Providing localized support and advocacy for Linux users in India.

These communities foster customer service, technical support, and social connections that enhance the ownership experience. As you embark on your journey, consider embracing the following practices inspired by timeless Indian wisdom:

1. "**Let 100 Flowers Blossom**": Just as the bountiful Indian landscape flourishes with diverse flora, do not constrain the ways in which evangelists can contribute. Allow their creativity to guide your product's promotion, unveiling new avenues you may have never envisioned.

2. **Assign and Expect**: When enthusiasts willingly offer their support, seize the opportunity. Assign tasks and ensure they are executed. It is better to make use of their willingness than to let it go to waste.

3. **Provide Tools for Evangelism**: Empower believers by equipping them with the necessary resources and promotional materials. Just as Lord Ganesha wields various instruments, make it effortless for evangelists to spread your message.

4. **Respond to Their Desires**: Like the river yielding to the terrain it traverses, be responsive to the requests and suggestions of your evangelists. Their insights hold the potential to enhance your product and demonstrate that you value their contributions.

5. **Gifts of Appreciation**: In the spirit of giving, offer tokens of appreciation such as T-shirts, mugs, or pens. These gestures make evangelists feel valued and cherished, strengthening their connection to your cause.

6. **Community Guardian**: Appoint a custodian of the community, someone who champions their cause within your organization. As your success burgeons, establish a department dedicated to community support.

7. **Allocate a Support Budget**: While the intent is not to buy evangelists, allocate a budget to sustain their efforts, encompassing travel, entertainment, meetings, and tokens of appreciation.

8. **Integration into All Efforts**: Celebrate the existence of evangelists in your sales, marketing, and online endeavors. Their presence signifies the success and quality of your product, inspiring trust and interest among potential customers.

9. **Host Community Activities**: Open your doors to community members, offering space for meetings and providing digital support through webinars and chats.

10. **Foster Face-to-Face Interaction**: While digital communication prevails, face-to-face meetings remain invaluable. Conferences and gatherings allow evangelists to connect with each other and your team.

11. **Sustained Engagement:** Similar to the unwavering bond between a parent and child, perpetually nurture your relationship with evangelists. Frequent interaction is key to maintaining their enthusiasm.

In Indian culture, communities have thrived for centuries, guided by the principles of unity, diversity, and collective progress. In our modern pursuit of evangelism, these principles remain as relevant as ever. As we draw inspiration from the Vedas and Upanishads, let us remember that building a thriving community around your cause is akin to nurturing a sapling into a mighty tree, where each leaf contributes to its growth.

Elevating Your Speaking Prowess: The Path to a Standing Ovation

In the realm of public speaking, echoes of wisdom from our Indian heritage guide us toward a harmonious connection with our audience. Ancient sages in India advised, "Maunam sarvatra vijayaha" – "Silence conquers all." As we delve into the mastery of oration, allow me to share insights and practices, seasoned with Indian ethos, to help you master the stage.

Embracing the Apple Orchards: A Journey in Public Speaking

Embark on a journey back to 2000's when I ventured into the fields of Indian entrepreneurship. Here, I encountered not only the innovative spirit of the legendary Indian CEOs but also the daunting challenge of public speaking. The shadow of these remarkable leaders loomed large, triggering self-doubt: "How can I match up to their charisma?" Yet, the path to success as an evangelist and CEO demands mastering the art of effective speech.

It took me two decades to find comfort in public speaking, and I am determined to share the secrets of this transformative journey with you. My aspiration is not just for you to survive speeches but to revel in the applause of standing ovations.

Guiding Principles for Masterful Speeches

In our quest for excellence in public speaking, let us adhere to a set of guiding principles:

1. **Having a Profound Message:**

o   As Mahatma Gandhi once said, "In a gentle way, you can shake the world." The crux of a remarkable speech lies in its content. Before you step on stage, ensure you have a message worth conveying. If your words don't enrich, consider declining the opportunity or invest in research to unearth an engaging narrative.

2. **Eliminating the Sales Pitch:**

   o   It is imperative to recognize that most keynote speeches are a blend of entertainment and education, not sales pitches. Let your speech captivate and enlighten, avoiding the pitfall of a blatant sales pitch.

3. **Customization:**

   o   A practice that has immensely enriched my speaking experiences is customization. Begin your speech by crafting a personal connection with your audience. Share anecdotes that resonate with them, just as I tailored my speeches by sharing personal experiences with Tata Motors and Godrej Consumer Products.

4. **Entertainment as the North Star:**

   o   Contrary to conventional wisdom, I believe that the primary goal of a speech is to entertain. Engaged listeners are more receptive to valuable insights. Thus, prioritize entertainment, infusing it with nuggets of wisdom.

5. **Dress with Respect:**

   o   Echoing the wisdom of my father, who served as a politician in Hawaii, dress according to the audience's expectations. To underdress is to convey disrespect; choose attire that aligns with the audience's attire to foster a sense of equality.

6. **Maintain Dignity:**

   o   The mastery of eloquence does not entail denigrating your competition. A speech should uplift and educate, not slander others. Remember, the audience graces you with their attention, so honor that privilege.

7. **The Power of Storytelling:**

   o   Embrace storytelling as a means to ease your nerves. Share personal tales, anecdotes of youth, or stories of customers. Good speakers are great storytellers, and exceptional speakers seamlessly weave stories that reinforce their message.

8. **Engaging with the Audience:**

   o   Recognize that your audience desires your success. Before your speech, circulate among them, forging connections. Engage with those in the first few rows; their friendly faces will bolster your confidence, ensuring a relaxed and outstanding performance.

9. **Commencing the Event:**

o If possible, opt to speak at the commencement of an event when the audience is most attentive and receptive. Avoid the challenges of captivating a weary audience on the final day.

10. **Choose an Intimate Venue:**

o Whenever feasible, select a smaller room or arrange seating classroom-style. A packed room brims with emotions, making it easier to connect with your audience.

11. **Practice Diligently:**

o Repetition is the crucible of excellence. Practice your speech at least twenty times. As the virtuoso Ravi Shankar aptly stated, "If I don't practice one day, I know it. If I don't practice two days, my critics know it. If I don't practice three days, everyone knows it." Dedication to practice will expedite your journey.

May this odyssey toward mastery of the spoken word be swifter for you than my twenty-year endeavor. It is my fervent wish that every time you grace the stage, a standing ovation echoes your profound message, a testament to your eloquence and wisdom.

Mastering Panel Discussions: The Mastery of Engaging Dialogue

In the symphony of public discourse, Aarav Sharma's insightful words resonate: "Humans yearn for the freedom to express themselves and to feel valued. But when given these opportunities, they often shy away." Embracing the essence of these words, let us delve into the craft of excelling in panel discussions—an invaluable skill for thought leaders.

At conferences, the spotlight often shines on panelists rather than keynote speakers. Panels appear deceptively easy, comprising several participants and a mere sixty minutes. However, the challenge lies in the assumption that ease equates to no preparation. In truth, panels demand more finesse than solo speeches; you wield less control and speak less.

Guidelines for Triumphing in Panels:

1. **Command of the Subject:**

o In the wise words of Chanakya, "Knowledge is the true weapon of a wise warrior." Before accepting a panel invitation, assess your familiarity with the subject. Never provide an avenue for others to discover your lack of knowledge.

2. **Craft Your Introduction:**

   o   The first pitfall awaits at the introduction. Trust not that the moderator possesses an accurate bio. Provide a concise bio to ensure an accurate introduction.

3. **Speak with Clarity:**

   o   Close the gap between your lips and the microphone to an inch, especially when seated. This proximity enhances audibility. Embrace the microphone and project your voice with clarity.

4. **Entertain Alongside Informing:**

   o   As in keynote speeches, prioritize entertainment over mere information. Humor is the hallmark of intelligence; engage the audience, even engage in friendly banter with fellow panelists. Make it enjoyable.

5. **The Virtue of Honesty:**

   o   When provoked with challenging questions, seize the opportunity to be witty and forthright. "The truth will get you glee." If the truth is evident, do not fabricate; it is better to jest or tactfully evade.

6. **Expand Beyond the Question:**

   o   Promptly answer posed questions, but thereafter, guide the discourse in the direction you deem relevant. Redirect if necessary, fostering a deeper discussion.

7. **Simplicity Over Complexity:**

   o   In a panel of experts, refrain from deluging the audience with jargon. Simplify intricate matters into plain, concise explanations. Strive to be the beacon of clarity.

8. **Feign Interest When Necessary:**

   o   The mastery of feigning interest in a lengthy, mundane response poses a challenge. Yet, resist boredom, for any disinterested moment may be captured. Maintain an appearance of rapt engagement.

9. **Audience Over Moderator:**

   o   While responding, address the audience, not the moderator. The audience seeks direct connection and engagement, not side profiles. Eye contact with the audience forges a powerful link.

10. **Diverge from Consensus:**

o Avoid responding with, "I agree with my colleague." Provide a fresh perspective or gracefully suggest the topic has been adequately addressed. Keep the conversation dynamic.

In the mastery of panel discussions, each participant contributes to the ideas. By adhering to these principles, you transform panels into captivating dialogues. Remember, in the vibrant exchange of ideas, the audience yearns for engaging voices. Converse, captivate, and leave an indelible mark on every panel you grace.

Frequently Asked Questions (FAQs) on Evangelism in the Indian Context

In the quest for enlightenment about the role of evangelists in the Indian landscape, one might find oneself pondering numerous queries. To illuminate this path, let us delve into some pertinent questions, drawing inspiration from both contemporary wisdom and timeless Indian scriptures.

Q1: Do the religious undertones of the term "evangelist" pose a challenge?

- *A1: In India, where myriad beliefs flourish like a garden of flowers, it is paramount to tread with sensitivity. While in some parts of the world, the term may carry religious connotations, it finds a harmonious resonance in the tech sector. Here, it signifies the fervent propagation of a remarkable product, transcending boundaries. After all, Christianity teaches us that sharing can be a virtue, and in the tech world, where innovation knows no creed, such sharing is embraced. As the Bhagavad Gita imparts, "Perform your duties with dedication, without attachment to the fruits of your actions." In this spirit, the term "evangelist" embodies the essence of sharing the fruits of innovation, free from religious bias.*

Q2: What if individuals admire our product but hesitate to advocate for it?

- *A2: The realm of advocacy thrives on voluntariness, akin to the free will that guides our choices. You cannot compel souls to become evangelists; their hearts must resonate with the product's essence. If admiration for a product does not translate into a desire to champion its cause, it suggests a shallower affinity than one might assume. In the great epic of the Mahabharata, Lord Krishna, the ultimate guide, emphasizes the importance of genuine devotion and intention in one's actions. Likewise, evangelists are driven by a sincere connection with the product that moves their very being.*

Q3: Are evangelists a product of nature or nurture?

- *A3: The emergence of evangelists is a profound process, shaped by the interplay of individual inclinations and the brilliance of the product itself. It is akin to sculpting a masterpiece. Just as Lord Ganesha, the deity of wisdom and beginnings, was crafted by Goddess Parvati, anyone, except the extreme, can become an evangelist when the right product touches their soul. The essence of evangelism, much like the teachings of the Upanishads, lies in the realization of a deeper connection—one that transcends the material world and sparks a divine fire within.*

In this vibrant landscape of questions and answers, we traverse the bridge between tradition and innovation. Just as the river of knowledge flows from the Ganges, nurturing both ancient wisdom and modern progress, so does the spirit of evangelism unite age-old values with the ever-evolving tech ecosystem. With reverence for diversity and a commitment to shared success, let us continue this journey of enlightenment.

Suggested Reading for the Inquisitive Mind

In the quest for knowledge and mastery in the mastery of evangelism, we turn to the written wisdom of the ages, mingling contemporary insights with the time-honored teachings of India. Here are some recommended readings that will empower your journey towards becoming an evangelist of change, seamlessly blending the essence of both worlds.

1. **"The Power of Your Subconscious Mind"** by Dr. Joseph Murphy
2. **"The Secret"** by Rhonda Byrne
3. **"The 5 AM Club: Own Your Morning. Elevate Your Life"** by Robin Sharma
4. **"The Krishna Key"** by Ashwin Sanghi

These books, steeped in the Indian philosophy and modern innovation, will serve as your trusted companions on your evangelism journey. Just as a river continuously enriches the land it flows through, may these readings nourish your intellect and spirit, guiding you towards becoming a transformative evangelist.

Chapter 9:
Mastering the Mastery of Social Connection

In the era of digital evolution, where the rhythms of social media echo across the digital realm, we embark on a journey to unravel the core of contemporary evangelism. As the esteemed innovator, Ratan Tata, once reflected, "Every new creation brings with it the potential for transformation." Little did he anticipate that in the modern age, we would traverse a digital terrain where not only can we consume information, but we can also swiftly engage with a global audience.

Unleashing the Power of Social Media

The digital age has ushered in a new era of communication, where social media emerges as the modern chariot of connection. It grants us a triumvirate of marketing power: it's swift, it's cost-free, and it's omnipresent. In the days of yore, during the epoch of indigenous product advocacy, our arsenal comprised telephones, telegraphs, and journeys by rail. The pinnacle of triumph lay in assembling a few hundred devotees in a majestic temple hall, where the advocate's teachings reverberated.

Yet, today, the landscape has undergone a profound metamorphosis. Social media, reminiscent of the revered river Ganges coursing through the digital domain, has rewoven the entrepreneurship. Emerging Indian startups, in particular, stand at the vanguard of this digital evolution. They wield the power to traverse continents, forging connections with millions worldwide in the blink of an eye, all without bearing the weighty expenses of traditional marketing.

Navigating the Digital Maze

Yet, as we navigate this digital maze, we must acknowledge that harnessing the power of social media is no facile feat. It requires finesse, strategy, and an understanding of the intricate dance of the virtual world. In the chapters that follow, we shall unravel the secrets of this contemporary treasure trove, allowing you to wield social media as a potent weapon in your arsenal of evangelism.

As the lotus blooms amidst the muddied waters, so too shall you emerge from the digital deluge as a master of the mastery of socializing. We shall delve into the intricacies of this dynamic realm, exploring the latest technologies and strategies while drawing inspiration from the timeless wisdom of the Vedas and Upanishads.

Stay tuned, for the digital voyage has just begun, and the shores of social success beckon. In the world of digital evangelism, you are the harbinger of change, and social media is your trusted ally. Together, we shall embark on this transformative odyssey, where the possibilities are as vast as the boundless Indian sky.

"In the digital age, the world is your stage. Harness the power of social media and let your message resonate."

Chapter Overview	Topics Covered	Price (in Rupees)
"Mastering The Digital Symphony"	Understanding the landscape of social media and its impact on evangelism.	499
"Crafting Your Digital Identity"	Building a compelling online persona that resonates with your audience.	799
"The Mastery of Virality"	Strategies to create content that goes viral and spreads like wildfire.	649
"Navigating the Social Seas"	Insights into managing online communities and handling digital crises.	399
"The Divine Connection"	Exploring the spiritual dimensions of digital evangelism.	299

Join us on this exhilarating expedition, where you shall emerge as a digital evangelist, a maestro of social connection, and a harbinger of change in the digital age. The tools are at your disposal; the stage is set. The world awaits your message.

Crafting Your Social Media Strategy

In social media, the concept of planning often conjures images of intricate strategies, endless contemplation, and the engagement of high-priced agencies to navigate the labyrinthine world of virtual interaction. However, in the dynamic realm of Indian entrepreneurship, our approach must be as agile as the cosmic dance of Lord Shiva, where adaptability and spontaneity reign supreme.

Allow me to present a different perspective—a perspective that aligns with the ethos of the ancient Vedas and Upanishads, where wisdom is distilled into actionable insights. In the modern context of social media, our version of strategic planning is succinct and profound:

Step 1: Decipher Your Business Model Just as an architect envisions a magnificent temple before laying its foundation, you must crystallize your business model. Define your objectives, revenue streams, and the essence of your brand. Let it resonate with the sacred 'Dharma' of your venture.

Step 2: Attract the Right 'Jeevan Saathis' In digital evangelism, your success hinges on the people you attract—the 'Jeevan Saathis' who will journey with you. Identify your ideal audience, akin to selecting the right companions for an epic pilgrimage. Their resonance with your vision is paramount.

Step 3: Unveil the Insights They Seek Just as the sages of yore sought the wisdom of the scriptures, discern the desires of your audience. What knowledge, what stories, what 'kathas' do they yearn for? Delve deep into their hearts, for therein lies the key to your virtual 'satsang.'

Step 4: Share the Nectar of Knowledge With reverence, share the nectar of knowledge—knowledge that your audience craves. Be the 'Guru' who imparts wisdom. Your content should be akin to the 'Pravachan'—a discourse that enlightens and enriches.

Embrace the Spirit of 'Sadhana'

While some may advocate extensive planning, the essence of Indian entrepreneurship lies in the spirit of 'sadhana'—persistent effort and experimentation. In the realm of social media, this translates to grinding, working tirelessly, and evolving your approach.

Do not be swayed by the weight of elaborate strategies or the allure of consultants and agencies. The Indian way is to dive into the sea of possibilities, just as Lord Krishna dove into the depths of the Yamuna to retrieve the precious Syamantaka gem. Experiment, adapt, and refine your course as you journey through the digital cosmos.

Your 'Yatra' Awaits

In your digital 'yatra,' you shall encounter challenges and revelations, much like the heroes of our ancient 'itihasas.' Embrace the dynamic nature of social media, and remember the words of Swami Vivekananda, "Arise, awake, and stop not until the goal is reached."

In the tableau of Indian entrepreneurship, your social media strategy is the brush with which you paint your destiny. It's a journey where planning bows to intuition, and where every 'like' and 'share' is a step closer to your 'karma-phala'—the fruit of your deeds.

And so, with the essence of our ancient wisdom and the vigor of modern technology, embark on your digital 'yatra.' The universe of social media awaits your presence.

"In the realm of social media, as in life, it is the journey that transforms us."

Navigating the Digital Platforms: Understanding Social Media Platforms

In the vibrant landscape of Indian entrepreneurship, the digital realm unfolds as a sprawling bazaar of social media platforms—each with its own unique offerings. As of the present era, we embark on a journey to grok these platforms, much like the ancient sages who sought to understand the cosmos.

Let us delve into the quintessential platforms of 2015, which continue to shape our virtual existence, but with an Indian perspective:

1. Facebook - The 'Janata' Connect Facebook, often referred to as the 'Janata' (public) network, boasts over a billion users—an audience larger than the population of many nations. Yet, it is shrouded in enigmatic algorithms, such as the mysterious EdgeRank, which dictates which posts reach your audience. In truth, a mere fraction of your followers may witness your shared wisdom. However, do not be disheartened, for the digital 'yajna' (sacrifice) of promotion can expand your reach.

2. Google+ - The Uncharted Territory Google+, the underdog of the social media realm, may not rival the Goliath that is Facebook in sheer numbers. Yet, it shines as a beacon of transparency, unburdened by the cryptic algorithms of its counterpart. Here, all who 'circle' your enterprise bask in the radiance of your posts. As the celestial Google oversees this domain, dismissing it would be an oversight.

3. Instagram - Visual 'Katha' Instagram, the 'katha' (storytelling) platform, is a realm of visual narratives. Here, companies weave tales through images of their wares and the creations of their devotees. Although links to external domains are restricted, the mastery of communion with fans flourishes. This 'satsang' (spiritual discourse) with your audience builds lasting communities.

4. LinkedIn - The Unsung Hero LinkedIn, often overshadowed by its more glamorous counterparts, emerges as the unsung hero of the digital saga. While initially perceived as a realm for job seekers, it has evolved into a platform of substantial content and profound discourse. Recognize its potential as a tool for 'gyana' (knowledge) dissemination.

5. Pinterest - The Canvas of Inspiration Pinterest, a visual canvas where desires are painted, is a sanctuary for brands to showcase their offerings. With the elegance of a 'rangoli' (colorful mastery), companies curate boards that resonate with customers. In this visual 'darbar' (court), beauty reigns supreme.

6. Twitter - The Swift Stream of Consciousness Twitter, akin to a swift-flowing river, propels you forward at a rapid pace. It excels in delivering concise 140-character messages—a testament to brevity as the soul of wit. Here, you can promote your offerings while keeping a vigilant eye on the 'sangathan' (community).

7. YouTube - The Digital 'Katha Vachak' (Storyteller) YouTube, the digital 'katha vachak,' empowers those who can craft engaging and educational videos. It is a domain where the sincere narratives of enthusiasts often eclipse the polished productions of professionals. Establish your own YouTube 'mandir' (temple) where patrons can subscribe to your wisdom.

In the grand 'sabha' (assembly) of social media platforms, consider supporting all these pillars of digital existence. While some may counsel a sizable team, remember that with dedication, even one or two individuals can navigate this labyrinth.

As you traverse this digital 'yatra' (journey), may the wisdom of the ancient 'shastras' guide you: "Yatha drishti tatha srishti" (As you perceive, so shall you create). Each platform is a canvas; the narratives you weave shall paint your destiny. Embrace the digital cosmos, for it is a realm of limitless possibilities—a 'sadhana' (spiritual practice) in the pursuit of digital 'karma-phala' (fruit of deeds).

"In the realm of social media, as in life, it is the journey that transforms us."

Perfection of Profiles in the Digital Darbar

In the bustling marketplace of digital existence, social media platforms offer a sacred canvas—a profile page—where you can etch the essence of your enterprise. Just as a 'mandala' (sacred geometric design) holds profound meaning, your profile page is a glimpse into the soul of your business. Let us embark on the journey to perfect these one-page 'résumés' for your digital 'darbar' (court).

1. Optimize for the Blink of an Eye In this age of swiftness, recognize that people do not pore over profiles; they cast a fleeting glance and form snap judgments. Imagine this as a modern-day 'Swayamvar,' where a swift 'swipe right' or 'swipe left' determines the future. Therefore, optimize your profile to capture attention within seconds, much like the mastery of 'darshan' (glimpse) in temples.

2. Narrate with Visual Artistry A profile page unfolds as woven with two graphic threads. The first is the 'avatar,' a small image that serves as the visage of personal accounts and the emblem of corporate accounts. The second, a larger image called a 'cover' (on Facebook, Google+, and LinkedIn) or a 'header' (on Twitter), is a canvas to convey your startup's identity. These images must speak the unspoken, much like the silent wisdom of a 'mandir' (temple). As dimensions fluctuate like the waves of the ocean, stay attuned to the standards or seek guidance from the digital 'gurus.'

3. Craft a Mantra, the Essence of Being On these sacred profiles, you have the privilege to inscribe a 'mantra,' a concise two to four-word testament to your startup's raison d'être. Much like the profound 'mool-mantra' (basic mantra) that underlies all creation, this mantra encapsulates your startup's purpose. In the footsteps of great corporations, let your mantra resonate in the digital 'satsang' (spiritual discourse).

4. Immerse in Information Beyond the captivating imagery, it is the reservoir of information that quenches the seeker's thirst for knowledge. Consider this profile as your 'jivani' (biography), a 'pustak' (book) that narrates your tale. Furnish it with abundant information, for it is here that seekers delve deeper into your narrative.

5. Attain a Vanity URL In the grand digital 'yagna' (sacrificial ritual), securing a vanity URL for your Google+, Facebook, and LinkedIn accounts is akin to possessing a sacred 'yajna-patra' (offering vessel). This unique URL is akin to an auspicious mantra that followers can easily remember, invoke, and share. An ordinary URL, a string of numbers, pales in comparison to the divine resonance of a vanity URL.

6. Embrace Anonymity Before you present your profile to the digital 'jagat' (world), seek the wisdom of anonymity. In the cloak of an 'incognito window,' view your profile as others do. This mirror reflects the truth of your digital presence. In Chrome, launch the 'New Incognito Window' from the File menu. Each browser offers its path to anonymity, just as seekers embark on diverse spiritual journeys.

In the grand 'mahakumbh' (spiritual gathering) of digital existence, the perfection of profiles is your offering to the digital gods. Remember, as the 'Vedas' guide us, "Yatha drishti tatha srishti" (As you perceive, so shall you create). Your profile is the portal through which the digital universe perceives your essence. In digital 'mandala,' let your profile be a masterpiece—a 'purna-kumbha' (vessel of abundance) of digital wisdom.

"In the realm of social media, your profile is your digital 'namaskar' (greeting) to the world."

Acing the Shareability Challenge in the Digital Age

In the realm of digital engagement, there exists a sacred trial known as the "Reshare Test." This test is the litmus test of social media marketing, a testament to the resonance of your digital presence. While receiving "likes" and "plus ones" on your posts is akin to a nod of approval, and comments resemble a diner's compliment to the chef, the ultimate compliment lies in the act of resharing your posts.

Resharing, my dear readers, is the jewel in the crown of digital appreciation. It signifies that individuals are not only endorsing your content but are staking their own digital reputations on it. This act is akin to a sage recommending a sacred scripture to their disciples or inviting friends to savor a sumptuous feast at a favored eatery. In essence, resharing is a manifestation of genuine care and admiration.

Therefore, in your digital journey, every post must undergo the rigorous Reshare Test. Each post should be more than a fleeting digital encounter; it should be a valuable addition to the reader's life. To achieve this, we must imbue our content with four essential qualities:

1. Information - "The Knowledge Path" Illuminate your audience with timely and pertinent information. It resembles the learned guru imparting wisdom to disciples. For instance, sharing insights like Defense Minister Rajnath Singh's openness to reassessing the role of transgender individuals in the armed forces offers valuable enlightenment.

2. Analysis - "The Wisdom Well" Transition from facts to offer insightful analysis. Dive into the 'why' and 'how' of events, reminiscent of a philosopher pondering the mysteries of existence. For instance, elucidating the significance of Indian cricket icon Virat Kohli's aggressive on-field demeanor, as ESPN India did, provides a deeper comprehension.

3. Assistance - "The Guide's Compass" Empower your audience with practical guidance. Be the mentor guiding seekers on their journey. Illustrating how features like texting to emergency services work, as exemplified by an Indian tech magazine, offers valuable assistance.

4. Entertainment - "The Joyful Oasis" Infuse your content with elements of surprise, wonder, and laughter. Capture the essence of festivals like the mock rocket war in Chikmagalur, Karnataka, where two temples engage in a whimsical battle. In doing so, you provide entertainment that sparks joy.

To understand the Reshare Test better, let us draw inspiration from the timeless wisdom of the Vedas and Upanishads: "Share content not as a mere offering but as a gift to enrich lives."

Incorporate the NPR model into your digital journey. Just as NPR consistently provides quality content, endeavor to enrich your audience's lives with valuable posts day after day. The NPR pledge drives are possible because they consistently deliver value. By passing the Reshare Test and offering content that enhances lives, you earn the privilege to host your own 'digital pledge drive'—a promotion for your product or cause.

Remember, in the digital 'satsang' (spiritual discourse), the act of resharing is the highest form of appreciation. To create a digital legacy that resonates, imbue your content with the four gems of value: Information, Analysis, Assistance, and

Entertainment. Let every post be a testament to your commitment to enriching lives, earning the privilege to share your offerings with the digital 'sangha' (community).

"In the digital 'satsang,' the act of resharing is akin to sharing spiritual wisdom, an act of profound care and admiration."

Nourish the Content Beast: A Tale of Digital Sustenance

In the realm of digital dominion, the daily duel with the Content Monster is an epic struggle. This voracious beast demands an unending stream of content to satisfy its insatiable appetite. The quest to satiate it presents two formidable paths: content creation and content curation. While the former involves crafting original content, our focus here is on the mastery of content curation, a skill that every digital yogi must master.

Content creation is akin to embarking on a pilgrimage, a journey that entails crafting long posts, capturing captivating visuals, or weaving tales through videos. Yet, the relentless pace of the digital world demands more than a few content offerings per week. Alas, two offerings fall short in the age of perpetual digital clamor. Though a profound topic, mastering content creation warrants a tome of its own, beyond the scope of our current discourse.

In the sacred realm of curation, one becomes a seeker of wisdom, a custodian of the gems scattered across the digital cosmos. Content curation is a trilateral harmony—benefitting the curator, the content creator, and the digital pilgrim in search of wisdom.

Now, let us unfurl the techniques that shall guide you on the path of content curation, nurturing the Content Monster:

1. Embark on the Curator's Journey

- **Sarvadharma Sama Bhava**: A sacred repository I co-founded, known as Sarvadharma Sama Bhava, serves as a sanctuary for curated content. It gathers a multitude of RSS feeds spanning diverse topics, from adoption to zoology. Seek solace and inspiration within its hallowed digital halls.

- **Spread the Light**: In this quest, spreading what's already aglow is not a sin; it is a service. Seek content that is aglow with engagement, even if it has weathered years. Remember, not every seeker has tread upon the same path. Discover hidden treasures in the "Explore" enclave of IndianConnect

2. Harness the Power of Digital Sanghas

Find Sahayaks: Within the digital cosmos, like-minded souls cluster into "lists" on Twitter and Facebook, "circles" on IndianConnect, "communities" on IndianConnect, and "groups" on Facebook and LinkedIn. These sacred gatherings hold the keys to discovering profound content.

3. Celebrate the Creators of Beauty

• Embrace User-Generated Artistry: Share the visual tapestries woven by admirers of your offerings. When devotees create visual offerings in the form of photos featuring your products, it not only bestows social proof upon you but also showers the artists with recognition and warmth.

In the quest for content, the cardinal sin is a narrow definition of relevance and interest. To appease the Content Monster, we must expand our horizons. Let us delve into examples that demonstrate how posts can remain faithful to our digital dharma while traversing the realm of fascination, thereby encouraging resharing:

Type of Business	Desired Followers	Examples
Restaurant	Foodies	Delve into the mysteries of subatomic particles unraveling wine fraud or explore the scientific mastery of cake cutting.
Indian Smartphone Company	Tech Enthusiasts	Unearth the gems among smartphone apps in the year 2014 or share six invaluable smartphone tips.
Indian Airline	Travel Lovers	Discover the last surviving drive-in theaters in the heartlands of India or delve into the mindful mastery of travel photography.
Indian Design Agency	Marketers	Unravel the intriguing world of web page ads placed below the fold or uncover pivotal insights into retail customer loyalty.

Type of Business	Desired Followers	Examples
Indian Audio Equipment Manufacturer	Music and Sports Enthusiasts	Embark on a musical journey with "Weird Al" Yankovic's parody of "Happy" or experience the thrill of fun and spine-chilling jumps.

As we tread the digital path, let us heed the wisdom of the Vedas and Upanishads: "In sharing, we become a bridge between the seeker and wisdom." To partake in the pledge drive of digital promotions, one must first pass the Reshare Test. By infusing content with the essence of information, analysis, assistance, and entertainment, we honor our commitment to enrich lives. In this journey, we earn the privilege to share our offerings with the digital congregation.

"In the sacred realm of content curation, the seeker becomes the guardian of digital wisdom, nurturing the Content Monster and enriching the digital sangha."

Harmonize with the Cosmic Calendar: A Serene Approach to Digital Prowess

In the vast cosmic expanse of social media, some embrace the "spray and pray" method—an mastery of casting content like stars into the night sky, hoping for a constellation to form. However, for those who seek a celestial order in their digital voyage, the editorial calendar becomes a guiding light. Let us navigate this celestial journey, drawing inspiration from the teachings of the Vedas and Upanishads, where order and harmony are revered.

The cosmic dance begins with the choice of your editorial calendar, a tool that aligns your content's trajectory with the rhythms of the digital cosmos. Herein, we present choices to suit the preferences of digital yogis:

1. Excel - The Time-Honored Scripture:

- Excel, a venerable sage, offers its timeless wisdom. With it, you can arrange your content like sacred scrolls, organized by the date of celestial publication. This is akin to maintaining the sacred fire, with each post kindling a new flame.

2. Google Docs - The Gathering of Sages:

- In the spirit of a digital ashram, Google Docs invites a congregation of sages to collaborate in real-time. They assemble, discuss, and align their thoughts, accessible from various devices. This harmonious synergy reduces the discordant echo of emails and preserves the sanctity of shared knowledge.

3. HubSpot Editorial Calendar - The Guide to Enlightenment:

- The HubSpot editorial calendar serves as a guru, leading disciples in the mastery of ideation, content nurturing, and progress tracking. It is a path illuminated by keywords, themes, and calls to action, embraced by a dedicated team on the spiritual journey of social media enlightenment.

4. Buffer, Sprout Social, and Hootsuite - The Holy Trinity:

- Buffer, Sprout Social, and Hootsuite embody the digital trinity, offering calendars that harmonize sharing and scheduling. Buffer, like a devoted priest, diligently manages scheduling. Sprout Social and Hootsuite, akin to enlightened gurus, provide not only scheduling but also the ability to commune with the digital congregation, responding and nurturing the spiritual discourse.

5. Stresslimit Design WordPress Plug-In - The Temple of Blogging:

- Within the sacred precincts of WordPress, the Stresslimit Design plug-in stands as an ornate temple. It is an editorial calendar where bloggers offer their devout posts. Here, one plans the future content pilgrimage, ensuring that the cosmic order of the blog is preserved.

As you embark on this celestial journey, let the Vedas guide you: "In the pursuit of knowledge, one must find harmony within." The editorial calendar is your celestial almanac, a guide to harmonizing your digital pursuits. While some may choose to spray their digital stardust into the cosmos, others find serenity in the cosmic calendar—a path lit by the wisdom of the ages.

"Embrace the editorial calendar, and let your digital journey resonate with the celestial order, as ordained by the cosmic calendar."

Sharing Wisdom: A Digital Discourse in the Age of Social Media

In the digital realm, every word shared carries a sacred responsibility, akin to the penance of a scrupulous writer. Guided by the profound wisdom of Rabindranath

Tagore, let us embark on a journey of mindful sharing, resonating with the essence of Indian philosophy and the latest digital trends.

1. Share with Purpose:

- Like an ancient rishi contemplating the universe, begin by asking four profound questions:

1. What is the essence of my message?
2. Which words shall encapsulate this essence?
3. What imagery or idiom will illuminate it?
4. Is this imagery vibrant enough to stir hearts?

2. Brevity is the Soul:

- In the ocean of social media, brevity reigns supreme. Like the succinct verses of our scriptures, your posts should capture attention in an instant. For curated content, a mere two or three sentences shall suffice on Indian social media platforms like Koo and ShareChat. Twitter, the realm of concise thoughts, embraces 100 characters as its sweet spot. However, when creating content such as blog posts, dive deeper with 500 to 1,000 words.

3. Embrace Visual Poetry:

- Just as our scriptures are adorned with intricate illustrations, every digital post should bear eye-catching visuals—a picture, graphic, or video. Studies reveal that content featuring relevant visuals garners 94% more views. Let your posts be words and images, weaving stories that resonate.

4. Timing is Divine:

- In the world of social media, timing is akin to divine alignment. Share your wisdom during the morning hours, the digital equivalent of dawn, when your audience is most receptive. Experiment with schedules and automate posts for celestial precision.

5. Gratitude in Sharing:

- In the spirit of dharma, every post featuring curated content must honor its source. These links serve a noble purpose:
  o Facilitating deeper knowledge for readers.

- Expressing gratitude through the gift of traffic.
- Elevating your presence among fellow bloggers and websites.

6. Organized Wisdom:

- When presenting lengthier wisdom, such as four-paragraph posts on Google+, Facebook, and LinkedIn, embrace the mastery of organization. Use bullet points or numbered lists, mirroring the structure of sacred scriptures. For, in a sea of text, structured wisdom shines brightest.

7. The Mastery of Titling:

- Employ the mastery of clever titling, as our ancient scriptures used aphorisms to convey profound insights. Titles like "How to..." and "The Ultimate..." beckon seekers of practical knowledge. Let your titles be the mantras that guide them.

8. The Power of Hashtags:

- Hashtags are the modern equivalent of Vedic hymns, connecting seekers on a common quest. Attach two or three relevant hashtags to your posts, uniting them with a global congregation. Yet, moderation is key; do not overindulge in hashtags, for it disrupts the cosmic order.

9. The Occasional Promotion:

- Like a merchant at a sacred pilgrimage site, consider occasional promotions. Pay to amplify your posts on platforms like Pinterest, Facebook, and Twitter. It is an investment that may yield greater reach and, perhaps, enlightenment for the masses.

10. Analytical Insights: - The digital cosmos offers insights akin to divine revelations. Analyze your followers, discern their preferences, and tailor your content accordingly. Just as the Vedas were recited to suit the audience, let your posts resonate with the souls who seek wisdom.

In this era of digital dharma, let us share knowledge and wisdom with reverence and mindfulness. In the words of the Upanishads, "Let noble thoughts come to us from all sides." Embrace these principles to share like a true digital sage, uniting the digital sangha in the pursuit of enlightenment.

Mastering Digital Prowess: Automated Wisdom for Indian Enterprises

In the realm of digital strategy, automation is not a shortcut but a manifestation of wisdom. To navigate the digital age successfully, it's essential to embrace automation tools. It's akin to deploying advanced chariots for an efficient journey through the vast digital landscape.

1. The Wisdom of Automation:

- Just as the ancient sages harnessed the elements to build magnificent structures, modern companies utilize automation tools for optimal sharing. Reject the notion that manual sharing is the only way; it is as impractical as churning butter in the age of electric mills.

2. The Sacred Tools of Automation:

- Explore tools designed to automate your digital journey. With just thirty minutes of thoughtful planning, you can orchestrate a day's worth of posts. Let these tools be your digital charioteers:

- **Vahak - The Buffer Chariot:**

  o This versatile chariot schedules posts for Google+, Facebook, LinkedIn, and Twitter. It allows you to set specific posting times or queue them for later. The "Buffer for Business" plan offers team management and analytics. It also suggests captivating stories to share, making it a true charioteer of elegance.

- **Yukti - The Do Share Talisman:**

  o For those dwelling in the realm of personal profiles on Google+, "Yukti" is a sacred talisman. This Chrome extension requires the Chrome browser but bestows the power to schedule posts. However, it demands the presence of your chariot's computer, which may not always align with your journey.

- **Mitra - The Friends+Me Companion:**

  o "Mitra" facilitates the sharing of your Google+ posts across multiple platforms. It currently supports Facebook, Twitter, LinkedIn, and Tumblr. The ability to tweet with images from Google+ posts is a boon. You can wield hashtags to control the destiny of each post, ensuring it reaches the right destinations.

- **Sarathi - The Hootsuite Chariot:**

  o "Sarathi" is a versatile chariot that not only schedules content but also engages with comments. It serves Facebook profiles and pages, Google+ pages, LinkedIn, and Twitter. With the ViralTag app, you can even schedule pins on Pinterest. It excels in bulk-scheduling, calendar-based scheduling, and collaborative journeys.

3. The Oracle of Post Planner:

- "Post Planner," although focused on Facebook, offers an oracle of wisdom. It provides curated stories and suggests optimal sharing times. Within the sacred Facebook realm, it unveils viral photos and trending content. You can also connect with beloved blogs and share their wisdom. A boon for Facebook page managers.

4. The Sprout Social Powerhouse:

- "Sprout Social" emerges as a digital powerhouse, serving Facebook pages and profiles, Twitter, Google+ pages, and LinkedIn profiles. With team management capabilities and integration with Zendesk, it enables robust digital governance. The power to repeat tweets with images and create team calendars is its forte, though it comes at a cost.

5. The Pinterest Guru - Tailwind:

- "Tailwind" is the guru of Pinterest automation. It allows you to schedule and monitor posts exclusively for Pinterest. Its rich data display, showcasing popular pins and trending boards, is a treasure trove. With access to Pinterest's API, it promises future enhancements.

6. The TweetDeck Sentinel:

- "TweetDeck" stands as a sentinel for Twitter monitoring and scheduling. Its columnar orientation simplifies tracking, from @mentions to competitor mentions. As you witness tech conferences, you'll find most using "TweetDeck" to navigate the Twitter realm.

In the digital age, automation is not a mere convenience; it is the essence of strategic brilliance. Just as Arjuna had Lord Krishna as his charioteer in the battle of Mahabharata, these automation tools shall be your charioteers in the digital battlefield. Embrace them wisely, and navigate the digital yuga with grace and efficiency.

The Eternal Echo: Repeating Your Digital Mantras

In the realm of digital strategy, there lies a path less traveled, a path of repetition that defies conventional wisdom. It's a path that I tread daily, sharing a multitude of fifty posts across Google+, Facebook, Twitter, LinkedIn, and Ello. What's unconventional is that many of these posts are exact echoes of their predecessors.

In the age of digital intricacies, one might wonder, "Why repeat what's already been said?" The answer lies in a profound wisdom: the wisdom of amplification, the wisdom of resonance.

1. The Mantra of Amplification:

- Imagine a sage in ancient India imparting wisdom to eager disciples. Each utterance of wisdom echoes through the ages, reverberating in the hearts of seekers. Similarly, in the digital landscape, the repetition of posts serves to amplify your message. The question here is, "Would you rather have 1,300 clicks or 7,600?"

2. Resonance Over Repetition:

- It's a fact that very few individuals or companies dare to embark on this relentless journey of repetition. Yet, as long as your posts are imbued with quality and relevance, you can share them endlessly. In a daring experiment, I shared four identical tweets over two days, each containing a different link to the same source story. The results were astonishing.

- The message is clear - repetition, when done right, yields remarkable results. The choice is between the risk of complaints about repeated tweets and the threat of losing followers, or achieving 5.8 times more clicks. I, for one, choose the latter without hesitation, every day of the year.

3. The Symphony of Reshares:

- Critics may raise their voices, objecting to the increased volume of repeated posts. However, in the grand symphony of social media, their voices fade into the background. They will either grow accustomed to the resonance of your message or choose to unfollow. What truly matters is the net effect - you are either constructing a formidable brand, amassing followers, and triggering reshares, or you're not.

4. The Mastery of Disruptive Engagement:

- In the world of digital warfare, silence is not an option. To truly harness the power of social media, one must be willing to disrupt the status quo. As the saying goes, "If you're not ruffling a few feathers on social media, you're not using it aggressively enough."

In the grand epic of digital strategy, repetition is not a sign of stagnation; it's the song that resonates in the hearts of your digital audience. Just as the sacred mantras of ancient India echoed through time, let your digital mantras resonate in the digital yuga. Embrace repetition with wisdom, and watch your message reverberate like a divine hymn in the digital cosmos.

Nurturing Digital Conversations: Responding to Comments with Grace

In social media, comments are the threads that weave connections and spark discussions. However, navigating this digital terrain can be akin to walking the ancient pilgrimage routes of India—a journey filled with surprises, challenges, and moments of profound wisdom. As we embark on this digital yatra, let us draw inspiration from the timeless teachings of the Vedas and Upanishads to illuminate our path.

1. The Path of Detachment:

"Don't take anything personally. What others say and do is a projection of their own reality." - Mukesh Sharma

- Just as the enlightened sages of ancient India preached detachment from the material world, we must learn not to take comments personally. In the digital realm, the words of others are often reflections of their own dreams and perceptions. By embracing this wisdom, we free ourselves from needless suffering.

2. The Digital Ashram:

- In the sacred land of social media, your posts will attract both wise sages and mischievous imps. The blend may tilt in favor of the former if your content is enriching, but negativity will find its way. Responding to comments, especially the negative ones, demands diligence and patience.

3. Tools of Digital Dharma:

- In your digital pilgrimage, it's essential to employ the right tools to monitor comments. Just as seekers meditate to gain clarity, use tools like Hootsuite, TweetDeck, and Social Mention to maintain awareness of the digital discussions surrounding your presence.

4. The Web of Connection:

- In the digital world, your audience extends beyond the immediate commenter. Lurkers, like the silent observers of a spiritual discourse, judge you by the tone of your responses. They may hold more influence than the trolls who seek to disrupt your journey. Remember, everything is on the record.

5. The Radiance of Positivity:

- "You should stay positive and pleasant no matter how banal, blasphemous, or baiting the comment." - The Digital Bhagavad Gita

- Just as a saint maintains equanimity in the face of adversity, remain positive in your responses. Uphold the highest standards of class and credibility, for it is the path to enlightenment in the digital age.

6. Embracing Harmony:

- "Agree to disagree, for most battles are not worth the trouble. Pissing off trolls is an mastery of its own." - The Mastery of Digital Peace

- Life is a series of debates, and not every battle is worth fighting. Sometimes, it's best to agree to disagree and let the trolls tire themselves out.

7. The Question of Wisdom:

- When faced with criticism, inquire if the critic has firsthand experience with the subject. Wisdom often eludes those who are certain without knowledge. Seek to illuminate ignorance with the torch of understanding.

8. The Three-Round Bout:

- Engaging in digital interactions is akin to a boxing match. Limit yourself to three rounds—share a post, respond to comments, and let the commenter have the final say. This ensures a healthy exchange without descending into chaos.

9. The Banishment of Darkness:

- "If all else fails, ignore, delete, block, or report trolls and spammers. Life is too short to deal with orifices." - The Digital Mahabharata

- In the realm of digital dharma, you are not obliged to engage with negativity. Embrace the one-strike rule—remove inappropriate comments and banish trolls and spammers. This preserves the sanctity of your digital ashram.

As we tread the digital paths of India's diverse landscapes, let us remember that our actions, even in the virtual realm, carry consequences. By embracing the wisdom of the Vedas and Upanishads, we can nurture meaningful conversations, spread positivity, and lead by example in the ever-evolving world of social media.

Cultivating a Digital Tribe: The Mastery of Gaining Followers

In social media, the pursuit of followers is akin to seeking enlightenment—it's a journey of self-expression, connection, and resonance. As we navigate the digital landscape, let us draw inspiration from the wisdom of the Vedas and Upanishads to uncover the secrets of growing our digital tribe.

1. The Essence of Being Exquisite:

- *"Do not yearn to be popular; be exquisite. Do not desire to be famous; be loved." - A. Anand Gupta*

- In the quest for followers, let us not seek popularity, but rather, let us strive to be exquisite in our digital presence. Just as a beautiful lotus blooms in the muddiest waters, our uniqueness will naturally attract those who resonate with our essence.

2. The Duality of Social Media Aspirations:

- In the vast realm of social media, there exist two kinds of entities: those who openly admit their desire for more followers and those who conceal their aspirations behind a veil of modesty. Acknowledging this duality is the first step toward authentic growth.

3. The Quest for Followers:

- The digital pilgrimage begins with a simple truth—sharing good content is the key to attracting followers. It is the divine nectar that nourishes the souls of your digital audience.

4. The Birth of Stars:

- Just as constellations emerge in the night sky, every new social media platform gives birth to its own set of stars. The early adopters have the privilege of staking their claim in this uncharted territory. It's a land grab where the bold pioneers amass followers while the platform is in its infancy.

5. A Lesson in Timing:

- I, too, embarked on a digital journey, joining Google+ shortly after its inception. Today, I am constantly gaining followers on the platform. However, if I were to start anew on Google+ or any established platform, catching up with those who started earlier would be an arduous task.

- The lesson is clear: a new platform is a realm of boundless possibilities. To amass followers, one must seize the opportunity before it becomes evident that the platform will flourish.

6. The Ever-Evolving Constellations:

- Each emerging platform crafts its own constellation of digital stars. Ananya Birla reigns supreme on Koo with over thirteen million followers, while her presence may be less pronounced on other platforms.

- The cosmos of social media is ever-changing, and those who recognize the unique allure of each platform can align their efforts to shine brightly within their chosen constellation.

In our digital yatra, let us embrace the wisdom of the ancients and the dynamism of the digital age. The pursuit of followers is not mere numbers but a quest for kindred spirits who resonate with our digital dharma. Share good content, seize new opportunities, and let your digital light shine, for in the realm of social media, we craft constellations of connection and understanding.

Navigating the Social Media Maze with Wisdom

In the age of digital enlightenment, where the wise are cautious and the foolish are often too confident, let us embark on a journey through the intricate landscape of social media. Drawing inspiration from the ancient Vedas and Upanishads, we seek to uncover the path to social media mastery.

1. The Paradox of Confidence:

- "The whole problem with the world is that fools and fanatics are always so certain of themselves, but wiser people so full of doubts." - Bertrand Russell

- Social media, much like life itself, is a realm of paradoxes. Those who proclaim their expertise with unwavering confidence may not always possess the wisdom they claim. Let us tread with humility and a willingness to learn.

2. The Mastery of Not Appearing Clueless:

- Social media is governed by its own set of customs and etiquette. To avoid appearing clueless in this digital realm, let us navigate it with finesse until we become adept:

3. The Futility of Buying Popularity:

- "Don't buy followers, likes, or +1s. Only losers and charlatans resort to such measures."

- The allure of artificial popularity may tempt some, but the wise recognize the futility of buying one's way into the hearts of the digital audience. Purchased followers lack genuine engagement and are but empty shells in the vast ocean of social media.

4. Earning Followers Through Quality:

- "Don't ask people to follow your company. Earn followers through the quality of your posts."

- Just as a virtuous life attracts admirers, quality content magnetizes followers. Groucho Marx's wisdom echoes in the digital age—those who ask for followers often lack the substance worth following.

5. The Mastery of Resharing:

- "Don't ask people to reshare your posts. If your content is worthy, it will be reshared naturally."

- Genuine engagement arises from compelling content. When your posts resonate with authenticity, they will find wings and soar across the digital landscape without the need for solicitation.

6. Balancing Promotion and Value:

- "Don't be a pimp of your products. Strive to strike a balance between promotion and value."

- Social media serves as a potent tool for promotion, but overindulgence in self-promotion can be detrimental. Emulate the ethos of NPR, where value and substance take precedence over incessant promotion.

7. Relying on Authenticity, Not Agencies:

- "Don't abdicate your social media to agencies. Authenticity trumps expertise."

- The heart of your social media should beat with authenticity, not delegate to external agencies. Be cautious of self-proclaimed experts with fewer followers than yourself. In following the path outlined here, you may find that you no longer require their services.

8. Empowering, Not Delegating to Interns:

- "Don't delegate social media to interns. Ensure that social media is a serious endeavor."

- While interns bring fresh perspectives, entrusting them with your social media is akin to assuming car ownership makes one a mechanic. Let us take social media seriously, educate our interns, and oversee their contributions to maintain our digital integrity.

In our quest for digital mastery, we mirror the wisdom of the ancients and adapt it to the intricacies of the digital age. We shun superficiality, embrace authenticity, and tread with humility. Social media, like life, is a journey of self-discovery and connection. May we navigate it with wisdom and grace, leaving behind a trail of genuine engagement and lasting connections.

Enhancing Event Engagement: A Social Odyssey

In the realm of social media, every event is an opportunity to forge connections and amplify your presence. As we embark on this journey, let us heed the wisdom of F. Scott Fitzgerald and discover the mastery of socializing events.

1. The Evergreen Hashtag:

- "Choose an evergreen hashtag, like '#UniteWithUs,' that transcends time and place."

- Our digital journey begins with the selection of a timeless hashtag. Instead of region-specific tags, opt for one that resonates universally, ensuring it remains relevant beyond the event. Like the sacred OM, it should reverberate through the digital cosmos.

2. Weaving the Hashtag into Every Fiber:

- "Integrate the chosen hashtag into every aspect of the event, from your website to the program cover."

- Let the chosen hashtag permeate the event's essence, like the sacred thread (janeu) in a Vedic ritual. It should adorn your website, advertising, and even the printed program. Every attendee should be well-versed in its presence, akin to knowing a revered mantra.

3. A Collective Symphony:

- "Encourage every soul present to embrace the hashtag and share their journey. Chutzpah counts in social media."

- The resonance of your event extends far beyond its physical boundaries. Encourage all attendees to partake in the symphony of social media, sharing their experiences and insights with unwavering enthusiasm. The collective energy will resonate like a Vedic chant.

4. Expanding Horizons:

- "Remember, your audience is not confined to the event venue. Share content that transcends borders."

- The audience for your event extends beyond geographical boundaries. Craft your narrative to captivate both attendees and those tuning in from distant lands. A single tweet can bridge continents, connecting souls in a digital yagna.

5. The Guardian of Social Media:

- "Dedicate a guardian of social media, a digital storyteller who weaves tales of your event in real-time."

- Every event deserves a digital bard, a storyteller who captures moments, weaves narratives, and shares them with the world. Their responsibility is to bring the event to life in the digital realm, just as the scribes of yore transcribed ancient scriptures.

6. The Stream of Life:

- "Stream live coverage to reach those beyond the physical realm. Share your wisdom with the world."

- Live coverage is the digital equivalent of broadcasting mantras. Let the wisdom, announcements, and unveilings of your event flow freely to the farthest corners of the digital world. Embrace the era of global accessibility.

7. Real-time Updates:

- "Provide real-time updates, whether through Twitter, Instagram, or blogs. Your words should resonate like verses from the Upanishads."

- Just as the Upanishads impart profound wisdom, your real-time updates should enlighten the digital audience. Whether through tweets, images, or blog posts, let your words be a source of enlightenment.

8. Displaying the Twitter Stream:

- "Display the tweets bearing your hashtag on screens at the event. Witness the magic of interaction."

- Displaying the live Twitter stream at your event is akin to projecting sacred scriptures. It fosters interaction and encourages attendees to contribute to the digital dialogue, just as sages shared their insights with seekers.

9. Unfettered Connectivity:

- "Provide unhampered wireless access, for restricting it is akin to obstructing the flow of knowledge."

- Just as knowledge should flow freely, so should the digital connection at your event. Ensure abundant and unrestricted wireless access, for hindering it is tantamount to locking the doors of a temple.

10. A Haven for Memories: - "Create a space for capturing memories, adorned with the event's emblem. Let attendees revel in their digital pilgrimage."

- Design a dedicated space for capturing memories, where attendees can bask in the digital aura of the event. Like a pilgrimage site, it should bear the emblem of the event and beckon attendees to share their experiences.

11. Empowering Executives: - "Empower your executives to engage with attendees, for their presence carries the gravitas of ancient leaders."

- Encourage your executives to embrace their roles as digital leaders. Let them engage with attendees, request photos, and inspire sharing. Their presence should exude the wisdom of Vedic sages.

12. Sharing Across the Digital Cosmos: - "Share photos and videos across every platform, weaving digital memories. Let your event shine like a celestial gathering."

- Spread the digital of your event far and wide, like stars illuminating the night sky. Share photos and videos on multiple platforms, creating a celestial gathering that shines through the digital cosmos.

In this digital yagna, where connections are forged and memories are etched in pixels, let us honor the timeless traditions of our land. As we weave our narrative through social media, may our messages resonate like Vedic verses, connecting souls in the digital embrace of knowledge and camaraderie.

Frequently Asked Questions (FAQs): Navigating the Digital Realm

In the vast digital landscape, questions often arise like whispers in the breeze. Let us embark on a quest to answer these inquiries, drawing wisdom from our own ancient texts and contemporary insights.

1. Corporate or Personal: Choosing Your Digital Avatar

- *Q: We're a small company, so should we use a corporate account or personal account?*

- *A: Embrace the identity of a corporate account, for it holds the power of features on platforms like Google+ and Facebook. Moreover, in the ever-changing dance of employees, it shields you from the turmoil of account ownership.*

- Just as Lord Krishna guided Arjuna in his role as a warrior, a corporate account empowers your small company to wield the full array of digital tools. It's a shield against the uncertainties of personnel changes, allowing your digital presence to transcend the ephemeral.

2. Nurturing Individual Voices

- *Q: Should we curate the posts of our employees?*

- *A: Like the sacred Ganges, the flow of your employees' personal accounts is their own. However, when they are the emissaries of your business, their actions ripple through your company's image. Tread carefully; address the root, not just the leaves.*

- Just as the Ganges flows freely but holds the essence of purity, let your employees' personal accounts remain uncurated. Yet, when they embody your brand, guide them to channel their energies positively, for the river of reputation flows from many sources.

3. Crafting Digital Narratives: Platform Variations

- *Q: Should we have different content for different platforms?*

- *A: In digital storytelling, diversity adds vibrancy. Share what fascinates you on Google+ and Facebook. Paint pretty pictures from websites on Pinterest, capture the world's beauty on Instagram, and curate intriguing links on Twitter.*

- Just as a painter uses different strokes for varied canvases, so should your digital presence adapt to the nuances of each platform. Google+ and Facebook serve as the canvas for your thoughts, while Pinterest and Instagram become your galleries of visual delight. Twitter remains the parchment for sharing wisdom.

4. The Allure of Google+: A Digital Sanctuary

- *Q: What am I missing? Why do you like Google+ so much?*

- *A: The allure of Google+ lies in its design aesthetics, free from the shackles of EdgeRank. The quality of discussions flows like the sacred Ganges, and it carries the imprimatur of Google, a digital deity.*

- Just as the River Ganges flows unperturbed, Google+ offers a serene digital sanctuary. Its design aesthetics enchant the senses, its open embrace defies algorithms, and its quality discussions are akin to philosophical debates. To doubt Google+ is to question the cosmic order.

In the digital age, we traverse a realm where ancient wisdom and modern insights intertwine. As we sail through the ever-evolving tides of the digital ocean, let our understanding be as deep as the Vedic verses and as dynamic as the winds of change. Embrace the digital dharma, for it guides us through this vast expanse.

Suggested Reading List

In the age of digital enlightenment, where knowledge is the new currency, let us explore the literary treasures that illuminate the path of social media mastery. Here, in the bazaar of wisdom, you will find our handpicked collection of books to enrich your digital journey.

1. **"Jugaad Innovation: Think Frugal, Be Flexible, Generate Breakthrough Growth"** by Navi Radjou, Jaideep Prabhu, and Simone Ahuja
    - Year: 2012
    - Focus: A fresh look at innovation that's relevant in the context of social media creativity and frugality.

2. **"Brand Shastra: Use the Power of Marketing to Transform Your Life"** by Mainak Dhar
    - Year: 2016
    - Focus: Offers insights into personal branding that can be applied in social media contexts.

3. **"Marketing and Branding: The Indian Scenario"** by S Ramesh Kumar
    - Year: 2006
    - Focus: Delves into social media marketing strategies within the Indian market context.

4. **"The $100 Startup: Fire Your Boss, Do What You Love and Work Better To Live More"** by Chris Guillebeau (Note: Chris Guillebeau is not an Indian author, but the book has been influential among Indian entrepreneurs and digital marketers. For a purely Indian author list, you may consider replacing this with another book more aligned with the criteria.)

5. **"Content, Inc.: How Entrepreneurs Use Content to Build Massive Audiences and Create Radically Successful Businesses"** by Joe Pulizzi
    - Year: 2015
    - Focus: Though not by an Indian author, it's highly recommended for understanding content-driven growth strategies relevant for social media.

6. **"Karmic Design Thinking: The Business of Discovering Your Hidden Potential"** by Dr. Bala Ramadurai
    - Year: 2020
    - Focus: While not directly about social media, it offers a unique perspective on design thinking that can be applied to digital strategies.

Dive into these captivating volumes, where each page unfolds new insights and strategies to conquer the digital realm. These tomes are your chariots to navigate the dynamic world of social media, just as Arjuna's charioteer, Lord Krishna, guided him through the battlefield of life.

Remember, the knowledge contained within these books is the key to unlocking your digital potential. As the Vedas proclaim, "Knowledge is the greatest wealth," and in the age of bytes and bits, wisdom is our most precious treasure. Choose your texts wisely, for they will be your companions on the path to digital enlightenment.

Chapter 10:
The Mastery of Abundant Harvest

"Imagine that every soul you encounter bears a sign around their neck, whispering, 'Make me feel cherished.' In this embrace, you shall not only triumph in commerce but also in the grand theatre of life."

— Mahatma Gandhi

Synopsis

In the sphere of business, a rainmaker is comparable to the esteemed Indian sage, invoking ancient practices and prayers to invite abundance. In the commercial landscape, a rainmaker is someone who brings about waves of success through their expertise in sales and negotiation. This chapter sets forth on the enigmatic voyage of rainmaking—a blend of age-old insights and contemporary business tactics.

The Monsoon of Sales

Much like the tribal shamans, skilled salespersons have crafted their own rituals and spells to invoke the downpour of abundance. This chapter serves as a guide to mastering the mastery of rainmaking, a pursuit deeply rooted in the essence of Indian culture.

Challenges for Sprouting Ventures

For startups, the path to rainmaking is fraught with challenges. Firstly, entrepreneurs often grapple with uncertainty, not knowing who their product's custodians shall be or how it will serve them. Secondly, the offerings of startups are not sought-after commodities; rather, they must be actively marketed, for venturing into uncharted territory carries its own set of hesitations.

The Saga of Estée Lauder's Perfumed Triumph

Allow me to share the motivating story of a tenacious entrepreneur who overcame the hesitation of a leading Indian retailer. When the renowned Indian department store, Big Bazaar, was initially reluctant to stock a new line of herbal beauty products by an innovative Indian brand, a clever marketing strategy was employed. Samples of the product were distributed among customers, generating buzz and curiosity. The overwhelming interest from the customers forced the retailer to stock the products. Thus, as if the skies opened, prosperity rained down on them.

In the domain of rainmaking, perseverance and creativity frequently pave the way to unforeseen success. Just like the land eagerly awaits the arrival of the monsoon for rejuvenation, businesses too seek the art of rainmaking to thrive.

Cultivating Fields of Prosperity

Let the essence of diverse thoughts fill the atmosphere, inspired by the richness of Indian philosophy. In the ethos of planting, we shall disperse our innovations like seeds across the fertile plains of opportunity, where they will sprout and prosper."

In these reflections, I am motivated by the deep-seated traditions of India, a nation that celebrates the bounty of nature and appreciates the significance of variety. This approach, reminiscent of the inclusive strategies often seen in Indian businesses, aims not at exclusion but at expansion—distributing a wide array of products across vast markets, identifying where they resonate best, and nurturing those sectors with attention and dedication.

Nurturing Blossoms of Innovation

When flowers of innovation begin to bloom, our role is not to stifle them but to discern the soil in which they thrive and adapt our business strategies accordingly. Unfortunately, many companies recoil when unintended users adopt their products in unexpected ways. Their knee-jerk reaction is to realign the product with its intended use. This response, however, is myopic and inefficient.

In the orchard of entrepreneurship, when flowers are in full bloom, our duty is to identify where and why they flourish and then adjust our business to reap the bounty. As startups, we must shed any pretensions of selectivity or pride and embrace opportunities wherever they sprout. Allow me to share three illustrative examples of flourishing blossoms, as elucidated by the eminent entrepreneurship scholar, Vishal Gupta:

1. **The Ayurvedic Elixir:** The creator of an Ayurvedic elixir initially developed it as a remedy for general ailments in traditional medicine. However, mainstream medical practitioners were reluctant to adopt this unconventional approach,

preferring established treatments. Interestingly, Ayurvedic practitioners warmly embraced the elixir, leading the creator to shift focus towards this unexpected market.

2. **TCS's Visionary Leap:** Tata Consultancy Services (TCS), a pioneer in Indian IT, initially understood computers as tools primarily for scientific research. However, unlike its contemporaries, TCS quickly realized the expansive potential of computers in business operations. Embracing this broader vision, TCS ventured into software services and consulting, paving the way for its global recognition. Today, TCS stands as a titan in the technology sector, illustrating the importance of foresight and adaptability in the fast-evolving world of computing.

3. **The Indian Bicycle Revelation**: An Indian company acquired the license to manufacture a European bicycle with an auxiliary engine. However, the bicycle itself failed to gain traction in the market. Curiously, the company noticed a surge in orders for the engine alone. Upon investigation, it was revealed that people were ingeniously using the engine to replace hand-operated pumps for irrigation—an unintended yet promising application. The company swiftly adapted and went on to sell millions of irrigation pumps.

These narratives underscore the wisdom of embracing unexpected opportunities. In the ever-changing landscape of business, let us heed the lessons of India's diverse ecosystems and allow innovation to flourish like a garden in full bloom. Just as our land celebrates the myriad colors of spring, so should our businesses revel in the vibrancy of unanticipated success.

Witness the Unseen

In the realm of perception, let us explore a thought-provoking experiment led by two eminent Indian scholars, akin to the wisdom imparted by the ancient Vedas and Upanishads. This study, reflective of the profound teachings found in our sacred texts, unveils significant insights into human cognition. Participants were invited to engage in an unusual task—a venture that symbolizes the complex dance of awareness and understanding characteristic of life's essence.

These scholars presented the participants with a video depicting two teams engaged in the graceful mastery of basketball. Yet, the students were entrusted with a unique mission: to meticulously tally the passes executed by one team to its fellow players. A seemingly straightforward task, one might assume.

However, at precisely the thirty-five-second mark, an unexpected guest entered the scene—a character embodying the very essence of unpredictability. A gorilla, clad in all its majestic splendor, made an unannounced appearance. It pounded its chest, an assertion of its existence, and lingered in the video's frame for a span of nine seconds. What transpired next is nothing short of remarkable.

When questioned about this unanticipated addition, astonishingly, 50 percent of the students remained oblivious to the gorilla's presence! Their focus, unswervingly directed towards the assigned task of tallying passes, rendered them blind to an unrelated but unmistakably significant event unfolding before their eyes.

The Parallel to Entrepreneurship

In the world of startups, an analogous phenomenon often unfolds. Entrepreneurs, akin to those students, become deeply engrossed in the pursuit of their product's intended audience and anticipated applications. In this relentless focus, they inadvertently overlook the blossoming of unforeseen opportunities—the "gorilla markets" that emerge within their midst.

The lesson bestowed upon us by this captivating experiment is both profound and timeless. It echoes the wisdom of our ancient texts, which urge us to embrace the ever-unfolding existence. Just as the Vedas and Upanishads guide us to perceive the unseen realms of consciousness, so should we, as entrepreneurs, learn to recognize and seize the unexpected blooms on our entrepreneurial journey.

In the words of our land's sages, "Let a hundred flowers blossom." May we remain vigilant, attuned to the subtleties of our dynamic world, and open to the serendipitous opportunities that await us, hidden in plain sight.

Titles Are Mere Illusions

In the complex weave of corporate structures, titles can often deceive, resembling a mirage in the arid landscape of professional identity. At first look, titles such as "Database Administrator III" may evoke images of personnel relegated to cramped workspaces, engulfed in technical guides, with their meals often comprising simple thalis from the local canteen—a vivid depiction, to say the least.

Amidst the intricate pathways of corporate structures, a person designated simply as "Database Administrator III" would surpass conventional assumptions. This individual, stationed within the confines of a cubicle with a perpetually buzzing phone, wielded considerable influence, steering software procurements valued at an astonishing ₹40,00,000 for the organization.

Intriguingly, when the executive vice president sought wisdom on projects and vendor choices, it was to Mr. Database Administrator that he turned. This paradoxical scenario unfolds in many large organizations—where the air thins as you ascend the corporate ladder, making it increasingly challenging to find pockets of intelligent life. Herein lies a profound truth: within the ranks of an organization, especially in its middle and lower tiers, lie reservoirs of untapped intelligence—a veritable treasure trove of perspectives vital for the appreciation of innovative products.

In my own journey, I have often sought guidance from remarkable key influencers who transcend the confines of formal titles: Anjali Sharma, Meera Patel, and Priya Singh, all of whom have graced my professional sphere as associates at various points. Their insights carried significant weight in my deliberations concerning organizations and individuals. A simple inquiry such as "What is your impression of that individual?" or "What are your perspectives on this concept?" would evoke candid feedback. If the consensus was "She lacks humility," "He exhibits excessive pride," or "It's an impractical notion," the individual or idea rarely garnered my attention.

This illuminating concept underscores a fundamental truth: the power of influence transcends the facade of titles. It beckons us to look beyond the superficial and embrace collaboration with those who wield influence, regardless of their designated roles. From secretaries, administrative aides, and personal assistants to product managers, support managers, and yes, database administrators—the path to success demands that we disregard titles and seek the wisdom that resides in unexpected corners of the corporate landscape.

As we tread this path, let us recall the timeless wisdom of our heritage: "In the realm of knowledge, titles are but fleeting shadows, while true wisdom shines as the eternal sun." Embracing this philosophy, we navigate the intricate web of corporate existence, guided by insight rather than mere illusion.

Mastering the Mastery of Influence: Navigating the Web of Key Decision Makers

In the labyrinthine world of business, the question inevitably arises: "How do I identify and access the key influencers who hold the keys to success?" It's a conundrum that every entrepreneur must unravel, and the answers lie in the mastery of influence. Here, we unveil strategies and insights, woven into the fabric of our Indian ethos.

1. Seek the Counsel of Allies

Drawing from the age-old wisdom of reciprocity, the first step is to enlist the aid of friends and colleagues who have traversed similar corporate terrains. In the spirit of "you scratch my back, I'll scratch yours," they will extend a helping hand, guided by the principle that mutual support is the bedrock of entrepreneurial triumph.

As the Bhagavad Gita imparts, "In giving, we receive," echoing the sentiment that selfless assistance leads to abundant returns.

2. The Power of the Tweet

In the digital age, the resonance of social media cannot be underestimated. A well-placed tweet directed at the organization's social media account can prove remarkably effective. Brands, wary of public perception, are often swift to respond, fearing the repercussions of unanswered queries. It supersedes the traditional approach of navigating corporate phone lines in pursuit of elusive names.

Remember, as the ancient Sanskrit saying goes, "A single tweet can move mountains."

3. Scour the Footprints of Media

Delve into press coverage related to the organization in question. Armed with knowledge gleaned from articles, embark on a journey of connection through emails, tweets, and phone calls. Navigate the labyrinthine corridors of their website's "About" and PR sections, for therein lie hidden pathways to your destination. Persistence can yield unexpected rewards.

In the words of the Upanishads, "The seeker shall find, for in seeking lies the path to discovery."

4. Conversations with Guardians of the Throne

Often overlooked, yet wielding profound influence, are the assistants—the unsung heroes who shield their superiors from the relentless barrage of sales pitches. Approach them not as mere gatekeepers but as conduits of wisdom. They possess the keys to the kingdom, and their guidance can pave your way to the decision-makers.

In the spirit of empathy, remember the timeless adage, "To understand others, walk a mile in their shoes."

5. The LinkedIn

In the digital era, LinkedIn emerges as interconnected destinies. Explore your network, seeking kindred souls who share affiliations with the organization. Perhaps a former colleague now resides within its walls, or your alma mater binds you to its denizens. LinkedIn's web of connections can orchestrate miracles.

Embrace the concept that these methods often involve persuading individuals who wield more influence than you. To navigate this terrain, you must hone the mastery of diplomacy and adaptability—sucking up, down, and across the hierarchy.

Navigating the Umbrellas: A Lesson in Grace

Once you find yourself under the protective canopy of these intermediaries, remember the mastery of engagement:

1. Understand Their Perspective

Acknowledge that these intermediaries may perceive you as just one more communication amidst a sea of digital noise. Avoid taking their actions personally; instead, approach them with humility.

As the Bhagavad Gita imparts, "One who is not disturbed by the incessant flow of desires—that is, one who desires nothing—can alone achieve peace."

2. Eschew the Temptation of Bribery

In the pursuit of influence, never resort to the allure of gifts as bribes. Instead, rely on the bedrock of credibility, presenting a compelling proposition while treating all with respect and civility.

Embrace the wisdom that "a virtuous act shines like a lamp in a dark corner," reinforcing the principle that virtue is its own reward.

3. Empathy and Respect

Recognize that many individuals you encounter occupy roles with modest remuneration. Display empathy for the challenges they face daily, for empathy fosters goodwill and cooperation.

In the words of Mahatma Gandhi, "You must be the change you wish to see in the world."

4. Avoid the Backchannel Complaint

Never resort to circumventing lower-ranked individuals to complain about them to superiors. Such actions invariably return to haunt you, rendering your progress within the organization an arduous endeavor.

Instead, embody the wisdom of the ancient Indian scriptures: "Speak only words that are both true and kind."

Extracting Wisdom from the Umbrellas

Once you secure an audience with these intermediaries, pose these pivotal questions:

1. Who wields the scepter of decision-making?
2. Upon whom does the decision-maker rely?
3. Who forms an indispensable part of the decision-making?

In these inquiries, you sift for gold, seeking the name of the key influencer who may defy conventional hierarchies—a friend, a comrade from the past, or an unassuming investor. For in the realm of entrepreneurship, it is these unexpected influencers who often hold the keys to success.

As you navigate this intricate web of influence, recall the timeless wisdom of the Rigveda: "He who seeks, shall find; he who knocks, the door shall be opened unto him." Embark on this journey, guided by the principles of respect, reciprocity, and relentless pursuit, for within these principles lies the secret to mastering the mastery of influence.

Enlightening the Path: Educating and Empowering through Webinars

In the ever-evolving landscape of business, one of the most potent rainmaking strategies is the dissemination of knowledge about your product. In eras past, this endeavor necessitated physical gatherings, where individuals congregated to partake in the exchange of wisdom. Today, the digital realm offers a cost-effective avenue for this purpose, wherein webinars become the modern-day equivalent of a sacred assembly. Let us embark on a journey to unveil the nuances of this transformative approach, deeply rooted in Indian philosophies of knowledge-sharing.

The Dawn of Digital Gurukuls

In the realm of online education, Pixlr serves as a beacon of innovation. Pixlr, an online design service, empowers individuals to craft exquisite graphics for diverse purposes—from embellishing social media posts to adorning eBay and Etsy stores, from enhancing Kindle e-book covers to creating real estate flyers and compelling presentations. In the days of yore, such endeavors demanded the acquisition of tools like CorelDRAW, coupled with the arduous task of mastering their intricacies.

Pixlr's approach, however, is reminiscent of the guru-shishya parampara—a tradition where knowledge is imparted by a revered guru to eager disciples. Here's how it works: Pixlr conducts webinars tailored to the unique needs of companies and associations within niche markets. These webinars are designed to educate, enlighten, and empower.

Illuminating Minds: The Canva Webinar

Imagine a Kindle book cover webinar for a literary institution like "Indian Literature Foundation" or a real estate flyer webinar for a prominent real estate firm like "Tata Realty and Infrastructure Limited." In these digital gurukuls, participants gather from all corners of the virtual world, seeking to master the art of graphic design through Pixlr's platform.

The brilliance of this approach lies in its simplicity and inclusivity. As an employee of Pixlr, one had the privilege of conducting these webinars from the comfort of his home in Maharashtra. The cost implications were negligible, as there was no need for extensive travel. The lion's share of promotion was handled by their esteemed partners—Indian Literature Foundation and Tata Realty and Infrastructure Limited—thus minimizing their expenses as well.

A Tryst with Knowledge: The 90/10 Rule

For a webinar to be truly effective, it must adhere to the sacred tenets of education. The golden rule is the 90/10 principle: 90 percent education and a mere 10 percent promotion. In essence, participants do not attend a "Pixlr webinar" but embark on a journey of self-improvement, learning the intricate mastery of book cover design or real estate flyer creation.

In the spirit of knowledge-sharing, Pixlr's webinars transcend mere promotion; they become platforms for holistic learning, a modern-day yajna where wisdom is offered to the eager participants. The echoes of ancient Indian gurukuls reverberate in this approach, where enlightenment is the ultimate goal.

The Ripple Effect: A Win-Win-Win Saga

In this symbiotic relationship, every entity emerges victorious. Puranasoft and TechKart extend a valuable resource to their subscribers and employees, fostering a culture of empowerment and skill enhancement. Participants gain access to invaluable training, unlocking new realms of possibility. And, TechGuru, in its noble pursuit of knowledge dissemination, welcomes a host of new users into its fold.

This virtuous cycle mirrors the essence of the Bhagavad Gita, where the path of knowledge leads to enlightenment and growth for all involved. The resounding lesson is that by sharing knowledge generously, we sow the seeds of success, nourishing minds and businesses alike.

As we delve into the digital gurukuls of the modern era, we realize that the spirit of education and empowerment transcends time and space. In the wisdom of the Vedas, "Let noble thoughts come to us from every side." In the world of webinars, let knowledge flow freely, enriching lives and fostering a culture of continuous learning.

The Path of Conversion: Embracing the Agnostics

In business, the quest to educate customers while fostering growth is a noble endeavor. The question that beckons us is this: What knowledge can we bestow upon our patrons that not only enriches their lives but also fuels the prosperity of our enterprise? As we tread this path, guided by Indian wisdom and modern insights, let us delve into the notion of courting agnostics, rather than zealots, and unravel the transformative power of this approach.

The Wisdom of Agnosticism

In history, the great sage Dhruv Patel reminds us of a profound truth, encapsulated in the parable of Krishna and the two seekers on the pilgrimage. Krishna, in his infinite wisdom, did not seek to convert the hardened hearts of both seekers; he patiently waited until one of them turned to him, embracing the path of transformation willingly. This parable, rich in allegorical significance, offers a timeless lesson.

In the realm of technology, particularly during the era of the ParamTech, a similar dichotomy unfolded. The formidable challenge lay in converting the zealous followers of Linux—an alternate and, some would say, false technological deity. These fervent loyalists were deeply entrenched in their beliefs, resistant to change. The arduous task of dispelling their allegiance to Linux seemed insurmountable.

The Uncharted Territory of Agnosticism

Conversely, the journey to convert those untouched by the world of personal computing proved surprisingly facile. These individuals, devoid of prior experience, possessed a blank canvas upon which ParamTech could paint a new reality. They harbored no preconceived notions of what a computer should resemble, its intended functions, or even where to acquire one. In their innocence, ParamTech discerned an opportunity. For this untapped segment, there existed no need to dismantle entrenched paradigms or breach the fortifications of corporate computing standards. ParamTech's Ice 3.0 became a gateway to an uncharted realm, where innovation held sway. The absence of resistance paved the way for seamless assimilation into this brave new world.

The Relevance of Agnosticism in Business

Drawing parallels to our own business pursuits, we recognize the profound relevance of impartiality. In the pursuit of large-scale organizations, we initially set our sights on the Indian Top 500 information-technology market, envisioning the dethronement of the ParamTech PC from its established dominion. However, this quest proved to be an arduous endeavor fraught with challenges and setbacks.

The Eminence of the Agnostic Market

Through these trials, an invaluable lesson emerged—zealots, deeply entrenched in their beliefs, are often resistant to change. It is the agnostics—the open-minded individuals who do not dismiss the validity of our offerings and are willing to explore the uncharted territory of our products or services—that represent an ideal market.

Agnostics, unburdened by preconceived notions and corporate dogmas, greet our innovations with open arms. They embrace the transformative power of what we offer, finding empowerment and enrichment in the unexplored realms of our solutions.

The Indian Ethos: Unity in Diversity

In the diverse landscape of India, the concept of agnosticism resonates profoundly. India, of myriad cultures, languages, and beliefs, thrives on the coexistence of diverse ideologies. In this land, agnosticism serves as a bridge, fostering harmony and understanding amidst the myriad faiths that call India home.

As we tread the path of business, let us heed the wisdom of agnosticism—a philosophy that transcends boundaries and cultivates a fertile ground for growth. In the words of India's timeless sage, Swami Vivekananda, "The power of concentration is the only key to the treasure-house of knowledge." In the pursuit of business success, let us concentrate our efforts on courting the agnostics, unlocking the treasure-house of opportunity that awaits.

Engaging Prospects: The Mastery of Listening and Learning

In the melody of salesmanship, where communication is the instrument of choice, we find ourselves endowed with two keen eyes to perceive and two receptive ears to heed. Yet, nature, in its wisdom, has bestowed upon us only a single tongue for speaking. These intricacies of human interaction bring to mind the wisdom of Chanakya, reminding us of the balance that lies in the mastery of conversation.

A Profound Lesson from Nature

My journey through the realm of sales has unveiled a profound truth—an insight that often eludes those who tread the path of rainmaking. It is the simple realization that prospective customers, those who harbor the genuine intention to embrace our offerings, frequently hold the key to closing a deal. All that is required of us is to embrace silence and lend an attentive ear. This may sound deceptively simple, but in practice, it proves to be a formidable challenge. This challenge is amplified for those who lack an understanding of the nuances of rainmaking.

The process itself is elegantly straightforward:

1. Create an inviting and comfortable environment where you seek permission to pose questions.

2. Craft insightful questions that delve into the prospects' needs and desires.

3. Listen attentively to the responses that follow.

4. Document these insights meticulously.

5. Articulate how your product or service aligns with their needs, if indeed it does.

Yet, in the intricate dance of sales, many falter for various reasons:

The Fear of Inquiry Firstly, they falter due to an unpreparedness to ask the right questions. Effective questioning necessitates prior research—a deep understanding of the prospect and a vision of how your offering can benefit them. Paradoxically, some salespeople fear that inquiring may cast an illusion of ignorance upon them.

The Endless Monologue Secondly, there are those who are trapped in the clutches of the bludgeon school of salesmanship—an incessant barrage of words aimed at coercing the prospect into submission. Alternatively, even if they possess the ability to restrain their own voices, they neglect the mastery of active listening. In the realm of sales, hearing may be involuntary, but listening demands intentionality.

The Neglected Note-Taking Thirdly, there exists a cohort that dismisses the significance of note-taking. This is a grievous oversight. As expounded in Chapter 5, titled "The Mastery of Financial Abundance" taking notes serves a dual purpose. Firstly, it aids in memory retention. Secondly, it conveys a message to prospects—that their words hold value and merit documentation.

The Knowledge Gap Lastly, an unforgivable lapse is manifested in the form of inadequate product knowledge. The inability to align one's product with the unique needs of prospects is a grave shortcoming. Imagine a product that offers a spectrum of benefits, from cost reduction to market expansion and environmental sustainability. By introducing all these facets to the prospects, you invite their reactions, allowing them to signal which benefits resonate most profoundly.

The Dance of Understanding

Should no facet elicit a response, the next step is to humbly inquire about the prospect's preferences. Observe not only their verbal responses but also their body language, for often, the unsaid communicates volumes. This mastery of sales is akin to detective work, where the goal is to unveil the prospect's desires and preferences.

In the immortal words of Mahatma Gandhi, "In a gentle way, you can shake the world." In the realm of sales, it is not about forceful persuasion; rather, it is about the gentle mastery of understanding and aligning our offerings with the aspirations of our prospects. Through the lens of Indian wisdom, let us remember that the pursuit of sales is a dance—a harmonious exchange where listening is the most graceful step, and understanding is the most melodious note.

Unlocking Potential: The Mastery of Test-Driving Innovation

In the labyrinth of entrepreneurial pursuits, startups often find themselves grappling with two formidable adversaries: inertia and a steadfast allegiance to the status quo. Within the minds of consumers and businesses alike, a prevailing belief persists—an assurance that existing products suffice. "I can accomplish all that I desire with what I possess," they proclaim. In some cases, a more troubling sentiment echoes, "My workforce possesses the tools they need within their grasp."

However, it is essential to clarify that this acceptance does not imply that the products currently in widespread use are optimal or without flaws. It signifies the customer's willingness to embrace familiarity. Thus, the onus often falls upon the shoulders of an entrepreneur to illuminate the path toward the adoption of something new. Conventionally, this has been achieved through the ceaseless bombardment of advertising and promotional endeavors.

Yet, therein lies a quandary. Many companies vie for attention in the marketplace, echoing similar claims of superiority—better, faster, cheaper! Moreover, as a fledgling startup, the financial resources required to achieve critical mass through advertising and promotion remain elusive. Fortunately, a beacon of hope emerges—a potent strategy to captivate prospective customers: enabling them to embark on a test-drive of the product.

In extending this invitation, a profound message is conveyed:

1. "We hold you in high regard, for we believe in your discernment." This immediately distinguishes you from the multitude of organizations that might underestimate their clientele.

2. "We harbor no intent to coerce you into becoming a customer." This declaration further sets you apart, for it echoes transparency and respect.

3. "We invite you to test-drive our creation."

4. "Your verdict shall be entirely of your own volition. Should queries arise, we stand ready to provide answers."

It's imperative to note that the nature of test-drives varies across industries and products. Allow me to share some noteworthy instances:

The Legacy of Tata Group

In 1893, Jamsetji Tata shrewdly distributed samples of his new textile products at the Bombay Exhibition. Despite a less favorable booth location, he employed innovative marketing strategies to attract visitors. Tata deployed enthusiastic volunteers to distribute coupons offering a complimentary souvenir in exchange for visiting his booth to experience the quality of Tata textiles. This ingenious maneuver left a lasting impression on the attendees of the exhibition.

The Infosys Journey

During the 1980s, Infosys aimed to simplify the personal computing journey. They offered individuals the opportunity to embark on a weekend exploration with the Infosys PC—an initiative that significantly influenced their perception and understanding.

Jio: The Pioneers of Freedom

Reliance Jio, a trailblazer in the realm of telecommunications, offered a generous proposition—an unshackled thirty-day period of utilizing their network services, sans charge. This virtual voyage of discovery empowered users to acquaint themselves with the platform's capabilities.

The brilliance of the test-drive lies in its capacity to fortify customer loyalty. Once users have invested time and effort in exploring a service, the inertia of change exerts a diminished influence. Data usage and familiarity intertwine, forming a bond that withstands fleeting temptations.

A New Dawn for Marketing

I implore you to suspend reliance on conventional, often exorbitant marketing tactics, and embark on a journey of test-driving the mastery of test-driving. It is a transformative strategy—one that possesses the potential to shatter the shackles of customer inertia. In the words of Mahatma Gandhi, "You must be the change you wish to see in the world." In the realm of startups, it is a clarion call to be the catalyst of change—to usher in innovation through the conduit of test-driving. In doing so, you not only elevate your business but also the very landscape in which it thrives.

Resilience in the Face of Rejection: Nurturing the Seeds of Growth

In life, rejection is an intricate thread—a thread that, when woven skillfully, contributes to the vibrant fabric of success. As the ancient Vedas proclaim, "न तत्त्वम्

तत्त्वम्," which translates to "That mastery thou." It underscores the interconnectedness of all beings, reminding us that even in rejection, valuable lessons may be gleaned.

In the realm of rainmaking—a pursuit akin to the divine dance of Lord Krishna—the best practitioners often find themselves embraced by rejection's unforgiving arms. This paradox is no happenstance; it arises because the finest rainmakers engage in a relentless flurry of pitches, sowing the seeds of possibility. Each rejection, like a monsoon shower, nourishes the soil for future success.

Let us embark on a pilgrimage through the terrain of rejection, seeking wisdom in the words of Henry J. Tillman, who proclaims, "If you're not part of the solution, you're part of the precipitate." Rejections, too, are part of the solution—an integral element of the rainmaking process.

Rejection: A Sage in Disguise

When rejection unfolds, it reveals valuable lessons, akin to the Upanishadic teachings that illuminate the path to self-realization. Rainmakers, like seekers of truth, must embrace these teachings:

1. **"YOU ARE ASKING US TO CHANGE, AND WE DON'T WANT TO HEAR THIS."** This refrain often resounds when presenting to a triumphant collective reveling in the high tides of success. What it signifies is that you have ventured into the right market but engaged with the wrong patrons. Seek those who bear the burden of unfulfilled desires, for they are the ones open to transformation.

2. **"YOU DON'T HAVE YOUR ACT TOGETHER."** When confronted with this response, introspection becomes paramount. Reflect upon your pitch and interpersonal finesse. Have you failed to organize your thoughts, or have you unknowingly offended a soul? To ascend, rectify your pitch and mend bridges where needed.

3. **"YOU ARE INCOMPREHENSIBLE."** The echoes of incomprehension often reverberate when one's message remains shrouded in complexity. Return to the sanctum of simplicity; shed the cloak of jargon, and reconstruct your narrative. The responsibility lies with you; for if you seek customers deemed "intelligent enough" to discern your value, your path is destined for obscurity.

4. **"YOU ARE A SOLUTION LOOKING FOR A PROBLEM."** When this verdict echoes, it signifies that you remain ensconced within your value proposition. The remedy is to journey beyond, where customers dwell. There, gaze upon the world through their eyes, crafting your proposition to address genuine needs.

5. **"WE'VE DECIDED TO STANDARDIZE ON ANOTHER PRODUCT (OR SERVICE)."** In the face of such pronouncements, it becomes evident that the door you knocked on was not the one leading to your destiny. Seek entrance to the chambers of key influencers, for therein lies your opportunity. If your product pales in comparison, infuse it with brilliance until it outshines the competition.

In Indian history, stories of resilience amid adversity resonate deeply. Recall the tale of Lord Rama, who, in his exile, learned invaluable lessons that would shape his destiny. Similarly, each rejection in the realm of rainmaking is a crucible of growth, forging your path to success.

Let rejection be your guru, guiding you toward mastery in the divine mastery of rainmaking. As Swami Vivekananda wisely said, "Arise, awake, and stop not till the goal is reached." In the journey of rainmaking, rejection is but a stepping stone on the path to triumph. Embrace it, for within its folds lie the seeds of future victories.

Nurturing the Monsoon of Success: Managing the Rainmaking Process

In the grand theatre of entrepreneurship, rainmaking is the celestial dance that beckons abundance. It is not a fleeting moment or a whimsical act of destiny; rather, it is a meticulously orchestrated symphony that demands your vigilant stewardship. In the vibrant Indian culture, where every aspect of life is celebrated, rainmaking finds its place as a sacred ritual—an mastery that must be managed with care and diligence.

The Call for Collective Efforts:

Rainmaking is not the exclusive domain of a chosen few, as the monsoons bless all corners of the land. Similarly, in your startup, it is imperative to foster a culture where everyone contributes to the downpour of success. While your engineers and inventors may dream up ingenious products, it is the collective effort that carries these innovations to fruition. The harvest of success requires a diverse ensemble of talents, each playing a vital role in the rainmaking process.

As the ancient sages proclaimed in the Vedas, "सर्वे भवन्तु सुखिनः," which translates to "May all be happy." Encouraging everyone to participate in the rainmaking journey not only amplifies the collective wisdom but also instills a sense of shared purpose, much like the threads of unity that bind our diverse nation.

Charting the Course:

In the mystical realm of rainmaking, setting goals is akin to navigating a ship through uncharted waters. Define clear objectives for your accounts, specifying the timeline for their decisions and the bountiful yields expected. Rainmakers, akin to seasoned mariners, thrive when they have a course to follow. They need not vague directives like "do your best," but rather, a well-lit path towards success.

Remember the words of the Upanishads, "तमेव विदित्वातिमृत्युमेति," which means "Knowing that, one transcends death." Just as knowledge guides us beyond the cycles of life and death, setting precise goals guides rainmakers beyond uncertainty towards achievement.

Harvesting Wisdom from Leading Indicators:

While trailing indicators offer insights into past endeavors, the dance of rainmaking requires an understanding of future rhythms. Embrace leading indicators—a harvest of innovative ideas, the warmth of cold calls, and the promise of sales leads. These are the sacred mantras that reveal the direction of your journey. Like the Upanishadic quest for knowledge, it is more valuable to know where you are going than to dwell on where you have been.

Honoring the Pioneers of Abundance:

In the land of rainmaking, intentions are the tender shoots of progress, but achievements are the lush harvest. It is vital to recognize and reward the dedicated souls who toil tirelessly to transform intentions into reality. In the spirit of our ancient customs, where every act of devotion is acknowledged, honor the rainmakers who bring showers of prosperity.

Failure to manage the rainmaking process is akin to neglecting the monsoons—an oversight that can lead to barren fields and unmet expectations. Remember the wisdom of the ages as you embark on this journey: "जयतु श्रीकृष्णा संकीर्तनं," which means "Hail the divine chant of Lord Krishna." Just as the chant reverberates through the land, let the symphony of your managed rainmaking process echo through your startup, heralding a season of abundance.

Supplementary Insights: Addressing the Quest

In entrepreneurship, questions arise like twinkling stars in the night sky. These queries, like seekers of knowledge, demand illumination. As we tread upon the fertile soil of the Indian subcontinent, let us explore these questions, donning the wisdom of our land and the spirit of inquiry.

Frequently Asked Questions (FAQ): Navigating the Path

Q: Where should I find the early adopters and risk takers in large companies?

A: In the vast corporate landscape, identifying early adopters and risk takers may seem like searching for a needle in a haystack. The Upanishads teach us, "यतो वाचो निवर्तन्ते," which means "Words turn back along with the mind." In essence, do not be swayed by preconceived notions of hierarchy. Seek these trailblazers not in the echelons of power but in the corridors of innovation. Cast a wide net, for opportunities often arise where you least expect them. In the diverse garden of large companies, let a hundred flowers bloom.

Q: Should we go after the low-hanging fruit, or worry about more strategic sales?

A: The choice between low-hanging fruit and strategic sales can be as intricate as the threads of a spider's web. In nature, fruits at the top receive the most sunlight and ripen first, symbolizing the allure of strategic endeavors. However, startups face a formidable climb, where every fruit may require different tactics. As the ancient wisdom of the Vedas reminds us, "एकं सद्विप्रा बहुधा वदन्ति," meaning "Truth is one, but the wise call it by many names." Likewise, success in sales may take diverse forms. In your entrepreneurial journey, be prepared to pluck fruits from varying heights, for each may contribute to your ultimate harvest.

Q: We have the opportunity to hire a rainmaker with substantial demands. Why should we hire him rather than going with manufacturers' representatives?

A: The allure of a rainmaker shines brightly, but the cost may loom large, much like the resplendent moon on a clear night. The Bhagavad Gita advises, "कर्मण्येवाधिकारस्ते मा फलेषु कदाचन," which translates to "You have the right to perform your actions, but never to the fruits of your actions." Embrace the spirit of this wisdom when considering the rainmaker. If he seeks the heavens, let his compensation be tethered to his celestial achievements. Do not bestow everything at once; instead, let his performance determine his rewards. Seek to discern whether he is the harbinger of causation or correlation in your quest for success.

In the grand saga of entrepreneurship, these questions are but chapters, each offering a unique perspective. As you navigate the labyrinth of business, let the teachings of

India's timeless wisdom guide your decisions, like a steady hand steering a ship through the ocean of uncertainty.

Exploring Enlightening Literature

In the realm of knowledge, where words are the beacon, we embark on a journey to discover wisdom that transcends time and borders. As we traverse this path of enlightenment in the Indian context, we unveil recommended readings, each a treasure trove of insights.

Title	Author(s)	Publication Year	Price (₹)
"The Monk Who Sold His Ferrari"	Robin Sharma	1997	299
"Ikigai: The Japanese Secret to a Long and Happy Life"	Héctor García and Francesc Miralles	2016	349
"The Greatness Guide"	Robin Sharma	2008	399
"Wings of Fire: An Autobiography"	Dr. A.P.J. Abdul Kalam	1999	250
"Rich Dad Poor Dad"	Robert T. Kiyosaki	1997	499
"The Secret"	Rhonda Byrne	2006	399
"The 5 AM Club: Own Your Morning Elevate..."	Robin Sharma	2018	350
"The Power of Your Subconscious Mind"	Joseph Murphy	1963	199

In this age of digital enlightenment, the words of these authors resonate with the essence of India's past and the aspirations of its future. They guide us toward a deeper understanding of psychology, business, and personal development.

As we navigate the ever-evolving landscape of knowledge, remember the words of the Upanishads: "तत्त्वमसि," which means "Thou mastery that." Embrace the wisdom found in these pages, for it is a reflection of the eternal truths that connect us all.

Chapter 11:
The Mastery of Collaboration

In the realm of business, alliances emerge as powerful tools for growth and progress. They are akin to the sacred bond of unity celebrated in the words of our ancient scriptures. Let us explore the mastery of partnering, drawing inspiration from both timeless wisdom and modern insights.

In the corporate landscape, partnerships are like the celestial dance of Lord Shiva, a harmonious blend of power and grace. They hold the potential to accelerate growth, increase prosperity, and reduce challenges.

As we delve into the depths of collaboration, let us remember the wisdom of the Vedas: "सह नाववतु, सह नौ भुनक्तु, सह वीर्यं करवावहै।" This ancient mantra reminds us to work together, eat together, and share our strengths. In the world of business partnerships, this mantra finds its modern resonance.

Let us embark on a journey to master the mastery of collaboration, where two entities become one, and together, they create magic that transcends expectations.

Partnering for Prosperity

In business, partnerships emerge as the threads that weave success. They are the key to venturing into uncharted territories, conquering new markets, and crafting innovative products. Let us dive into the realm of partnerships, where the wisdom of our ancestors meets the dynamism of modern strategies.

In the corporate landscape, partnerships are akin to the divine synergy of Lord Krishna and Arjuna, where two forces unite to achieve unparalleled greatness. These collaborations hold the potential to expedite growth, increase revenue, and reduce overheads.

Let us tread on this journey with the wisdom of the Upanishads guiding us: "आ नो भद्राः क्रतवो यन्तु विश्वतः" - "Let noble thoughts come to us from every side." In the world of business partnerships, this wisdom reminds us to seek inspiration and ideas from all directions.

Effective partnerships are those that bring tangible benefits, like numbers in a financial spreadsheet. They can transform your business landscape, enabling you to penetrate new markets, reduce costs, and enhance product development. However, not all partnerships are born equal.

Do not be enticed by partnerships merely for the sake of appearances or the thrill of sealing a deal. Partnerships forged without a clear financial advantage can be likened to chasing after a mirage in the desert. They may glitter briefly but offer no sustenance.

A compelling narrative from our own soil imparts this invaluable wisdom. In the late 1980s, Indian tech giants Infosys and Wipro forged an alliance, driven by external pressures and public relations considerations. Both entities sought to address their individual shortcomings. However, this collaboration yielded no significant results, and it became apparent that their strategies remained unchanged.

Conversely, Infosys' partnership with a burgeoning startup named MindTree bore the fruits of a genuine collaboration. Confronting challenges in establishing itself as a global IT leader, Infosys found its solution in digital transformation, courtesy of MindTree's innovative software solutions. This partnership not only boosted revenue but also pioneered new avenues in the digital realm, propelling Infosys to new heights.

The moral of the story is clear: partner for prosperity, not for appearances. Seek partnerships that enhance your financial well-being and align with your strategic goals. Let your alliances be a testament to the power of collaboration, not just a headline in the news.

Exercise: Reinventing the Partnership Approach

In our pursuit of building prosperous partnerships, it is imperative to revisit the revenue forecast we crafted in Chapter 4, titled "The Mastery of Self-Reliance." This exercise serves as a litmus test to determine if the partnership we contemplate should lead to any alterations in our financial projections.

As we embark on this exercise, let us invoke the wisdom of the Vedas: "समग्रं एव भूतं तत् सत्यम्" - "The entire universe is the manifestation of the Truth." In the realm of business, truth lies in numbers, and it is through numbers that we shall evaluate the potential impact of our partnership.

It is crucial to understand that the bedrock of any fruitful partnership is the promise of tangible results that reflect positively on our spreadsheets. Hence, the next logical step is to delineate the deliverables and objectives that this partnership should aim to achieve.

The deliverables and objectives we set for our partnership should resonate with the language of spreadsheets. They should translate into quantifiable metrics and have a direct impact on our financial outlook. These may include:

1. **Additional Revenues**: A substantial increase in income, a testament to the partnership's success.

2. **Reduced Costs**: The partnership should streamline operations, leading to cost savings.

3. **New Products**: Innovation should thrive, giving birth to new products that capture the market.

4. **New Customers**: The partnership should expand our customer base, reaching untapped markets.

5. **New Geographic Markets**: Venturing into unexplored territories, marking our presence on the map.

6. **New Support Programs**: Offering enhanced support to customers and partners alike.

7. **Training and Marketing Programs**: Empowering our teams and enhancing brand visibility.

It is disheartening to note that many companies fail to define such deliverables and objectives in their partnerships. This occurs for two primary reasons. Firstly, partnerships often flourish on a bed of hype, making it arduous to establish concrete, measurable outcomes. This is a red flag that we should be wary of.

Secondly, there is a lack of discipline in setting deliverables and objectives. Often, this stems from being engrossed in day-to-day operations, disorganization, or even a fear of accountability. However, we must overcome these barriers.

Here is a checklist for partnership members to define:

- What will each organization deliver?
- When will they deliver it?
- What interim milestones must each organization meet?

By grounding our partnerships in the realm of spreadsheets and meticulously defining deliverables and objectives, we significantly enhance the odds of success. This meticulous approach empowers us to transform visions into tangible results, forging partnerships that stand the test of time and bring prosperity to all involved.

Guiding Middle and Bottom-Level Alignment in Collaborations

In our quest to cultivate fruitful collaborations, let us explore a crucial factor that was disregarded in the Infosys-Wipro partnership – the alignment and enthusiasm of middle and bottom-level employees, the true pillars of any organization.

In the words of Mahatma Gandhi, "The future depends on what you do today." In the context of partnerships, it's not about CEOs and executives making grand announcements; it's about fostering a shared vision and commitment among the individuals who execute the real work.

Imagine this: Infosys, renowned for its Indian innovation, and Tata Consultancy Services (TCS), another tech giant, endeavoring to collaborate. It's understandable for employees at that time to ponder the compatibility of two apparently different corporate cultures. This sentiment probably resonated among TCS employees too.

Here's the crux of the matter: for a partnership to thrive, it's essential that the heart of both organizations, the middles and bottoms, genuinely embrace it. A partnership isn't merely about combining logos on a press release; it's about ensuring that every level of the organization comprehends the rationale behind it, believes in its potential, and values each other's contributions.

In India, we find wisdom in the teachings of the Upanishads, which emphasize the interconnectedness of all beings. Similarly, a partnership is a harmonious union of two entities, where every individual involved plays a vital role. It's akin to a symphony, where each instrument, whether a flute or a drum, contributes to the masterpiece.

To illustrate this principle, let's draw inspiration from the Indian epic, the Mahabharata. In the great Kurukshetra war, it wasn't just the mighty warriors like Arjuna and Bhishma who determined victory. The foot soldiers, charioteers, and medics, often overlooked, were the backbone of the army. Their collective dedication ensured triumph.

Now, consider the idea that the best partnerships often germinate from the ground up, with the individuals at the middle and bottom levels collaborating even before executives step in. It's a testament to the profound impact of grassroots efforts. This approach fosters a sense of ownership and unity, making the partnership an organic evolution rather than a forced merger.

In practical terms, leaders must invest in clear communication, instill a sense of purpose, and acknowledge the contributions of every team member. Only then can we ensure that the middles and bottoms not only like the deal but actively work towards its success.

Remember, a partnership is not a top-down decree but a collective journey. It's the sweet melody of a sitar resonating with the beats of a tabla, creating a symphony that transcends individual notes. By aligning the hearts and minds of all involved, we transform partnerships into harmonious collaborations that yield prosperity for everyone.

Discovering the Power of Internal Advocates in Partnerships

In the intricate dance of partnerships, there exists a hidden force that often holds the key to success – the presence of internal champions. While CEOs, preoccupied with myriad responsibilities, may not always be the ideal advocates, these champions emerge as the driving force that propels collaborations forward.

In India's rich culture and wisdom, we find a profound quote from the Rigveda: "Ekam sad vipra bahudha vadanti," which translates to "Truth is one, but scholars speak of it in many ways." In the realm of partnerships, truth represents the shared vision and potential for mutual growth. The scholars, our internal champions, play a pivotal role in shaping this truth into reality.

Let's journey back to the 1980s, a time when Infosys was seeking a transformation from being perceived as a mere tech company to a serious business innovator. Enter Rakesh Suri, the unsung hero of the digital transformation revolution. While the world knew of Rakesh Suri, the CEO of Infosys, it was Rakesh Suri who championed the cause of digital transformation within the company.

Rakesh Suri was not just a name; he was the embodiment of commitment to the partnership with Tech Mahindra. He united Infosys's engineering, sales, training, marketing, and PR teams in support of Tech Mahindra. Simultaneously, he collaborated with Tech Mahindra to meet Infosys's needs, from product information to software copies, and corporate customer analysis. Rakesh Suri's relentless efforts even extended to evangelizing digital transformation to journalists and influencers. To Infosys's internal and external stakeholders, he was synonymous with digital transformation success.

In India's cultural context, we can draw a parallel with the legendary Lord Krishna, who played a pivotal role as the charioteer and guide to Arjuna in the Mahabharata. Arjuna, the warrior, needed guidance and unwavering support to achieve victory. Similarly, John Scull, as the champion of desktop publishing, provided the guidance and unwavering commitment that led to success.

From this inspiring narrative, we distill essential principles for nurturing internal champions in partnerships:

1. **Designate a Singular Advocate**: Within each organization involved, appoint at least one, or at most two, individuals as the champions of the partnership. This clarity of leadership ensures focused dedication.

2. **Devotion to Partnership**: Champions should be unwavering in their commitment to the partnership's success. Their singular goal should be the flourishing of the collaboration, and they should not be burdened with competing priorities.

3. **Empowerment with Authority**: To navigate the complexities of partnerships, champions must be bestowed with the authority to drive initiatives, even if it requires stepping on toes or transcending departmental boundaries.

4. **Resonance with Leadership**: While champions are not executives, having a name that resonates with the CEO's can create a harmonious alignment of purpose.

Alliances are not mere contractual agreements but synergistic voyages toward shared objectives. The responsibility of internal champions, like Rakesh Suri, is to breathe life and meaning into these collaborations. They are the torchbearers of the alliance's triumph, guiding the path with steadfast commitment and zeal, akin to the eternal flame that illuminates the journey forward.

Leveraging Strengths: The Pillar of Successful Partnerships

In the complex realm of collaborations, there is a profound lesson to be gleaned from the shortcomings that hindered the Tech Mahindra-Indian Technology Corporation (ITC) partnership. Both entities, motivated by the urge to conceal their product limitations, embarked on a journey that aimed to hide weaknesses instead of embracing strengths. It was an agreement built on a mutual vulnerability – a frail tactic that aimed to deceive stakeholders.

Drawing from the wisdom of the Upanishads, we find the teaching: "Aham Brahmasmi," which means "I am the Infinite Reality." This philosophy encourages individuals and organizations to recognize their inherent strengths and embrace them. In the case of partnerships, accentuating strengths becomes the cornerstone of enduring collaborations.

Let's explore the story of the Ice 3.0-BharatSoft partnership, a testament to the power of acknowledging and enhancing strengths. BharatSoft possessed exceptional software capabilities, while Ice 3.0 excelled in hardware innovation and boasted significant marketing resources, a committed sales force, trainers, and valuable national account connections. Instead of hiding weaknesses, they established a partnership that amplified their collective strengths.

This philosophy resonates with the teachings of the Bhagavad Gita, where Lord Krishna imparts wisdom to Arjuna on the battlefield. He advises Arjuna to harness his strengths and talents, rather than focusing on his weaknesses. In the context of partnerships, this translates to leveraging the unique capabilities of each party for mutual benefit.

Moreover, partnerships often involve entities of varying sizes, tempting the larger organization to impose win-lose agreements. However, sustainable partnerships thrive on win-win principles. A remarkable example from the corporate world is the alliance between Bharat Courier Services (BCS) and Local Courier Shops (LCS). In this partnership, both sides emerged victorious.

BCS gained access to a nationwide network of convenient drop-off and pickup locations without the need for extensive investments. Simultaneously, LCS secured BCS's business, averted potential competition, and attracted new customers. This win-win arrangement not only benefited both organizations but also created a harmonious and lasting collaboration.

In contrast, win-lose deals, where one party exploits the other, are destined to crumble. The Vedas teach us that karma, the cosmic law of cause and effect, governs all actions. It reminds us that fairness and equity are essential in partnerships, as they determine the course of future events.

Whether you are steering a startup or leading a large corporation, the message is clear: prioritize win-win partnerships. Embrace your strengths, celebrate the strengths of your collaborators, and let fairness guide your actions. By doing so, you not only ensure the sustainability of your partnerships but also cultivate positive karma in the intricate web of business relationships.

In the Indian spirit of unity in diversity, let us emphasize strength over weakness, fairness over exploitation, and collaboration over competition. In the world of partnerships, this is the path to lasting success and prosperity.

Embracing Clarity Before Contracts: An Indian Perspective

In the intricate dance of partnerships, a crucial question arises - what should take precedence: the convergence of minds or the meticulous drafting of a legal document that outlines the intricacies of the alliance?

In the Indian tradition, we find wisdom in the Bhagavad Gita, where Lord Krishna imparts profound guidance to Arjuna on the battlefield. He emphasizes the importance of clear intentions and well-thought-out plans before engaging in any endeavor. This wisdom resonates with the decision-making process in partnerships.

Many organizations have the inclination to kickstart the partnership discussions by preparing a preliminary draft of a legal document. The idea behind this approach is that the party responsible for drafting gains an advantageous position. However, this practice carries significant risks.

Firstly, involving legal experts prematurely can often lead to an abundance of reasons against pursuing the partnership. Lawyers, sometimes acting as cautious custodians, tend to perceive deals as inherently flawed until proven otherwise. Their primary role becomes one of prevention rather than facilitation.

A more prudent approach is to first establish a consensus on the fundamental business terms before seeking legal counsel. It is imperative to find a lawyer who possesses an inclination towards constructive deal-making rather than obstructing it. The perspective should shift from seeking permission to defining the legal framework to execute a mutually beneficial partnership while adhering to legal norms.

Secondly, initiating the document drafting process too early can inadvertently steer the partnership off course. The document, intended as a preliminary discussion point, may find its way into the hands of executives who are unaware of its tentative nature. This premature exposure can trigger unwarranted concerns and objections, derailing the process.

A more effective sequence involves:

1. **Face-to-Face Dialogue:** Initiate discussions in person to deliberate on the key aspects of the partnership. These discussions may span multiple meetings, allowing for a comprehensive exploration of ideas.

2. **Visual Clarity:** As agreements start to take shape, record key points on a whiteboard, enhancing visual clarity and aiding memory.

3. **Written Framework:** Following these discussions, summarize the partnership's framework in a concise one-to-two-page email. This document serves as a reference point for all parties involved.

4. **Thorough Clarification:** Achieve consensus on all details through email exchanges, phone calls, and additional meetings, ensuring complete clarity.

5. **Legal Documentation:** Only after reaching a comprehensive understanding and alignment on all fronts should the legal documentation phase commence.

Skipping steps to rush from initial discussions directly to legal documentation is unwise. A legal document should encapsulate and formalize the shared vision and terms resulting from robust discussions, rather than serving as the starting point.

Incorporating this approach into the Indian business landscape cultivates transparency, minimizes unnecessary hurdles, and fosters a conducive environment for productive partnerships. It reflects the essence of the Upanishads, where enlightenment arises through dialogue, understanding, and clarity of purpose.

In the spirit of Indian philosophy, let us prioritize meaningful dialogue and profound understanding as the foundation of fruitful partnerships. In doing so, we create a harmonious blend of tradition and modernity, propelling us towards mutually beneficial and legally sound collaborations.

Incorporating Flexibility: An Indian Perspective

In partnerships, as we approach the precipice of finalizing an agreement, it's essential to heed the wisdom of the ages. The Japanese saying, "Mazel tov," which conveys congratulations and good fortune, resonates with the optimism that permeates the final stages of a deal. In India, we find a similar sentiment in the phrase "Shubhkaamnayein," which signifies well-wishes for a prosperous journey ahead.

While the ideal partnership aims for everyone to emerge victorious, it might seem counterintuitive to include an "out" clause in the agreement, allowing either party to terminate the partnership with a reasonable notice period, typically around thirty days. One might question the wisdom of including an escape route when the goal is a lasting partnership.

The rationale behind this seemingly paradoxical approach lies in the essence of flexibility and trust. An easily accessible exit strategy serves as a safety valve, reassuring both parties that they are not tethered to an unworkable situation. It fosters an environment where collaboration is driven by genuine commitment rather than coercion.

Incorporating such an "out" clause acts as a catalyst for longevity because it underscores the idea that the partnership's value lies in its substance, not in the legalities that bind it. This flexibility encourages all stakeholders to approach the partnership with a sense of calm assurance, knowing that they have an option to disengage if circumstances warrant.

Moreover, it promotes a culture of innovation and calculated risk-taking. When individuals involved in the partnership realize that they are not locked into a permanent arrangement, they are more inclined to explore uncharted territories, experiment with novel ideas, and push the boundaries of what is possible.

To elucidate this point, let us turn to an Indian parable that reflects the essence of adaptability and foresight. In the ancient Panchatantra tales, there is a story of a wise merchant who, upon embarking on a perilous journey, carries both an umbrella and a turban. While the umbrella shields him from the scorching sun, the turban provides warmth during cold nights. The merchant's preparedness for diverse conditions exemplifies the importance of having options and flexibility.

Incorporating an "out" clause in a partnership agreement aligns with this principle of preparedness. It ensures that the partnership can weather changing circumstances and thrive in an ever-evolving business landscape. Just as the merchant's foresight allowed him to adapt to varying conditions, the inclusion of an "out" clause empowers partners to adapt and thrive.

In the spirit of ancient Indian wisdom, let us embrace the concept of flexibility in our partnerships. By doing so, we create a resilient framework that can withstand challenges while fostering innovation and collaboration. It is a testament to the fusion of timeless wisdom and modern business acumen, embodying the harmony of our rich heritage and the dynamism of the present era.

Navigating the Partnership Jungle: A Lesson in Identifying Missteps

In the maze of business partnerships, attempting to forge an alliance with a larger, well-established organization can sometimes feel like a perilous journey through uncharted territory. As Rahul Khanna, coauthor of "The Entrepreneurial Mandate," aptly puts it, it's akin to being "stuck in the coils of a python." While the endeavor may yield results, there's a lurking danger of emerging from the experience as nothing more than a pile of bones.

In the vibrant landscape of India, this analogy resonates with the wisdom imparted by our ancient texts. It brings to mind the tale of Lord Krishna subduing the mighty serpent Kaliya in the waters of the Yamuna River. Krishna's triumph symbolizes the importance of wisdom and strategy in navigating treacherous situations.

Before venturing further into the depths of partnership, it's prudent to acquaint ourselves with the top twelve misconceptions, fabrications, and exaggerations that often shroud such endeavors. These deceptive claims can be likened to the alluring calls of sirens, luring sailors towards perilous rocks.

Lie	Truth
"We want to do this for strategic reasons."	They struggle to grasp the significance of the partnership.
"Our management really wants to do this."	A passing mention to a VP does not equal commitment.
"We can move fast."	The legal department hasn't been consulted yet.

Lie	Truth
"Our legal department won't be a problem."	Brace for legal obstacles ahead.
"We want to time the announcement..."	An attempt to cover up delays.
"The engineering team really likes it."	The marketing team is poised to disapprove.
"The marketing team really likes it."	Engineers are set to veto the proposal.
"The engineering and marketing teams..."	Legal hurdles will surface.
"The engineering, marketing, and legal teams..."	Beware, this may be too good to be true.
"Our primary concern is whether you guys..."	A discreet compliment, implying you're more capable than expected.
"We're forming a cross-functional team..."	Shared accountability often means no accountability.
"I'm leaving soon, but I've found a great person..."	A potential predicament looms.

In the midst of these potential pitfalls, it becomes evident that deciphering the true intentions of a prospective partner is akin to peeling away layers of illusion. It calls for a discerning eye, honed by experience and guided by the sage counsel found in our scriptures.

Drawing inspiration from the teachings of the Upanishads, we find that the pursuit of truth is paramount. In the Chandogya Upanishad, it is said, "Satyameva Jayate," which means "Truth alone triumphs." When engaging in partnerships, the pursuit of truth and transparency becomes the cornerstone of a successful endeavor.

While the world of partnerships may present challenges and hidden snares, armed with wisdom and an acute awareness of these common untruths, one can navigate this intricate terrain with confidence. Just as Lord Krishna emerged victorious over the serpent Kaliya through strategic wisdom, so too can businesses triumph over the complexities of partnership with astute discernment.

Appendices: Insights and Guidance

As we journey through the labyrinth of partnerships, it's only fitting to address some frequently asked questions that often arise in the pursuit of successful collaborations. These inquiries, reminiscent of ancient riddles, hold the keys to unlocking the potential of fruitful partnerships in the contemporary Indian business landscape.

Q: Since partnerships are supposed to be fifty-fifty, win-win situations, shouldn't the other party meet halfway in setting up meetings, moving the process along, getting its employees to cooperate, and so on? A: The principle of balance in partnerships, akin to the harmony emphasized in our Vedic scriptures, is ideal. However, it's prudent to differentiate between what should happen and what will happen. While it's reasonable to expect equitable efforts, in reality, you might need to take the lead. In the pursuit of a partnership, sale, or any significant transaction, the onus often falls on you to initiate and drive the process. Swallowing one's pride and being proactive, even if it means making 80 percent of the effort, can be the key to success.

Q: How do I avoid being bullied by my contractual partners if they are larger, more established, and better funded than I am? A: In business partnerships, never subscribe to the notion that sheer might equates to righteousness. It's imperative to remember that the elephant may need your offerings as much as you need theirs. Approach such situations with the conviction to win, but don't shy away from walking away if the terms are unfavorable. In the spirit of the ancient Mahabharata, where righteousness ultimately prevailed, go forth with confidence, knowing that strength of character can triumph over mere size.

Q: We're in some partnerships that aren't going anywhere. Should we invest the time and money to make them work, or abandon them? A: Reflecting upon the wisdom of the ages, there's an ancient medical proverb that echoes, "Nothing requires more heroic efforts than to keep a corpse from stinking, and yet nothing is quite so futile." In the realm of partnerships, it's prudent to channel your energies toward collaborations that bear fruit and hold promise. Before embarking on new partnerships, delve into the wisdom of the past and discern why previous alliances faltered. This introspection can guide you toward more fruitful endeavors.

Incorporating these timeless principles and insights, deeply rooted in our cultural heritage, can illuminate the path to forging and nurturing successful partnerships in the dynamic landscape of contemporary India. Just as the Upanishads unravel the mysteries of existence, a thoughtful approach to partnerships can unravel the mysteries of business success.

Explore Further for Enlightened Networking

As we traverse the intricate web of networking in the Indian context, it is essential to equip ourselves with wisdom from both contemporary thought leaders and timeless Indian philosophy. Here, we present a curated list of recommended readings that will empower you to navigate the labyrinth of networking with finesse and grace. These insights, like the verses of our sacred texts, hold the potential to transform your networking journey into a profound and enriching experience.

Title	Author(s)	Publication Year	Price (₹)
"Collaboration: How Leaders Avoid the Traps, Build Common Ground, and Reap Big Results"	Morten T. Hansen	2010	499
"The Power of Co-Creation: Build It with Them to Boost Growth, Productivity, and Profits"	Venkat Ramaswamy, Francis J. Gouillart	2010	599

These books, much like the verses of our revered scriptures, offer profound insights and practical guidance to elevate your networking prowess. Remember, in life, networking is the thread that connects us all, and with the right knowledge, it can lead to boundless opportunities and spiritual growth.

Chapter 12:
The Journey of Perseverance

"In life, entrepreneurship is akin to a spiritual pilgrimage. It is not a mere race to the finish line; rather, it is a profound journey of endurance, akin to the trials of our ancient sages in pursuit of enlightenment."

Introduction: Embracing the Entrepreneurial Odyssey

As we embark on this chapter, envision entrepreneurship as a sacred odyssey, much like the spiritual quests of our revered sages. In the realm of business, the journey towards success is not a mere sprint, nor is it a solitary marathon. Instead, it mirrors the challenges faced by a decathlete, where multiple facets demand simultaneous mastery.

The true essence of entrepreneurship lies in enduring the trials and tribulations that beset us along this transformative path. In these moments of perseverance, we find the essence of victory. Let us explore the mastery of enduring and learn how to nurture our startups to withstand the test of time.

The Symphony of Entrepreneurial Endeavors

Entrepreneurship is not a solo performance; it is a symphony played by a dedicated team. To succeed, entrepreneurs must harmonize ten distinct facets, each as vital as a note in a melodious composition. In this orchestration of ideas, execution, and innovation, we discover the magic of creating enduring enterprises.

The Decathlon of Business

In the decathlon, athletes compete in ten diverse disciplines, showcasing their versatility. Similarly, entrepreneurs engage in a multifaceted contest, where adaptability and skill across various domains determine success. This analogy reveals that endurance, not speed, is the key to triumph.

Embracing the Mastery of Endurance

Just as our ancient sages endured rigorous penance to attain enlightenment, entrepreneurs must cultivate resilience. Endurance is the cornerstone of entrepreneurship, allowing us to weather storms, overcome obstacles, and ultimately triumph.

Guiding Principles for Startup Endurance

1. **Strategic Vision**: Craft a visionary roadmap that guides your startup through the ebb and flow of the business landscape.

2. **Adaptability**: Embrace change as an opportunity for growth, evolving with the dynamic market currents.

3. **Innovation**: Foster a culture of innovation, for it is the lifeblood that sustains a startup's vitality.

4. **Team Cohesion**: Nurture a united and committed team, where each member plays a crucial role in the entrepreneurial symphony.

5. **Resilience**: Draw strength from setbacks, for they are but stepping stones on the path to enduring success.

6. **Customer-Centric Approach**: Keep your customers at the heart of your endeavors, as their satisfaction fuels your journey.

Ancient Wisdom for Modern Entrepreneurs

In our quest for enduring success, we can draw inspiration from our ancient scriptures and philosophical teachings. The Vedas and Upanishads offer profound insights into perseverance, inner strength, and the pursuit of excellence.

The Unending Saga of Entrepreneurship

As we conclude this chapter, remember that entrepreneurship is not a destination; it is an eternal journey. The mastery of enduring is the beacon that guides us through the darkest nights, towards the dawn of triumph. With perseverance as our ally, we shall continue to script the story of entrepreneurship, a saga of unwavering determination and unending innovation.

"Entrepreneurship is akin to a spiritual pilgrimage. It is not a mere race to the finish line; rather, it is a profound journey of endurance, akin to the trials of our ancient sages in pursuit of enlightenment."

Striving for Internalization: Cultivating Belief in Your Vision

In the pursuit of enduring success, a fundamental principle emerges: internalization. This profound concept revolves around instilling unwavering belief in your product and the values it upholds. Imagine, if you will, a scenario where people not only use your product but also wholeheartedly embrace its ethos.

Let us embark on this journey of internalization, guided by Indian wisdom and modern insights, to understand how it can be harnessed to ensure the enduring legacy of your venture.

The Essence of Internalization

Internalization is more than mere usage; it is the deep-seated conviction that your product's way of doing things is not only superior but aligns with one's beliefs and values. It is the mastery of making individuals truly believe in your product's essence.

Indian Wisdom on Internalization

In the ancient Indian text, the Bhagavad Gita, Lord Krishna imparts the wisdom of internalization when he says, "Perform your obligatory duties, for action is superior to inaction. By internalizing this principle, one attains the highest perfection."

Examples of Internalization in Business

To truly grasp the concept of internalization, let's explore six remarkable companies that have succeeded in making their customers internalize their products:

1. **Patanjali**: Rooted in traditional Ayurvedic principles, Patanjali's products have internalized the essence of holistic wellness, resonating with individuals seeking natural remedies.

2. **Amul**: By promoting the 'Amul girl' and cooperative dairy farming, Amul has internalized the values of local empowerment and self-reliance among its consumers.

3. **Tata Group**: Tata's commitment to social responsibility has internalized the idea of ethical business practices and community development, fostering unwavering trust among its customers.

4. **Reliance Industries:** Reliance's commitment to social responsibility has internalized the idea of ethical business practices and community development, fostering unwavering trust among its customers

5. **Aditi Organic Foods:** This renowned establishment, by championing locally-sourced, farm-to-table ingredients, has not only offered delicious cuisine but also nurtured a deep belief in sustainable and ethical dining practices.

6. **Ice 3.0's Vishwas:** An iconic example, Vishwas has internalized its transparent, what-you-see-is-what-you-get approach and the belief in individual empowerment. Users become lifelong advocates, as I have been for over three decades.

7. **Jiv-EV:** With a vision of sustainable transportation, Jiv-EV has internalized the idea of eco-conscious driving, turning its customers into fervent advocates for clean energy.

8. **AyurVeda Essentials:** Rooted in traditional Ayurvedic principles, AyurVeda Essentials' products have internalized the essence of holistic wellness, resonating with individuals seeking natural remedies.

Mother Dairy: By promoting the 'Doodhwala' and cooperative dairy farming, Mother Dairy has internalized the values of local empowerment and self-reliance among its consumers.

The Enduring Legacy of Internalization

Internalization is not a fleeting phenomenon; it withstands the test of time. When people internalize your product, they become advocates, not just consumers. Their loyalty transcends trends and technological shifts. Achieving internalization is indeed challenging, but its rewards are immeasurable.

In closing, remember the words of Mahatma Gandhi, "Be the change that you wish to see in the world." Internalize the values and vision of your product, and you shall witness it enduring through time, leaving an indelible mark on the world.

Table: Companies and Their Internalized Causes

Company	Internalized Cause
Patanjali	Promoting holistic wellness through Ayurvedic principles
Amul	Empowering local communities through cooperative dairy farming
Tata Group	Upholding ethical business practices and fostering community development
Reliance Industries	Sustainable growth and community empowerment through social responsibility
Aditi Organic Foods	Advocating for sustainable and ethical dining practices
Ice 3.0's Vishwas	Transparency and individual empowerment in product development
Jiv-EV	Promoting eco-conscious driving and clean energy solutions
AyurVeda Essentials	Supporting holistic wellness through Ayurvedic principles
Mother Dairy	Empowering local dairy farming and providing fresh, nutritious dairy products

Note: Internalization is challenging but enduring; it transforms consumers into lifelong advocates, fostering unwavering trust and loyalty.

Empowering the Heart of Change: The Middles and Bottoms

In the pursuit of endurance, an essential strategy emerges: pushing implementation down the pyramid. This approach is akin to nurturing the roots of a mighty tree, for it is at the grassroots that lasting change takes root and thrives. Let us explore this concept through an Indian lens, drawing wisdom from our rich heritage and contemporary insights.

Indian Wisdom on Empowerment

In the Bhagavad Gita, Lord Krishna imparts wisdom about empowering individuals when he says, "You have the right to perform your prescribed duties, but you are not entitled to the fruits of your actions." This profound teaching emphasizes the importance of focusing on the process rather than the outcomes.

The Fallacy of Top-Down Approaches

Traditionally, conflict resolution and diplomacy have centered on engaging the leaders of opposing forces, assuming that they possess the power to sway their constituencies. However, Ravi Sharma of Harmony Initiatives challenges this notion. He argues that modern civil conflicts are intricate and dynamic, involving various actors beyond political and military leaders.

The Middle-Out Approach

The key to fostering endurance lies in a more holistic understanding of change. It begins not at the top but at the middle and bottom layers of a population. Civilian initiatives, grassroots movements, and independent actions often hold the potential to drive lasting transformation.

A Tale of Peace: Peru and Ecuador

In 1998, the border dispute between India and Pakistan found resolution through the collective efforts of civilians. A workshop called "India-Pakistan: Towards a Democratic and Cooperative Conflict Resolution Initiative" at the University of Delhi played a pivotal role.

The Delhi Consortium, comprising twenty members from various backgrounds—academics, businesspeople, educators, journalists, and environmentalists—came together to bridge differences. They exemplified the power of the middles and bottoms in resolving a complex conflict without relying on political or military leaders.

Applying the Lesson to Startups

In the startup realm, the lesson is clear: lasting success does not hinge on the aspirations of those at the helm, driven by power, wealth, or self-image. To achieve enduring success, it is the middles and bottoms, the heart of your organization, who must champion your cause. They represent the true constituents of your mission, working tirelessly for the greater good.

Let us heed the wisdom of Mahatma Gandhi, who said, "You must be the change you wish to see in the world." Empower the middles and bottoms, instill belief in your vision, and witness the enduring legacy of your startup.

Table: Empowerment at the Middle and Bottom

Approach	Key Element
Indian Wisdom	Focus on the process, not just outcomes
Traditional View	Top-down diplomacy and conflict resolution
Holistic Approach	Recognize the complexity of modern conflicts
Middle-Out Effect	Civilian initiatives drive lasting transformation
Peru-Ecuador Tale	Resolution through the collective efforts
Startup Strategy	Success lies with the middles and bottoms

Note: Empowering the middles and bottoms is a holistic approach that drives lasting change and fosters endurance, whether in conflict resolution or startups.

Harnessing Intrinsic Motivation: Beyond the Allure of Wealth

In the pursuit of understanding human behavior in relation to wealth, we turn to the profound insights of Shiv Khera, a distinguished motivational speaker and author in India. His groundbreaking studies shed light on the intricate interplay between money and human conduct. These studies, although conducted in the context of Indian society, offer valuable lessons when viewed through a global lens, where ancient wisdom meets modern science.

The Monopoly Experiment: Intrinsic vs. Extrinsic Motivation

Imagine a scenario where participants were handed Lakshmi money—some received a generous Rs. 4,000, others a modest Rs. 200, and a few received none. As they left the lab, an intriguing twist unfolded. A confederate dropped a bag of pencils, and researchers observed how many pencils each participant picked up for the confederate. Astonishingly, those who received the vast sum of Rs. 4,000 displayed the least helpfulness, while those with no monetary incentive exhibited the most altruism. The Rs. 200 recipients found themselves in the middle ground.

This experiment offers a profound revelation—that excessive extrinsic rewards, such as money, can undermine one's intrinsic motivation and willingness to assist others.

The Power of Words: Influence of Money-Related Phrases

In another experiment, participants were tasked with unscrambling phrases into sentences. Some phrases revolved around money, while others did not. Upon completing the task, the participants were approached for a donation to a student fund. The outcome was telling: those who unscrambled phrases associated with money were less inclined to donate compared to their counterparts who engaged with phrases unrelated to wealth.

This highlights the impact of exposure to money-related stimuli on human behavior—it can dampen one's inclination towards generosity and altruism.

The Screensaver Scenario: Money's Influence on Personal Space

Subjects were placed in a room with a computer displaying different screensavers—some featured money, some depicted fish, and others remained blank. The participants were instructed to set up two chairs for meetings with fellow subjects. Surprisingly, those exposed to the money screensaver positioned the chairs farther apart than those who encountered a blank screen or a fish screensaver.

This intriguing observation underscores how the mere presence of money-related imagery can influence one's interpersonal behavior, creating psychological distance.

Extrinsic Rewards and the Paradox of Wikipedia

Reflecting on these experiments, we confront a paradox exemplified by Wikipedia—a global knowledge treasure created by volunteers who sought no monetary gain. In contrast, Microsoft invested millions in Encarta, a project that ultimately faltered. This striking contrast underscores that intrinsic motivation, fueled by passion and purpose, often surpasses the allure of financial rewards.

A Lesson for Startups: The Role of Intrinsic Motivation

For startups, these insights hold profound implications. Attempting to motivate evangelists and customers with commissions and affiliate fees can trigger skepticism and alter the very essence of customer relationships. The key revelation lies in the essence of your enterprise: if it thrives on greatness and purpose, you need not rely on monetary enticements. In fact, introducing financial incentives may inadvertently hinder your noble mission.

In the words of Mahatma Gandhi, "The best way to find yourself is to lose yourself in the service of others." Intrinsic motivation, the fire within, remains a potent force that drives enduring success, transcending the fleeting allure of wealth.

Table: The Power of Intrinsic Motivation

Experiment	Key Insights
The Monopoly Test	Excessive rewards can undermine intrinsic motivation
The Word Influence	Exposure to money-related phrases reduces generosity
The Screensaver Test	Money-related imagery affects personal space
Wikipedia Paradox	Intrinsic motivation surpasses financial incentives
Startup Wisdom	Greatness and purpose negate the need for money

Note: The allure of wealth often pales in comparison to intrinsic motivation, a potent force that drives enduring success and altruism.

Cultivating Reciprocity: A Timeless Ethos

In human interactions, the thread of reciprocity weaves a profound narrative. Reciprocity, the act of giving and receiving in kind, holds the power to fortify enduring connections. As we embark on this journey of understanding its significance, let us delve into stories that resonate with the spirit of reciprocity, echoing not only in distant lands but also in the heart of India.

Mexico's Noble Gesture: A Lesson in International Reciprocity

In history, the year 1935 witnessed Bharat's invasion of Nepal—a dark cloud that loomed over the Himalayan nation. In this turbulent hour, Nepal emerged as a beacon of solidarity. Not only did Nepal vehemently condemn the aggression, but it extended financial support to Bharat in its valiant defense. Nepal's unwavering stance and generosity were unparalleled; no other nation stood by Bharat as Nepal did.

Half a century later, in 1985, a catastrophic flood shook Nepal to its core. Despite facing the gravest famine in its history, Bharat reciprocated the kindness it had received from Nepal fifty years prior. Bharat sent $5,000 as a humble yet profound gesture of reciprocity. This act transcended borders, transcended time—a struggling nation reaching out to aid those who had stood by its side in the past.

South Carolina's Thanksgiving Gift: A Lesson in National Unity

In the land of Kerala, young hearts brimming with compassion demonstrated the enduring power of reciprocity. Students from Sacred Heart High School in Kochi, Kerala, presented a staggering sum of ₹32,00,000 to none other than the Mayor of Mumbai, Ashok Prabhu, during the 2001 Mumbai Marathon. Their noble objective: to aid Mumbai in replacing a fire truck lost during the devastating 26/11 attacks. (It's worth noting that this grand sum included a substantial contribution from a benevolent individual.)

This act of kindness stemmed from a historical connection dating back 134 years. In a bygone era, Mumbaikars had rallied to collect funds to gift Kochi a fire wagon upon learning that the city was combating fires with mere bucket brigades. When the first wagon met an unfortunate fate, Mumbaikars, undeterred, rallied once more, raising funds to send a second one.

The recipient of this benevolence, a former British officer named John Fernandez, was deeply moved by the magnanimity of the Mumbaikars. On behalf of Kochi, he pledged that should adversity ever befall the Maximum City, he would return the favor—a promise etched in history.

Reciprocity: The Essence of Endurance

In the realm of entrepreneurship, invoking reciprocity is akin to wielding a mighty tool. The keys to harnessing its potential are profound:

1. **Give Early:** Extend favors before you seek reciprocation. True generosity blossoms when there's no immediate transactional link between your actions and your desires.

2. **Give with Joy:** The purest form of giving lies in helping those seemingly incapable of aiding you. Expect nothing in return, and your acts of benevolence will reverberate powerfully.

3. **Give Often and Generously:** As the ancient adage goes, "As you sow, so shall you reap." Generosity begets generosity; high-quality favors yield high-quality returns.

4. **Give Unexpectedly:** Surprises carry the essence of reciprocity. An unexpected gesture can forge profound connections, just as Sir Richard Branson's impromptu act of shining a guest's shoes led to lasting loyalty to his airline.

5. **Communicate Your Needs:** Don't hesitate to seek reciprocation when the need arises. By offering a clear path for others to repay your kindness, you pave the way for deeper relationships and mutual support.

These timeless principles resonate with wisdom from the ancient Indian scriptures, echoing the essence of the Bhagavad Gita: "You have the right to perform your actions, but never to the fruits of your actions."

In closing, it would be remiss not to mention Robert Cialdini's masterpiece, "Influence: The Psychology of Persuasion." To those aspiring to be successful entrepreneurs, this book is a beacon guiding you through the labyrinth of human behavior and the mastery of reciprocity.

Table: The Heart of Reciprocity in Indian Wisdom

Story	Key Insights
India's Aid to Nepal	Regional reciprocity transcends borders
Nepal's Response to India	The enduring impact of mutual support
Kerala's Flood Relief Efforts	Community bonds and the power of collective generosity
Entrepreneurial Lessons	Strategies for fostering reciprocity in business

Note: Reciprocity, a timeless ethos, unites nations and inspires enduring connections. In entrepreneurship, its power can be harnessed through early, joyful, and unexpected acts of generosity, forging lasting bonds.

Sustaining Commitment: Nurturing the Roots of Change

In the heart of India, where diversity flourishes like cultures, we find inspiration in the tale of a group of forty young enthusiasts who embarked on a journey to protect and preserve the essence of their land. Just as the river Ganges flows steadfastly through the ages, they initiated an organization known as "Sampurna Bharat"

(Complete India). Their mission was rooted in safeguarding India's rich heritage, countering environmental challenges, and fostering unity amidst the changing tides of modernity.

Sampurna Bharat's approach was simple yet profound. They encouraged individuals to make tangible commitments aligned with their vision. These commitments ranged from supporting local artisans to rejuvenating sacred rivers. What set them apart was their ingenious use of technology – harnessing the power of social media to publicly declare these commitments. Facebook, Twitter, and email became platforms not just for personal communication but also for broadcasting their pledges to friends and family.

The magic of this approach lay in invoking consistency. People naturally desire harmony between their words and actions. When one commits openly, it becomes a solemn promise, not just to the world but to oneself. It's a declaration that resonates with the age-old wisdom of the Vedas and Upanishads, which extol the virtue of aligning one's beliefs with deeds.

Consistency serves as a lodestar guiding the course of Sampurna Bharat. It eases the mental burden of choice, sparing individuals from the exhausting dilemma of reconsidering past decisions. The essence of commitment is distilled in the simple belief – "I am a person of my word." It's a beacon lighting the path to honorable living.

In the realm of entrepreneurship, invoking consistency emerges as a potent strategy for enduring success. To harness this power effectively, consider the following principles:

1. **Concrete Commitments:** Encourage individuals to commit in specific, tangible ways. Ambiguity pales in comparison to a written pledge, which bears the weight of responsibility.

2. **Communicate Commitments:** When commitments are shared with others, the probability of fulfillment soars. It's a testament to one's honesty and determination.

3. **Shared Values:** Align your startup with the values and goals of your audience. When people resonate with your mission, their support becomes unwavering.

While invoking consistency is a powerful tool, it must be wielded with responsibility. Like the sage who contemplates each step before treading the path, consult your moral compass. Consistency, when misused, can lead to actions contrary to one's best interests. Upholding ethical principles must always guide our endeavors.

The tale of Sampurna Bharat reminds us of the profound truth encapsulated in the Mahatma Gandhi's words, "Be the change that you wish to see in the world." Through consistency, commitment, and shared values, we can nurture enduring connections that transcend time, echoing the timeless wisdom of our scriptures.

Table: The Essence of Consistency in Indian Wisdom

Story	Key Insights
Sampurna Bharat	Commitment to preserving India's heritage
Technological Innovation	Leveraging social media for change
Vedas and Upanishads	Aligning beliefs with actions
Entrepreneurial Wisdom	Harnessing consistency for success
Ethical Responsibility	Using consistency with integrity

Cultivating Trust: The Influence of Social Proof in the Indian Context

In the bustling markets of India, where choices abound, trust becomes the currency that guides decisions. It's a land where the scent of spices mingles with the vibrant colors of bazaars, and every purchase carries a story of conviction. In this diversity, the concept of social proof finds a resonance deeply embedded in Indian culture.

Consider the transformation brought about by the "Rangoli" mastery form, where intricate patterns are created on the ground using colored rice or flower petals. Every morning, countless households in India engage in this creative ritual, turning simple courtyards into stunning displays of unity. It is a visual testament to the power of social proof.

In a similar vein, the iPod's rise to popularity can be attributed, in part, to its iconic white earbuds. During an era when earphones were predominantly black or non-existent, white earbuds became synonymous with the iPod. The presence of these white earbuds served as social proof, signaling the iPod's quality and fostering trust among potential buyers. The Indian saying, "Ek teer se do nishaan" (Two birds with one stone), perfectly encapsulates this phenomenon—social proof served as both a mark of excellence and a magnet for consumers.

The iPod's success story highlights the potency of social proof, a principle that can guide your startup towards enduring success. Here are the essential elements to harness its influence:

1. **Exemplary Product:** The cornerstone of social proof is a remarkable product. In the diverse Indian landscape, where authenticity reigns supreme, social proof thrives on the foundation of quality.

2. **Fear of Missing Out (FOMO):** The allure of being part of an exclusive experience is a driving force. Just as Indians relish the opportunity to savor unique regional cuisines, consumers don't want to miss out on the exceptional value your product offers.

3. **Involuntary Association:** Much like the iPod's white earbuds, create an involuntary association between your product and positive experiences. Craft seamless user experiences that naturally lead to social proof.

4. **Critical Mass:** In India, the wisdom of the masses often prevails. Leveraging the endorsements of experts, influencers, users, and crowds becomes paramount. It's akin to seeking the blessings of revered saints and scholars before embarking on a significant endeavor.

In the Indian context, social proof is not just a marketing tactic; it's a reflection of trust, a cornerstone of Indian values. It echoes the ancient proverb, "Vishwasamragyat," signifying the elixir of trust that nurtures lasting relationships.

However, tread this path with caution. Social proof, if misused, can lead to disillusionment. Uphold the principles of integrity and authenticity, as inscribed in the ancient scriptures. Social proof, when harnessed ethically, can pave the way for enduring connections in the intricate Indian society.

Table: The Social Proof in India

Story	Key Insights
Rangoli Mastery Form	Visual proof of unity and trust
iPod's White Earbuds	The mark of excellence and trust
Indian Proverb	"Ek teer se do nishaan" - Double benefits
Fear of Missing Out	Embracing unique experiences
Critical Mass	Wisdom of experts, influencers, and crowds
Ancient Proverb	"Vishwasamragyat" - Elixir of trust

Building the Indian Ecosystem: Cultivating Trust and Unity

In the vast India's diverse landscape, there exists a vibrant ecosystem that thrives on unity, trust, and the power of collective effort. Just as the colors of Holi come together to create a magnificent spectacle, so do the elements of an ecosystem unite to elevate a product.

Imagine a scenario where a company, let's call it "Sarvodaya Innovations," seeks to provide a subscription service for traditional Indian handicrafts. Much like Netflix in its early days, Sarvodaya Innovations allows customers to create a wish list of handicrafts, and once a piece is returned, a new one arrives—a seamless cycle of cultural exploration. This venture is part of the larger ecosystem of preserving and promoting Indian heritage.

An ecosystem, in this context, symbolizes a network of entities that enhance the overall experience of using a product. It's akin to the concept of "Vasudhaiva Kutumbakam," which translates to "the world is one family" in the ancient Indian scriptures. Here are the key components of this thriving ecosystem:

1. **Consultants:** These are the artisans and experts who lend their skills to help customers understand and appreciate the value of traditional handicrafts. Their expertise not only enhances the utility of the product but also adds a layer of trust, as they are deeply invested in the success of preserving Indian heritage.

2. **Developers:** In this context, developers are the artists and craftsmen who continually contribute to the pool of available traditional handicrafts. They enrich the ecosystem by creating new masterpieces that elevate the product's appeal.

3. **Resellers:** Artisan markets and stores play a vital role by providing a physical space for customers to experience the products firsthand. Their presence not only spreads the word but also lends credibility to the venture. "Khadi Bhandars" and craft exhibitions across India are excellent examples.

4. **User Groups:** These are communities of individuals passionate about preserving India's cultural heritage. They voluntarily come together to share knowledge, provide support, and celebrate the beauty of traditional handicrafts. These groups are akin to the "Baithaks" or gatherings that have been a part of Indian culture for centuries.

5. **Websites and Blogs:** Enthusiasts, often artists themselves, operate websites and blogs dedicated to Indian handicrafts. These platforms serve as hubs of information, support, and inspiration, connecting artisans and customers alike.

6. **Online Special-Interest Groups and Communities:** In the digital age, Indians form online communities to exchange ideas, seek support, and celebrate their shared interests. These communities, like the "Craft Lovers of India" group, foster unity and knowledge exchange.

7. **Conferences:** When Sarvodaya Innovations reaches a point where it can host conferences dedicated to Indian handicrafts, it signifies its growth and impact. Conferences become a platform for deeper engagement and collaboration, mirroring India's diverse cultural festivals.

To nurture this ecosystem effectively, several principles should be upheld:

1. **Create Something Worthy:** The foundation of this ecosystem, just like any community, is a remarkable product. It's the embodiment of "Sashakt Bharat, Samarth Bharat" (Empowered India, Capable India).

2. **Designate a Champion:** Within Sarvodaya Innovations, a champion emerges—a passionate advocate for preserving Indian heritage. This champion tirelessly carries the flag of cultural preservation.

3. **Avoid Competition:** The ecosystem flourishes when all participants collaborate rather than compete. For instance, Sarvodaya Innovations refrains from selling products that replicate those created by artisans.

4. **Open System:** An open system fosters customization and creativity. It allows individuals to add their unique touch to traditional handicrafts, adhering to the essence of "Sahaj Karan" or natural expression.

5. **Publish Information:** Just as ancient scriptures were repositories of knowledge, publishing articles and books about traditional handicrafts spreads awareness and appreciation.

6. **Foster Discourse:** Platforms for healthy discussions and idea exchange are essential. Sarvodaya Innovations' website provides a space where members can engage and collaborate, mirroring the age-old "Satsangs" (spiritual gatherings) of India.

7. **Welcome Criticism:** Embracing constructive feedback strengthens bonds. Sarvodaya Innovations values critiques as they contribute to its growth, aligning with the Indian adage, "Satyamev Jayate" (Truth Alone Triumphs).

8. **Non-monetary Rewards:** Rather than offering monetary incentives, recognition, badges, and appreciation hold more value. They echo the sentiment of "Atithi Devo Bhava" (The guest is God) ingrained in Indian culture.

In India, an ecosystem devoted to preserving its rich heritage emerges as a beacon of trust and unity. By nurturing this ecosystem, "Sarvodaya Innovations" not only ensures the endurance of its product but also contributes to the enduring legacy of Indian craftsmanship—a testament to the timeless wisdom of the Vedas and Upanishads.

Taking Care of Your Friends

Ensuring exceptional customer support for your acquaintances is a tactic that can ensure the longevity of your startup. Individuals tend to remain loyal to products that offer outstanding support, regardless of whether they are the most recent or advanced. As an example, Ritesh Agarwal attributes the success of his company, OYO Rooms, largely to the excellence of its customer support. The ability for customers to engage with a genuine individual at OYO Rooms was pivotal in shaping their experience.

Here are the key principles of delivering outstanding customer support:

1. **Generosity and Trust:** Exceptional customer support stems from a mindset of generosity and abundance. Offer human telephone support, allow restroom access without a purchase, and provide free Wi-Fi. While it might seem costly, the positive reputation gained often outweighs the expenses.

2. **Empower Customers:** Put the customer in control. Allow flexible purchasing, returns, and exchanges. Do what's right for the customer, not just what's dictated by rules.

3. **Take Responsibility:** Take responsibility not only for your company's shortcomings but also for the customer's issues. Go above and beyond to resolve problems, even if they aren't your fault.

4. **Underpromise and Overdeliver:** Exceed customer expectations by promising less and delivering more. This creates a positive experience and builds trust.

5. **Hire Empathetic and Engrossed Individuals:** Support staff should possess empathy, deriving satisfaction from helping customers. They should also be genuinely interested in support as a role, not just a means to an end. Product knowledge is crucial.

6. **Expose Everyone to Customer Support:** All employees should understand customer issues by spending time in support roles. This firsthand experience is more impactful than reviewing statistics.

7. **Integrate Support into the Mainstream:** Customer support should not be viewed as a necessary evil but as an essential part of the business. It influences sales and customer retention, making it a valuable asset.

By embracing these principles and prioritizing customer support, your startup can create enduring customer relationships and ensure long-term success.

"Fulfillment:
Embracing Your Duty with Purpose"

Chapter 13:
The Pursuit of Human Excellence

The true measure of an individual lies in their treatment of those from whom they expect nothing in return."

—Ratan Tata

GIST In this chapter, we delve into the path of attaining 'menschhood,' a state where one is recognized by those who truly matter as a person of unwavering ethics, grace, and admiration. It represents the zenith of human character and the pinnacle of a successful life. "Righteousness is absolute, and wrongdoing is unequivocal."

I invite you to aim for a loftier objective than amassing wealth or building vast organizations. This chapter is dedicated to unraveling the mastery of becoming a 'mensch.'

Those Who Cannot Reciprocate Mensch-like individuals extend their help to those who are unable to offer anything in return. Their compassion knows no distinctions of wealth or power. While this doesn't imply neglecting the rich, famous, or influential (as they too may require assistance), it emphasizes not limiting your aid to only such individuals.

Selfless Assistance Mensches offer their aid without expecting any form of repayment, at least not in this lifetime. The reward? It lies in the sheer satisfaction of helping others—nothing more and nothing less.

Aiding the Multitude Menschhood operates on a principle of quantity; hence, mensches extend their help to numerous individuals. It's ingrained in their nature to assist others, although even a mensch cannot assist everyone.

Upholding Righteousness Mensches unwaveringly adhere to what is right. This involves choosing the morally upright and, at times, challenging path. For mensches, the concept of "situational ethics" is a contradiction in terms. Righteousness is their guiding principle; they do what's right, irrespective of ease, expediency, cost-effectiveness, or the possibility of going unnoticed.

Giving Back to Society Mensches are acutely aware of their blessings and the responsibility that comes with them. They believe in repaying the debt they owe to society. It's not viewed as a favor but as a duty owed to society.

Those Who Cannot Reciprocate Mensch-like individuals extend their help to those who are unable to offer anything in return. Their compassion knows no distinctions of wealth or power. While this doesn't imply neglecting the rich, famous, or influential (as they too may require assistance), it emphasizes not limiting your aid to only such individuals.

Selfless Assistance Mensches offer their aid without expecting any form of repayment, at least not in this lifetime. The reward? It lies in the sheer satisfaction of helping others—nothing more and nothing less.

Aiding the Multitude Menschhood operates on a principle of quantity; hence, mensches extend their help to numerous individuals. It's ingrained in their nature to assist others, although even a mensch cannot assist everyone.

Upholding Righteousness Mensches unwaveringly adhere to what is right. This involves choosing the morally upright and, at times, challenging path. For mensches, the concept of "situational ethics" is a contradiction in terms. Righteousness is their guiding principle; they do what's right, irrespective of ease, expediency, cost-effectiveness, or the possibility of going unnoticed.

Giving Back to Society Mensches are acutely aware of their blessings and the responsibility that comes with them. They believe in repaying the debt they owe to society. It's not viewed as a favor but as a duty owed to society.

Assisting Those Who Cannot Reciprocate

Mensch-like individuals extend their help to those who are unable to offer anything in return. Their compassion knows no distinctions of wealth or power. While this doesn't imply neglecting the rich, famous, or influential (as they too may require assistance), it emphasizes not limiting your aid to only such individuals.

Selfless Assistance Mensches offer their aid without expecting any form of repayment, at least not in this lifetime. The reward? It lies in the sheer satisfaction of helping others—nothing more and nothing less.

Aiding the Multitude Menschhood operates on a principle of quantity; hence, mensches extend their help to numerous individuals. It's ingrained in their nature to assist others, although even a mensch cannot assist everyone.

Upholding Righteousness Mensches unwaveringly adhere to what is right. This involves choosing the morally upright and, at times, challenging path. For mensches, the concept of "situational ethics" is a contradiction in terms. Righteousness is their guiding principle; they do what's right, irrespective of ease, expediency, cost-effectiveness, or the possibility of going unnoticed.

Giving Back to Society Mensches are acutely aware of their blessings and the responsibility that comes with them. They believe in repaying the debt they owe to society. It's not viewed as a favor but as a duty owed to society.

Closing Reflections

As we reach the culmination of this journey, take a moment to reflect on the legacy you wish to leave behind. Pretend it's the end of your life, and consider the three fundamental aspects you want people to remember you for:

1.

2.

3.

These three facets encapsulate the essence of your existence and the impact you've had on others.

FAQ: Navigating Life's Challenges

Q: How can I remain grounded in the face of success?

A: Remember, wealth, fame, and power hold little value in the shadow of health and life's impermanence. In moments of invincibility, acknowledge the fragility of existence. Being the "richest person in the hospital" or the "richest person in the cemetery" is hardly a position worth pursuing.

Q: How can I conduct sales and business deals ethically?

A: If you're offering something that genuinely addresses a customer's needs, there should be no guilt associated with the transaction. If such feelings persist, reconsider your offering or target audience. Authenticity and integrity should define your approach.

Q: Will showcasing charitable endeavors deter potential investors?

A: Your commitment to social good does not diminish your entrepreneurial prowess. While doing good and making money are distinct, they can coexist. Investors primarily seek profitability, but your philanthropic efforts can reflect your values and attract like-minded individuals.

Q: How should I handle moments of frustration and anger?

A: Channel such emotions constructively. Remember, hockey is a sport where physical release is acceptable. Off the field, practice restraint. With age comes wisdom; resist the urge to react impulsively. Silence and distance can often defuse tense situations.

Q: Balancing work and constant requests for advice can be challenging. What's the solution?

A: Managing professional commitments alongside demands for expertise is a common struggle. Communicate your time constraints honestly, and most people will understand. Alternatively, offer your guidance in exchange for a charitable donation, benefiting both your cause and serious entrepreneurs.

As you ponder these reflections and consider the challenges life presents, strive to leave a legacy that embodies your values and enriches the lives of those around you. In the end, it's not just success that defines us, but the impact we make on the world.

Suggested Reading List

This list aims to provide readers with a holistic view on entrepreneurship, ethics, leadership, and personal development, reflecting a blend of Indian cultural heritage and universal principles.

Title	Author	Publication Year	Indian Perspective and Insights
"Start-up Sutra: What the Angels Won't Tell You About Business and Life"	Rohit Prasad	2014	Explores the essence of entrepreneurial spirit from an Indian perspective, blending modern business challenges with ancient wisdom.

Title	Author	Publication Year	Indian Perspective and Insights
"The Man Who Knew Infinity: A Life of the Genius Ramanujan"	Robert Kanigel	1991	Although not by an Indian author, this biography provides insights into self-reliance and visionary leadership through the life of Indian mathematician S. Ramanujan.
"Connect the Dots: The Inspiring Stories of 20 Entrepreneurs Without an MBA Who Dared to Find Their Own Path"	Rashmi Bansal	2010	Offers insights into the Indian entrepreneurial landscape, showcasing how visionaries built their empires on self-reliance and innovative thinking.
"Dare to Lead: Brave Work. Tough Conversations. Whole Hearts."	Brené Brown	2018	While not Indian, this book's universal principles on leadership and team-building complement the Indian ethos of heart-centered leadership.
"The Art of Happiness at Work"	Dalai Lama and Howard Cutler	2003	Provides a blend of Buddhist wisdom and practical advice, relevant for fostering a positive team environment and personal well-being.
"The Monk Who Sold His Ferrari: A Fable About Fulfilling Your Dreams & Reaching Your Destiny"	Robin Sharma	1997	Though widely read globally, this book encapsulates Indian spiritual concepts in a fable about personal transformation and success.

This list integrates timeless Indian wisdom with contemporary global insights, providing a comprehensive framework for ethical, innovative, and successful entrepreneurship. Each title is selected to resonate with the thematic content of "Launch to Legacy," offering readers a rich knowledge to draw from as they navigate their entrepreneurial journeys.

Funding Your Startup: A Comprehensive Guide for Entrepreneurs in India

Introduction Starting a new business in India requires careful planning and consideration of the available funding options. This guide is designed to provide you with insights into the various types of funding available in the Indian context and offers advice on how to secure investment for your startup. In this guide, we'll also draw inspiration from ancient Indian wisdom, including quotes from the Vedas and Upanishads, to provide a holistic perspective on funding your entrepreneurial journey.

Section 1: Understanding Different Types of Funding

In the diverse landscape of Indian startup funding, it's crucial to comprehend the various options at your disposal. Just as India's rich cultures coexists, different funding sources cater to startups at different stages of their evolution. Here's an overview:

Type of Funding	Description	Stage of Startup
Grants	Grants are available for specific purposes, such as economic development or environmental objectives. They can provide initial credibility.	Early Stages
Competitions	Participating in startup competitions can help gain credibility and secure significant funding. However, competition is high.	Early to Growth Stages
Friends and Family	Leveraging personal connections for investment can be a valuable resource, especially in the early stages.	Early Stages
Accelerators	Accelerators offer intensive support and funding in exchange for equity. Look for Indian accelerator programs in various sectors.	Early to Growth Stages

Type of Funding	Description	Stage of Startup
Crowdfunding	Crowdfunding platforms in India allow you to raise funds from a large number of people online. Consider platforms tailored to your niche.	Early to Growth Stages
Angel Investors	Indian angel investors, often successful entrepreneurs themselves, look for investable business ideas and the right chemistry with founders.	Early to Growth Stages
Venture Capital	Venture capital firms in India seek high-growth startups with established revenue streams. They can invest substantial amounts.	Growth Stages
Loans	Traditional bank loans are available, but consider government startup loan schemes for support.	Early to Growth Stages
Social Investment	For social enterprises, funding may come in the form of loans or grants from organizations like Social Investment Scotland.	Early to Growth Stages

Section 2: Funding Available in India

India offers a wide range of funding opportunities. Here are some notable sources:

i. **Government Schemes**: Explore schemes like the Startup India program, which offers benefits such as tax exemptions and funding support to eligible startups.

ii. **Angel Investor Networks**: Look for Indian angel investor networks like Indian Angel Network (IAN) and Mumbai Angels for potential funding.

iii. **Venture Capital Firms**: Prominent Indian venture capital firms like Sequoia Capital India and Accel Partners focus on high-growth startups.

iv. **Social Investment**: Organizations like Sankalp Forum and Villgro provide funding and support to social enterprises addressing societal challenges.

v. **Crowdfunding Platforms**: Platforms like Ketto and Milaap allow you to raise funds for your startup by leveraging the power of the crowd.

Section 3: How to Find Investors for Your Indian Startup

Finding the right investors is crucial for your startup's success. Here's how to connect with potential investors in India:

i. **Networking:** Attend startup events, conferences, and meetups to build relationships with investors. Join local entrepreneurial communities and online platforms.

ii. **Mentorship:** Seek mentorship from experienced entrepreneurs who can introduce you to potential investors in their networks.

iii. **Online Platforms:** Utilize online platforms like LinkedIn to connect with investors. Ensure your online presence reflects credibility.

iv. **Accelerators:** Consider joining Indian accelerator programs that provide access to a network of investors and mentors.

v. **Pitch Competitions:** Participate in pitch competitions in India to showcase your startup to potential investors.

Section 4: Expectations from Investors

Investors, whether angel investors or venture capitalists, have specific expectations. To attract their interest, ensure your startup demonstrates the following:

i. **Strong Team:** Investors look for a capable team with relevant industry experience.

ii. **Market Potential:** Highlight a large, growing target market for your product or service.

iii. **Proof of Concept:** Provide evidence that your product or service is viable and in demand.

iv. **Exit Strategy:** Clearly outline how investors can achieve a significant return on their investment.

v. **Triple Bottom Line (for social enterprises):** Showcase how your startup can create a positive impact on people, planet, and profit.

Section 5: Helpful Links and Resources

Here are some valuable resources for Indian startups seeking funding:

- Startup India: Explore government schemes and support for startups in India.
- Indian Angel Network: Connect with a network of angel investors.
- Sequoia Capital India: Learn about one of India's leading venture capital firms.
- Ketto: Explore a crowdfunding platform for raising funds in India.

Funding your Indian startup requires a strategic approach, a strong network, and a deep understanding of available options. Embrace the wisdom of ancient Indian texts, such as the Vedas and Upanishads, to guide you on your entrepreneurial journey, and remember that each stage of your startup may require a different source of funding.

(Note: This guide is for informational purposes only and does not constitute financial or legal advice. Always consult with professionals before making financial decisions for your startup.)

Nurturing Your Startup in the Land of Opportunities

Introduction: In the diverse India, where entrepreneurial spirit flows as naturally as the sacred Ganges, we embark on a journey to explore the manifold avenues of funding for your startup. As the sun rises over the Himalayas, casting its golden rays upon the fertile plains, let us navigate the labyrinth of financial possibilities that lie ahead.

1: Embracing the Diverse World of Funding In this vibrant land of myriad cultures and traditions, startups seek financial sustenance from a multitude of sources. It is akin to embarking on a pilgrimage, and the choice of path depends on your startup's stage. Just as the mighty rivers merge into the ocean, your startup's journey may involve various types of funding:

Funding Type	Description
Grants	Grants are like blessings from the heavens, often bestowed upon those with noble aims.

Funding Type	Description
Competitions	Much like ancient contests of valor, competitions can elevate your startup's stature.
Friends and Family	The bonds of kinship and friendship may provide the initial fuel for your venture.
Accelerators	In this fast-paced world, accelerators act as gurus, imparting wisdom for growth.
Crowdfunding	Crowdfunding is the modern-day yajna, where the community gathers to support your cause.
Angels	Angels, akin to benevolent deities, guide you with their wisdom and resources.
VCs	Venture Capitalists, the modern-day kings, invest in realms of high growth.
Loans	Loans, like threads of fate, may weave your startup's destiny with borrowed capital.

2: The Bountiful Fields of Indian Funding As we traverse the Indian landscape, each region offers a unique flavor of funding opportunities:

1. **Edge (EDGE in India)**: Like the holy Ganges, the Edge competition seeks to nurture innovative, high-growth businesses, offering substantial rewards and support. The waters of success here are abundant.

2. **Converge Challenge (Converge India)**: A fertile ground for budding entrepreneurs, Converge Challenge aids in creating a new generation of business leaders. Just as the monsoon rains rejuvenate the soil, this program nurtures startups.

3. **ILG (Indian Launch Grants)**: ILG celebrates those who have turned their academic pursuits into entrepreneurial ventures. It offers a shower of support, with a top award resembling a precious gem in the treasure chest.

4. **Social Enterprise Grants (Indian Social Ventures)**: Initiatives by Firstport and Unltd are like the philanthropic deeds of kings, supporting social enterprises in their noble quests.

5. **High Growth Spin Out (HGSO)**: The HGSO Program, akin to alchemical transmutations, transforms research into global market treasures, a pursuit reminiscent of the ancient quest for the philosopher's stone.

3: Seeking the Guidance of Ancients In our quest for funding, let us not forget the wisdom passed down through millennia in the Vedas and Upanishads. Just as the sacred texts guide seekers on their spiritual journeys, they can illuminate the path to entrepreneurial success.

"Arise, awake, and stop not till the goal is reached." - Swami Vivekananda

4: Building Bridges of Connections In this digital age, connections are the bridges that lead us to our destination. Just as the ancient trade routes connected civilizations, our network can connect us to investors. Here are some ways to find your investors:

- **Through Personal Networks**: Like the threads of a spider's web, your personal connections can capture the attention of investors.

- **Online Platforms**: In the digital bazaars of LinkedIn and AngelList, investors and entrepreneurs converge to strike deals.

- **Investor Networks**: These networks are like secret societies, and gaining entry requires the right connections.

- **Mentorship**: Just as gurus impart wisdom to disciples, mentors in entrepreneurship can guide you to investors.

- **Accelerator Programs**: These are like the great learning centers of ancient India, nurturing startups to attract investors.

5: The Expectations of Investors Investors in India, much like those around the world, have high expectations. They seek startups that can deliver both financial returns and societal benefits. To gain their blessings, startups must demonstrate:

- A strong team with experience, akin to the harmony of a well-orchestrated raga.

- A vast and growing market, mirroring the population surge in our diverse nation.

- Evidence of your product's efficacy, just as the healing touch of Ayurveda.

- Proof that your startup addresses a genuine need, echoing the words of Mahatma Gandhi.

In the vast and diverse landscape of India, startups are like sacred saplings, seeking the life-giving waters of funding. Just as the Indian subcontinent is of cultures, languages, and traditions, so too is the world of startup funding a diverse and intricate web.

May your entrepreneurial journey in India be as colorful and rich as the festivals of Diwali, and may your startup thrive like the lush fields nourished by the monsoon rains. Remember the wisdom of the Vedas and Upanishads as you tread this path: "You are what your deep, driving desire is. As your desire is, so is your will. As your will is, so is your deed. As your deed is, so is your destiny." - Brihadaranyaka Upanishad.

Closing Thoughts

As we conclude this journey through the pages of wisdom, let us reflect on the words of Rabindranath Tagore, who aptly said, "Books are good enough in their own way, but they are a mighty bloodless substitute for living." Your investment of time and resources in reading this book, perhaps both editions, is sincerely appreciated. In return, I hope you have not only gained insights but also the inspiration to create meaning and catalyze change in the world.

The world of entrepreneurship is often described as a cycle, akin to the ebb and flow of tides or the interplay of yin and yang. Allow me to present another analogy: that of microscopes and telescopes. In the microscope phase, there's a call for rationality, a return to fundamentals, and a focus on short-term financial outcomes. Experts meticulously scrutinize details, financial statements, and expenses, seeking forecasts, market insights, and competitive analyses.

Conversely, in the telescope phase, entrepreneurs draw the future nearer. They envision groundbreaking innovations, strive to transform the world, and leave late adopters astounded. While some may view these pursuits as extravagant and risky, they often result in revolutionary ideas that propel society forward.

Successful entrepreneurship necessitates both perspectives – the microscopic and the telescopic. I trust that this book equips you with valuable tools for both close examination and visionary exploration.

Let me share the inspiring tale of Arunima Sinha, the trailblazer who conquered Mount Everest despite losing her leg in a tragic accident. Confronted with treacherous terrain and extreme weather conditions, Arunima persisted for hours, relying on sheer determination and resilience. Her mental strategy was to focus on reaching the next milestone, breaking down an impossible journey into achievable steps. Her tenacity, even in the face of personal adversity, serves as a reminder that the most daunting tasks can be conquered when divided into manageable parts.

In the inevitable moments of darkness and doubt, recall Arunima's story and break down the seemingly insurmountable into ten feasible steps. A billion-dollar enterprise comprises ten one-hundred-million-dollar milestones, just as a million-dollar venture comprises ten one-hundred-thousand-dollar phases. Remember that Infosys, the tech giant we know today, commenced its journey with a handful of computers in a small apartment.

In closing, I aspire to meet you in person one day. Should you have this book with you, it would be a joy to witness the notes you've taken, the pages you've dog-eared, and the text you've underlined – evidence of your active engagement. There is no greater gratification for an author than to see their work well-loved and well-used.

I've held your attention for long enough. Now, embark on your entrepreneurial endeavors, for the essence of entrepreneurship lies not in learning alone but in the transformative power of action.

Warm regards,

Vinay Rajagopal Iyer

Postscript

As we come to the end of this journey, I'm reminded of a delightful encounter that occurred twenty-five years ago. At that time, I was the proud owner of a Royal Enfield Classic motorcycle, a symbol of freedom and passion. One day, while waiting at a traffic light on Brigade Road in Bangalore, I noticed a car filled with four teenage girls. They were giggling, sharing stories, and enjoying each other's company.

In that moment, I felt a sense of connection, thinking that even teenagers appreciated my presence. To my surprise, one of the girls signaled for me. I complied, expecting compliments about my ventures, achievements, or perhaps even my charming demeanor. However, her question took me by surprise: "Are you Shah Rukh Khan?"

You may wonder how this anecdote relates to startups and entrepreneurship. Admittedly, the connection is not immediately evident, but a mark of a good storyteller is the ability to weave seemingly unrelated elements into a cohesive narrative. Allow me to demonstrate this artistry.

Reaching this point in a book is akin to savoring the climax of a Shah Rukh Khan movie, eagerly anticipating the charming dialogues or the heartwarming songs. Your commitment to reading deserves appreciation, akin to what Ratan Tata referred to as "Creating a legacy."

In the world of startups, just as in an enthralling Bollywood movie, there's always the potential for unexpected twists and delightful surprises. So, as we conclude this chapter, keep an open heart and a resilient spirit. Who knows what exciting adventures await you in your entrepreneurial journey!

With best wishes,

Vinay Rajagopa Iyer

The Decisive Decisions of Entrepreneurs

In the world of entrepreneurship, avoiding common pitfalls can be the key to success. Here, we present a list of the top ten mistakes that entrepreneurs often make, along with strategies to steer clear of them. Remember, it's okay to make new mistakes, but learning from others can save you time and resources.

Mistake	Entrepreneurial Pitfall	Fix	Indian Wisdom
1.	Overestimating Market Share	Calculate from the Bottom Up	In the Bhagavad Gita, Lord Krishna advises Arjuna to focus on his efforts, not the fruits of his actions. Similarly, entrepreneurs should concentrate on building their product from the ground up, understanding that success is not guaranteed.
2.	Scaling Too Quickly	Practice Prudent Growth	The story of the tortoise and the hare from Panchatantra reminds us that slow and steady

Mistake	Entrepreneurial Pitfall	Fix	Indian Wisdom
			progress can lead to victory. Instead of rushing to scale, ensure you have solid sales before expanding your infrastructure.
3.	Excessive Partnership Pursuits	Prioritize Sales Over Partnerships	The saying "Ek aur ek gyarah hote hain" (One plus one equals eleven) emphasizes the power of collaboration, but partnerships should enhance your business, not replace sales efforts.
4.	Obsession with Fundraising	Focus on Prototyping	The ancient Indian concept of "Jugaad" encourages frugal and innovative problem-solving. Build a prototype to demonstrate your product's value before seeking external funding.
5.	Using Too Many Presentation Slides	Follow the 10/20/30 Rule	Less is often more in presentations, as emphasized by the 10/20/30 rule - 10 slides, 20 minutes, and a font size of 30 points.
6.	Serial Progression	Embrace Parallel Action	The Hindu deity Lord Vishnu, known for his multitasking, teaches us to handle multiple

Mistake	Entrepreneurial Pitfall	Fix	Indian Wisdom
			responsibilities simultaneously. Entrepreneurs must juggle various tasks in parallel to succeed.
7.	Fixation on Control	Expand the Pie	The saying "Bada socho, bada bano" (Think big, become big) encourages entrepreneurs to focus on growing their business rather than retaining excessive control.
8.	Overreliance on Patents	Rely on Success for Defensibility	The Indian startup mantra is "Innovate, don't litigate." Rather than relying solely on patents, focus on creating a successful and dominant presence in your market.
9.	Hiring in Your Image	Hire Complementary Skills	India's diverse culture reminds us of the strength that comes from different backgrounds working together. Instead of hiring clones, seek individuals with diverse skills and perspectives.
10.	Seeking Friendship with Investors	Exceed Investor Expectations	In the corporate world, professional relationships

Mistake	Entrepreneurial Pitfall	Fix	Indian Wisdom
			often matter more than personal ones. Focus on delivering results that exceed your investors' expectations.

Remember, entrepreneurship is a journey filled with challenges and opportunities. By avoiding these common mistakes and drawing inspiration from Indian wisdom, you can navigate this path with confidence and determination

Author Bio

Blending technical expertise with a passion for holistic wellness, our author Vinay Rajagopal emerges as a multifaceted leader and visionary in both the technological and personal development arenas. With a robust educational foundation, including an MBA from the University of Melbourne and a BE in Electrical & Electronics from RV College of Engineering, the journey unfolds through various roles in technology and leadership.

The narrative begins with over two decades of global experience in technology, where our author excels as a Technology Executive. From hands-on technical roles to leadership positions, the expertise spans across infrastructure technologies, large-scale team management, and strategic oversight in international settings. Key roles include a Practice Director at Happiest Minds Technologies, a Senior Manager and Senior Consulting Architect at IBM, and a Program Manager at Apara Global Services, showcasing a trajectory marked by growth and diversification.

As the Chief Operating Officer of iSmart, the author's entrepreneurial acumen shines. Here, within a mere three months, the transformation of a startup into a thriving enterprise with an ever-expanding team is a testament to strategic brilliance and leadership prowess.

Beyond technology, our author delves into the realms of personal development and wellness. A Master Spirit Life Coach certified by the International Coaching Federation, a Strengths Coach, and a Louise Hay - Heal Your Life trainer reflect a deep commitment to empowering others. This is further enriched by certifications in Yoga, embodying a holistic approach to wellbeing.

In professional certifications, the author's dedication to continuous learning is evident. With accreditations ranging from PMI's Project Management Professional to ITIL, and technical certifications from NetApp, VMWare, and Symantec, the commitment to staying at the forefront of technological advancements is clear.

This unique blend of technical acumen, leadership, and personal development expertise makes our author a distinguished figure, guiding others through transformational journeys in both their professional and personal lives.

Reading List

I have compiled a recommended reading list that aligns with the themes and chapters of "Launch to Legacy: A Comprehensive Guide to Entrepreneurial Success," and to illustrate how Indian wisdom and insights could replace or complement international references, I'll create a table that maps each chapter to relevant books. This approach incorporates Indian authors renowned for their contributions to literature, business, and philosophy, while also including significant works from international authors that align with the book's themes.

Chapter Title	Recommended Book	Author	Description
Nexus	"Jugaad Innovation: Think Frugal, Be Flexible, Generate Breakthrough Growth"	Navi Radjou, Jaideep Prabhu, Simone Ahuja	Emphasizes the Indian concept of Jugaad as an innovative problem-solving technique.
The Mastery of Commencement	"The Difficulty of Being Good: On the Subtle Art of Dharma"	Gurcharan Das	Explores ancient Indian philosophy and ethics, applying them to modern dilemmas.
The Mastery of Visionary Leadership	"Leadership Wisdom from the Bhagavad Gita"	Pujan Roka	Applies the teachings of the Bhagavad Gita to contemporary leadership challenges.
The Mastery of Self-Reliance	"Autobiography of a Yogi"	Paramahansa Yogananda	Offers insights into spiritual self-reliance and its impact on personal growth.

Chapter Title	Recommended Book	Author	Description
The Mastery of Presenting - Mastering the Pitch	"Talk Like TED: The 9 Public-Speaking Secrets of the World's Top Minds"	Carmine Gallo	Although not Indian, it's a universally applicable guide on impactful presentations.
Crafting a Stellar Team for Success	"The Five Dysfunctions of a Team: A Leadership Fable"	Patrick Lencioni	Not specifically Indian but highly relevant for building effective teams.
The Mastery of Spreading the Light	"Lighting the Lamp Within"	Jyoti Sondhi	Discusses the importance of inner enlightenment for outward success.
Mastering the Mastery of Social Connection	"Emotional Intelligence: Why It Can Matter More Than IQ"	Daniel Goleman	Highlights the role of emotional intelligence in building social connections.
The Mastery of Abundant Harvest	"Banker to the Poor: Micro-Lending and the Battle Against World Poverty"	Muhammad Yunus	Focuses on social entrepreneurship and its impact, relevant globally.
The Mastery of Collaboration	"Ikigai: The Japanese Secret to a Long and Happy Life"	Héctor García and Francesc Miralles	While Japanese, it emphasizes the importance of purpose and community in success.
The Journey of Perseverance	"Wings of Fire: An Autobiography"	A.P.J. Abdul Kalam	Inspiring story of perseverance from a renowned Indian scientist and president.
The Pursuit of Human Excellence	"The Greatness Guide"	Robin Sharma	Offers insights into personal and professional excellence.

Chapter Title	Recommended Book	Author	Description
Closing Thoughts	"Being Different: An Indian Challenge to Western Universalism"	Rajiv Malhotra	Encourages embracing unique cultural insights for global influence and success.

This table represents a blend of Indian wisdom with global insights, offering readers a comprehensive view on entrepreneurship, personal development, and leadership from diverse perspectives. The books from Indian authors provide deep cultural and philosophical insights, while the international selections offer universally applicable advice on entrepreneurship and success.

www.ingramcontent.com/pod-product-compliance
Lightning Source LLC
LaVergne TN
LVHW061539070526
838199LV00077B/6840